Intimate Relations

Intimate Relations

MURRAY S. DAVIS

FP
THE FREE PRESS
A Division of Macmillan Publishing Co., Inc.
New York
Collier Macmillan Publishers
London

The Free Press
A Division of Macmillan Publishing Co., Inc.
866 Third Avenue
New York, New York 10022

Collier–Macmillan Canada Ltd., Toronto, Ontario

Library of Congress Catalog Card Number: 73–1859

Printed in the United States of America

printing number
1 2 3 4 5 6 7 8 9 10

Library of Congress Cataloging in Publication Data
Davis, Murray S.   1940–
    Intimate relations.
    Originally presented as the author's thesis,
Brandeis, 1969.
    Includes bibliographical references.
    1. Interpersonal relations.   2. Intimacy
(Psychology)   I. Title. [DNLM: 1. Interpersonal
relations. 2. Psychology, Social. HM132 D263i 1973]
HM132.D38 1973   301.11   73–1859
ISBN 0–02–907020–1

ACKNOWLEDGMENTS

Chapter 7, "Betrothal," in *The Life and Work of Sigmund Freud*, edited by Ernest Jones, Volume 1. Copyright © 1953 by Ernest Jones.

On Old Age and on Friendship by Cicero, translated by Frank Copley. Published by The University of Michigan Press.

The Art of Love by Ovid, translated by R. Humphries. Published by Indiana University Press.

Ethics by Aristotle, translated by J. A. K. Thomson. Copyright 1953 by Humanities Press, Inc., New York. Published outside the United States by George Allen & Unwin Ltd, London. "Sunday Will Never Be the Same" by Gene Pistilli & Terry Cashman, © 1966 and 1967 Pamco Music Inc.—1973 ABC/ Dunhill Music, Inc., Los Angeles. Used by permission.

Excerpts from "When Illness Follows a 'Giving Up'" by Jane Brody, April 7, 1968; "Breakthrough by 'The Boys in the Band'" by Rex Reed, May 12, 1968; "Review of George Painter's André Gide" by Enid Starkie, June 23, 1968; "Autumn Brings Bicycle Traffic Jams to Central Park Paths," August 12, 1968; "Young Unmarrieds Find a New Way of Life," April 6, 1969 © 1968/69 by The New York Times Company. Reprinted by permission.

To the Brandeis University Sociology Department 1964–1969 who taught me that a social scientist need not be irrelevant to himself or his society.

Contents

Preface

THERE HAS BEEN a spate of books recently designed to change
the way people relate to one another, but this is not one of them.
These books have been moralistic and melioristic on the one hand,
or cynical and strategical on the other. The former tell the reader
how to fix the *mechanism* of his intimate relations: "If only he
would stop playing games with his intimate, be more honest,
bring his feelings out into the open, touch his intimate more..."
The latter tell the reader how to win the *game* of his intimate
relations: "If only he would learn to use skillfully the various
tactics (strategic increases of affection, strategic withdrawals of
affection, etc.) necessary to seduce the other player into yielding
to his goals (sex, marriage, etc.)..."

Intimate Relations differs considerably from these other books.
It is *not* the interpersonal equivalent of *Popular Mechanics* or
Winning Poker. It does *not* see intimacy as a solemn and significant enigma or as an unserious and unreal contest. It does *not*
assert that intimates should be more noble than they are or that
intimates are actually less noble than they think they are. It is
not designed to change the way people relate to one another, but
only to inform them about the way they do in fact relate to one

another. I have tried to write a book about intimate relations that would be enlightening without being moralistic or cynical. I hope this book will neither improve nor impair the intimate relations of anyone who reads it—except insofar as awareness gives distance, and distance gives choice.

Numerous books on intimate relations are being written today because accelerating social change has drastically eroded the bonds that tied individuals together in the past, causing them to seek outside advice on how to reestablish these bonds (doing consciously, as it were, what their ancestors did spontaneously). I will call this present social sickness—one of whose symptoms is the large number of treatments published—*erosis.*

Erosis seems to be the appropriate name for this disorder since most of those who have dealt with it have assumed that the individual's basic difficulty in relating to others stems from a malfunction of his love faculty (taking "love" in its largest sense to mean "a concern for others"). Some have traced its etiology to the atrophy of the individual's ability to love and have suggested he can cure all his interpersonal ailments through more love. Others have traced its etiology to the hypertrophy of the individual's ability to love and have suggested he can cure all his interpersonal ailments through less love It would not be difficult to discover why both these therapies for interpersonal problems have been advocated today by tracing them back to their respective economic, social, historical, philosophical, and ultimately religious roots, but to do so would take us far afield from interpersonal relations themselves.

I believe both the more-love and the less-love therapies for interpersonal problems are deficient. Neither of their diagnoses will prove adequate and neither of their prescriptions will prove effective because they are not grounded on an understanding of the fundamental processes of interpersonal relations. They will ultimately fail, I think, because they treat only the surface symptoms of the sickness of our time and not its underlying pathology. This underlying pathology lies not in the individual himself—if it did, it would perhaps respond to the treatment of more love or less love; rather, it lies in the nature of the individual's *relationships* with others—and whatever treatment these *relationships* may need must be of a quite different sort.

Since the discussion of this malaise of modern society seems so far to have produced few tangible results, I propose that we shift its central locus away from the psychological concept of "love" and toward the sociological concept of "intimate relations," and that instead of prematurely formulating panaceas for the problems of intimates, we establish a *science* of the relations of intimates. Only after we come to understand how intimates interact with each other can we begin to formulate effective solutions for their problems. In Chapter 3, I have designated a name for this science of intimate relations—PHILEMICS, the study of all behaviors through which two interacting individuals construct and communicate an intimate relation. It will describe and analyze the intimate relation in its own right and look at its variation, stresses, and strains under different social environments.

This is not to say that the problems of intimate relations are unimportant and can be ignored until that hypothetical time when the science of philemics reaches maturity, when we understand the processes of intimate relations fully and can then—at last—turn our attention to their problems; for it is the very problems of intimate relations themselves that constitute the major source of clues to their processes. (In fact, what many people now consider the overall "problem" of intimate relations stems mostly from their misconception of the specific problems of intimate relations. Much of this book is devoted to describing the large number of problems that are *intrinsic* to the processes of intimate relations and so are ultimately *unsolvable*. It is my belief that the so-called crisis of intimate relations today is due to the increasing disparity between the rising expectation that all their problems can be solved and the intractable fact that many of them simply cannot be solved. Only by accepting the little tragedies of intimate relations as inherently necessary can the big tragedy of their breakup be avoided.)

I view science not as the study of some phenomenon that uses quantitative methods but as the study of some phenomenon that uncovers its basic building blocks and interrelates them systematically until the complexity of the phenomenon itself is approached. I have modeled the science of philemics on this conception of science. Thus, my discussion within each chapter of a single dimension of the intimate relation moves from the simple to the complex, from the obvious to the obscure, from the pure to the problematic; my discussion throughout all the chapters (in Part One) of the overall development of the intimate relation moves from its outer, surface aspects to its inner, essential ones. Those who want to consume only the phenomenological core of intimacy may skip directly to Chapter 6. This book, however, is written for those who find equal savor and delight in its behavioral rind.

It used to be said that politics is the fundamental science of human happiness, but I believe this honor should be reserved for philemics. Without satisfactory intimate relations, an individual would be unhappy in the most benign utopia; with them, he would be able to find some happiness even in the most oppressive totalitarian society.

I have omitted three major topics usually found in books on intimate relations. I discuss *sex* here only peripherally, as this labyrinthine subject needs separate treatment; I discuss *gender* only when I cannot avoid it, for I am attempting here to investigate intimate relations on a level of abstraction high enough to render inconsequential the sex roles of those who enter into them; finally, I discuss *emotions* as little as possible, feeling that the passionate side of intimate relations has already been documented extensively and that its hitherto neglected nonpassionate parts should be given at least equal attention.

Without sex, gender, and emotions, is there anything left of intimate relations to be discussed? I am optimistic that the reader of this book will come to agree that there is.

One problem with this kind of book is that some of its examples will inevitably sound dated. Intimate relations cannot be portrayed convincingly except in terms of the language through which most of their processes take place, and this language is inherently in flux. The rhetoric of intimate relations changes faster than most other specialized rhetorics in our society because this essentially esoteric mode of communication is continually disseminated to the public through the mass media and other media of information diffusion. The ingroup distinguishes itself from the outgroup in part through its unique language. To maintain its customary distance from the outgroup, then, the ingroup must develop a new language as soon as the outgroup learns and adopts its old language. Hence the rapid turnover of the clichés through which intimates communicate about their relationship.

This particular book is based on research initiated in the late 1960s. Some of its examples, therefore, have already gone out of date. Although others of them will eventually become obsolete, I feel confident that the general principles they illustrate will not.

I cannot acknowledge all those whose germinal insights into intimate relations contributed to the gestation of this book; however, I would like to thank those who contributed the largest amount to its postnatal care: Professor Barrie Thorne (Michigan State) and Hannah Marshall (Northern Illinois), who read previous drafts; N.D., who helped me with the editing; Professors Morris Schwartz, Larry Rosenberg, Jerome Boime, and James Klee (Brandeis), who were indulgent of my idiosyncracies and receptive to the experimental character of my research; the Department of Sociology of Northern Illinois University, which assumed some of the copying costs; and Professor Donald Levine (Chicago), who provided the sponsorship necessary to see the manuscript into publication.

Most of all, I would like to thank my acquaintances, friends, and loves who, though aware I was often objectively detached from our relationship, decided to maintain it nonetheless.

Introduction

INTIMACY DEFINED AND DIFFERENTIATED

ALTHOUGH it is customary to begin with a definition of one's subject matter, I will not do so because *intimacy*[1] is much too complex a concept to be defined succinctly. The whole of this book, in fact, may be seen as an extended definition of intimacy in the sense that it will consist of an enumeration of the many specific behaviors in which intimacy inheres (taking "behavior" in its widest meaning to include internal movements of the mind —"experiences"—as well as external actions of the body). For the present, *intimate behavior* will be defined, simply and tautologically, as that which most people in a particular society consider to be intimate behavior. The book's theme will be wound around this circular starting point. I will focus especially on the behaviors that are considered intimate in modern American society; however, since many of these behaviors are also considered intimate in other urbanized societies, I will illustrate them with materials drawn from a variety of cosmopolitan cultures past and present.

A few more technical definitions and distinctions of the terms I will be using here must be made at the outset. An *intimate relation* (often popularly called a *personal relation* or, by social scientists, a *primary relation*) is an ongoing social interaction between individuals that consists of a large number of intimate behaviors. I will restrict the discussion to those intimate relations in which the interacting individuals are relatively equal in status and power (to exclude such unequal relationships as mother–child) and in which the interacting individuals reciprocate each other's intimate behaviors (to exclude such one-sided relationships as psychiatrist–patient). I will further restrict this discussion to two-person relationships, although occasionally I will consider the ways in which the various intimacies of an individual can come into conflict. In brief, I will be describing the intimate behaviors that essentially characterize *intimates*, those relatively equal pairs of interacting individuals who reciprocate numerous intimate behaviors.

There are four species of the genus intimates: friends, lovers, spouses, and siblings. *Friends* are intimates insofar as they engage in all intimate behaviors except sexually related ones. *Lovers* are intimates insofar as they engage in sexually related intimate behaviors; they may be engaging in other intimate behaviors as well.[2] *Spouses* are intimates insofar as they (by having become officially related) share a common future of potential intimate behaviors, though they may not be currently engaging in many intimate behaviors. *Siblings* are intimates insofar as they (by having been officially related) share a common past of intimate behaviors, though they too may not be currently engaging in many intimate behaviors. (Since I will be concerned mostly with the evolution of intimate relations through the accumulation of more and more intimate behaviors, only passing reference will be made to siblings, who have been reciprocating many intimate behaviors almost since birth.) Except in the few cases where such distinctions are crucial, I will stress the behavioral similarities among these species of intimates while deemphasizing the differences, although I will often describe a particular intimate behavior in terms of the species that specializes in it more than the others.

I will contrast intimates with nonintimates, the latter being those pairs of interacting individuals who do not reciprocate a large number of intimate behaviors. There are four species of the genus nonintimates: strangers, role-relations, acquaintances, and enemies. *Strangers* are nonintimates insofar as they engage in scarcely any reciprocal behaviors at all beyond merely responding to each other's general social existence when they are in each other's presence.[3] *Role relations* (often called *secondary relations*) are nonintimates insofar as they engage in only a few narrowly prescribed, reciprocal behaviors between segments of themselves. If they add intimate behaviors to their core activities, as when a clerk gives a "personal touch" to his relations with a customer ("How are you today, Mr. Jones? Come for your usual pack of tobacco?"), they are considered as being friendly, i.e., friendlike. *Acquaintances* are nonintimates insofar as they engage in few intimate behaviors, though they have met each other at least once as particular whole persons instead of encountering each other merely as general persons (strangers) or segmental persons (role-relations). They include those pairs of ex-strangers and ex-role-relations who, beyond merely registering their particular personal existence with each other in this way, either do not intend to matriculate for advanced degrees of intimacy, or are in the process of acquiring intimacy credits, or have dropped out before graduating as fully certified intimates, or are alumni of an intimate relation they have allowed to lapse. Finally, *enemies* are nonintimates insofar as they engage in numerous intimate behaviors that they counterdefine with numerous anti-intimate behaviors. Like friends and lovers but unlike acquaintances, enemies are oriented almost entirely to each other; unlike friends and lovers, however, enemies violently dislike this obsessive orientation and wish to destroy each other in order to be rid of it.

The flow charts on page xx will serve to diagram the conception of *sociable mobility* between relationships of nonintimate status and relationships of intimate status to be used in this book. Solid lines represent relatively frequent movements; broken lines represent relatively infrequent movements.

INTIMACY SITUATED IN HISTORY

From the sociological point of view, the most important event in the history of intimate or personal relations was the transforma

SOCIABLE MOBILITY FLOW CHARTS

Upward Mobility

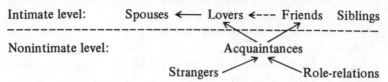

Downward Mobility

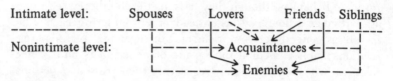

tion of social life from that based on gemeinschaft (community) to that based on gesellschaft (society).[4] It is this historical circumstance that accentuated the factors that, we shall see, pull the person apart, motivate him to search for intimates, and put problems in his path.

Such urbanization has occurred several times in the West: in Classical Greece, in the Roman Empire, and in the Renaissance. During each of these periods, personal relations became problematic enough to engage the attention of such social commentators as Plato, Aristotle, Cicero, Montaigne, and Bacon. The most recent and most extensive period of urbanization, since the eighteenth century, has resulted in an eruption of interest in personal relations both in the abstract, by such philosophers as Thoreau, Emerson, Nietzsche, Simmel, Buber, Schutz, and Sartre,[5] and in the concrete, by such novelists as Choderlos de Laclos, Stendhal, Tolstoy, Forster, and Nabokov.[6]

This transformation of social life from gemeinschaft to gesellschaft brought about a change in both persons and relations. On the one hand, each person began to behave in a way that differed considerably from the behavior of others, while he began to con-

ceive of himself as an entity distinct from them—in short, he became more of a unique individual; on the other hand, others began to relate to him through only one of his segmental aspects or
social positions, while they began to conceive of him as only one
of the many possible recipients of these relations—in short, he
became more of a replaceable role player. As the social pressures
on the person both to be unique and to be replaceable became increasingly contradictory, he became increasingly subject to psychological stress. As a result, every person in gesellschaft came to
feel a growing need to relieve the intensifying tension of an individuality that was being simultaneously heightened and flat-
tened, a growing need for new social forms of personal relations
through which he could return to that relatively tranquil psychological state enjoyed by his ancestors in gemeinschaft.[7] E. M.
Forster wrote in the early part of the twentieth century:

> London was but a foretaste of this nomadic civilization
> which is altering human nature so profoundly, and throws
> upon personal relations a stress greater than they have
> ever borne before. Under cosmopolitanism, if it comes,
> we shall receive no help from the earth. Trees and
> meadows and mountains will only be a spectacle, and the
> binding force that they once exercised on character must
> be entrusted to Love alone. May Love be equal to the
> task![8]

In society, each person (to one degree or another) does not
merely endure the psychological dis-ease this isolation engenders,
while waiting for the millennium to return him to the Garden of
Gemeinschaft in which his psychological equilibrium will be re-
stored; rather, each person (with differing degrees of success) actively attempts to reconstruct around himself the community he
feels he lacks—or at least a small-scale version of it, consisting
of his personal relations. In this sense, we are all social planners
and community organizers. In rebuilding our kleinen-gemein-
schaften (microcommunities), we are renewing ourselves.

The relatively few personal relations in which a person participates by choice consist of holistic, multifaceted interactions that contrast with the segmental, single-faceted interactions of the relatively many role-relations in which he participates by necessity. In order to offset the tendency of his poorly integrated social roles to disintegrate him into incompatible psychological parts, a person will try to interact with those who will relate to him as an individual and as a whole. Personal relations provide a person with psychological coherence insofar as they supply to his inner life the continuity that is often lacking in his outer life. In other words, a person can counteract the tendency of his role-relations to pull him apart by engaging in personal relations that help him to "pull himself together."[9] Although a person does not want his ego to disintegrate under the conflicting demands of most of his interaction partners, he does want it to dissolve under the sympathetic understanding of a few of his interaction partners. By being accepted in his personal relations as a unique totality, a person can overcome his isolation and merge with others into a larger unit, with all the increased relief, security, and power that membership in such a supraindividual entity provides. In urbanized societies, then, personal relations permit a person to have his individuality and lose it, too.

Potentially, personal relations in mobile societies can be more satisfying than relations with others in static communities, for the mere fact that a person comes into contact with more people increases the probability that he will encounter those with whom he can interact extremely well. Whereas in the community a person found his set of close associates to be ready-made, in the society he now finds that he must *make* his own friends, loves, and spouse. In gesellschaft, personal relations can be more selective, but they must also be more deliberate. In attempting to construct his personal relations, societal man must deal with difficulties of which his communal counterparts were scarcely aware. Since he is no longer attached to others by the connective tissues that tied members of the community together, he must now forge new links for himself. He must now deliberately activate the unifying forces the already unified members of the community merely experienced passively. How the isolated individuals of gesellschaft, in order both to strengthen and to surrender their individuality, attempt to combine into larger social units by deliberately activating certain unifying forces, and how their compound creations can become unstable and break down, are the subjects of this book.

INTIMACY ANALYZED PHILOGENETICALLY

Thus the relation between intimates is composed of elementary intimate behaviors, and individuals who want to engage in an intimate relation must generate certain social forces to fasten themselves together. Since these integrating social forces are inherent in the elementary intimate behaviors, individuals who wish to become intimates must come to interact by way of an increasing number of these basic binding behaviors.

Chapters 1 through 6 all begin with a brief consideration of how urbanization has transformed each of six dimensions of social interaction into a crucial aspect of intimate relations. Each chapter describes in detail how individuals who wish to become intimates must construct their relation on each dimension out of certain component intimate behaviors, and concludes with a summary of the fundamental fusion force intimates generate on each dimension out of these atomistic intimate actions. The sequence of these six chapters corresponds roughly to the order in which those who become intimates activate these forces and to the increasing integrating power of these forces (*philogenesis*). This sequence also approximates a concentric analysis of intimate relations from outer to inner behaviors.

Moreover, every chapter contains a section called "Complications," which considers the factors that interfere with the easy functioning of the simple processes of coordinated intimate interaction treated in its earlier sections. It is at these problematic points in intimate relations that dissatisfactions and disagreements occur.

Chapter 1 treats the dimension of *probability*—in particular, the opportunities to begin an intimate relation that strangers who wish to become at least acquaintances must seize. Chapter 2 treats the dimension of *congregation*—in particular, the ways of perceiving and achieving their bodily copresence that acquaintances who wish to become intimates must develop. Chapter 3 treats the dimension of *communication*—in particular, the modes of signaling their relationship level that acquaintances who wish to become intimates must use. Chapter 4 treats the dimension of *information*—in particular, the concealed personal characteristics that acquaintances who wish to become intimates must reveal and learn. Chapter 5 treats the dimension of *ecology*—in particular, the favors that aid transactions with, and resistance to, their environment that acquaintances who wish to become intimates must exchange. Chapter 6 treats the dimension of *intersubjectivity*—in particular, the couplings of their self-components that acquaintances who wish to become intimates must effect.

The essential characteristic of all man-made constructions, unfortunately, is that they are constantly crumbling and are often destroyed—and personal relations are no exception. Accordingly, Chapter 7 treats the decay of social ties between those who have become intimates, as well as the techniques they use to attempt to rejuvenate their relationship. Finally, Chapter 8 treats the accumulation of counterintimate forces, as well as the techniques used by those whose intimacy is incurably ill to disconnect themselves completely from their decomposing relationship.

A NOTE ON RESOURCES

The concepts that constitute the body of this book were derived from my observations of my own intimate relations and of the intimate relations of those I have known. Merely to record any of these observations, however, would have been a solipsistic exercise, for I often found it difficult to tell the lover from the looker. Since I had hoped to write a generalized sociology and not a jargonized autobiography, I have tried to take some precautions against the temptation to elevate my own peculiar style of interpersonal relations into a universal feature of social life. Whenever possible—and it was not always possible—I have tried to illustrate my own observations with the words, phrases, experiences, opinions, or findings of others. I felt far more confidence in the universality of each of my observations if I could find at least one other person who saw things the same way I did. I hope the reader will be the third.

Proverbs, maxims, and unnumbered but attributed quotations in the text were found in the following works of general reference: *A New Dictionary of Quotations on Historical Principles from Ancient and Modern Sources* (New York: Alfred Knopf, 1942); *A World Treasury of Proverbs from Twenty-Five Languages* (New York: Random House, 1946); *The Macmillan Book of Proverbs, Maxims, and Famous Phrases* (New York: Macmillan, 1948); *Dictionary of American Maxims* (New York: Philosophical Library, 1955); *A Treasury of Friendship* (New York: David McKay, 1957); *The Home Book of Quotations* (New York: Dodd, Mead & Co., 1958); *The Quotation Dictionary* (New York: Macmillan, 1962); *The Home Book of American Quotations* (New York: Dodd, Mead & Co., 1967).

Intimate Relations

PART ONE

Architecture

CHAPTER 1

Pickups

THE READER can best prepare himself for this chapter by recalling precisely how he first met those who now are or who once were his intimates. He will find that they fall into two groups: those, like his childhood friends, whom he has known so long that he can no longer recall how he first met them, and those who were at one time strangers to him and whom he can recall coming to know at a specific time and place. The metamorphosis of the small community into the mass society has inverted the relative frequencies of these two types of first encounters so much that the latter now vastly predominates over the former. The great amount of geographic mobility in gesellschaft, which at present in America occurs especially when a person has finished his high school and/or his college years, disperses those who have grown up with one another and brings together those who have not. Under the conditions of gesellschaft, then, the primal encounters between the previously unacquainted are a critical phase in personal relations.[1] In this chapter, I will focus on the *pickup*, in which strangers intend some degree of intimacy to be the outcome of their acquaintance, although I will also consider those first encounters that occur without such intimate intent. I will begin by considering the simplest (though most difficult to accomplish) case, in which one stranger's attempt to meet another

3

is unexpedited by anything in the situation itself, then continue by discriminating the situational factors that facilitate first encounters, and finally end by pointing out the problems that often prevent one stranger from meeting another. In other words, I will begin by considering the cases in which the probability of a successful pickup is unknown but is unlikely to be very high, then continue by analyzing the factors that raise the probability of success, and finally end by pointing out the factors that lower the probability of success.

UNFACILITATED FIRST ENCOUNTERS

In order for one stranger to pick up another successfully, he must accomplish six tasks: (1) determine whether a particular other possesses the *qualifiers* that make it worth his while to bother to begin; (2) determine whether the other is *cleared* for an encounter and a relationship; (3) find an *opener* that engages the other's attention; (4) discover an *integrating topic* that interests the other as well as himself; (5) project a *come-on self* that will induce the other to want to continue the present encounter and seek future ones; (6) finally, schedule a *second encounter*.

The inception of love relationships differs from the inception of friendships because potential lovers usually begin by being exclusively interested in each other's qualifiers (1), then seek to initiate (2) (3) and sustain (4) (5) (6) their interaction; whereas potential friends usually begin with interest in their integrating topics (4) and then notice with whom it is that they are interacting in so self-sustaining a manner.

1. One stranger will consider another to be profitable enough to attempt to pick up if the latter exhibits the *qualifiers* that make him a potential candidate for an intimate relation. Qualifiers may be manifest or latent. Manifest qualifiers, such as status symbols or physical beauty, are the visible aspects of a person that attract strangers. Manifest qualifiers are usually appreciated not so much in themselves but as the surface symptoms of less visible and more valuable personality characteristics. A particular cut and style of clothing implies that it would be worn

only by a particular cut and style of person.[2] These latent qualifiers of personality, such as perceptivity or sensitivity, are the
invisible aspects of a person that, when confirmed or discovered
during the course of the first encounter, entice strangers to attempt
to sustain the present interaction and to seek further interactions.

The attractive power of any particular qualifier may be broad-
banded, pulling in a wide variety of strangers, or narrow-banded,
pulling in only those with tastes for the exotic. The attractiveness
of a person is the sum total of all of his qualifiers.

2. Even though the stranger may have the appearance of a desirable candidate for an intimate relation, however, the person
who would like to pick him up must ascertain whether he is
cleared for one. Before the encounter begins, the potential accoster must determine whether the other is likely to be available for
a pickup. If the pretty girl a boy is watching embraces the person
sitting next to her, he may decide that she would probably prefer
not to meet him at the moment. The potential accoster must also
determine, during the course of the first encounter, whether the
other is likely to be available for a protracted relationship. If a
boy discovers that the girl with whom he has started a conversation is leaving town shortly or already has a lover or a husband,
he may decide that the encounter and their potential relationship
is not worth pursuing.

3. An *opener* is the subject pursued by one stranger who has
decided to approach another, not because he is interested in it,
but merely to gain the other's attention and to legitimize his being
within conversational (as well as mugging or raping) distance,
while allowing the latter time to gather his wits and examine his
assailant in order to see if he is safe and sane. The accoster will
continue the opener in order to keep the communication channels
open until he can find a topic of common interest and determine
whether it is both desirable and possible to continue the encounter. The following openers suffer from the fact that their intrinsic
interest is small and their viable lifetime is short. They seem as
uninspired in practice as they do in print. An accoster must use
them, however, if he can come up with none of the more felicitous openers discussed in the next section.

The most common opener consists of requesting a service or

providing one unasked. Thus, a person may ask for the time, a light, a cigarette, change, or directions, and he may provide such unrequested services as opening a door, returning a lost item, or helping to gather up spilled groceries. Unfortunately, a service usually does not lead easily onto the next phase of the encounter, the topic of common interest, and the time it takes is usually too short in which to find one. However, the willingness of the person approached to create unnecessary extensions of the service ("I hear they've been having a coin shortage") indicates his willingness to prolong the interaction. In Western societies, at least, the weather is often employed to open an encounter because it is always available, noncontroversial, and affects everyone ("Looks like rain"). But the weather is not usually an engrossing subject in itself (unless it is extreme or the strangers happen to be meteorologists), and it does not lead easily onto one. Again, however, the willingness of the person accosted to create unnecessary extensions of the opener ("Yes, it does. This is the rainiest summer we've had in years") indicates his willingness to prolong the interaction. Finally, the opener may consist of a direct request for an encounter ("Hello. May I join you?"). But this opener not only fails to solve the problem of the transition to the next encounter phase, it also reveals the accoster's desire for an encounter before he can decide whether one is possible, and it forces the accostee to accept or reject the proffered encounter before he has time to decide whether one is desirable.

4. If the opener has successfully gained the attention of the approached, the approacher can begin the search for topics of common interest, or *integrating topics,* which he usually attempts to generate by asking the other a series of questions. He may ask about residence ("Do you live around here?"), previous residence ("Where are you from?"), occupation ("What do you do?"), or present activities ("What are you doing here?"). The accoster hopes one of the accostee's replies will explode him into enthused spontaneity ("Oh! You lived in Berkeley. I used to live there too. Did you know...?"). If the accoster's flare-up sets off a chain reaction in the accostee, all sorts of integrating topics might then fall out ("Know her? She was my best friend. If you knew her,

you must also know..."). Those who are skilled in the early phases of personal relations know to ask open-ended questions rather than those that can be answered yes or no or in a single word, in order to encourage the accostee to reply at length, thereby providing the accoster with more raw materials to mine for more integrating topics ("What did you think of Berkeley?" is a more effective question than "Did you like Berkeley?"). The degree to which the accostee aids the accoster in the search for integrating topics indicates the former's desire to continue the encounter. Other measures of the accostee's interest in extending the interaction are the degree to which he replies to the accoster's searching questions and the degree to which he makes his own inquiries of the accoster in return. Regardless of the overt questions asked and answered, the covert question actually asked and answered is, "Do you want our encounter to continue?"

5. The approacher has only a brief interval at the beginning of a pickup in which to create that first impression on the basis of which the person he approaches determines the desirability of continuing the encounter. The approacher's opener and proposed integrating topics constitute that sample of his total personality from which the person he approaches will extrapolate a probable picture of him as a whole. The latter will then evaluate this picture relative to some ideal version of what an intimate of his should be like, and decide to continue or discontinue the encounter accordingly. For instance, he will consider the accosting stranger who makes one witty remark as likely to be a witty person; if he likes witty people, he will be favorably disposed to further their affair. Plutarch provides an example of someone who did:

> When Anacharsis came to Athens, he knocked at Solon's door and told him that he, being a stranger in town, would like to be his guest and become his friend. "It is better to make friends at home," said Solon. "Then you that are at home make friends with me." replied Anacharsis. Solon, somewhat surprised at the readiness of the repartee, received him kindly, and took him in for some time.[3]

The accoster, of course, is aware that the partial self he reveals is being generalized to his whole self. Consequently, he is likely to attempt to put forward only those of his features he hopes the other will like. His strategy is to keep the other from ending the encounter until he himself is able to show more of his self. In other words, he plays for time in order to provide the other with a larger sample of his self, one he feels is more indicative of his intricacy and worth. One tactic to keep the encounter going is to be agreeable, to seem to accept and approve of all of the other's responses. Thus a smile or nod can convince the other that he has finally found someone who appreciates him fully. (Those who are accomplished in the art of being agreeable even know how to disagree in order to reveal a higher consensus about common values, the importance of the topic, etc.)

This tactic is necessary to keep the other interesting, but it is not sufficient. The accoster must not only be receptive to the accostee's manifestations of self, he must also come on with a self of his own. If he wants the other to continue the encounter and seek future ones, he must discover a *come-on self* the other approves. He may, in fact, be forced to try on various come-on selves until he finds the appropriate one, as does Prevan in Pierre Choderlos de Laclos's eighteenth-century novel, *Dangerous Liaisons:*

> After the usual vague remarks, Prevan soon made himself master of the conversation and successively tried different tones to see which ones would please me. I refused that of sentiment, as not believing in it; I stopped his gaiety with my seriousness, because it seemed to me too light for a beginning; he fell back on delicate friendship, and it was under that commonplace flat that we began our reciprocal attack.[4]

The following two examples from J. P. Donleavy's *The Ginger Man* provide concrete illustrations of many of the themes presented in the rather abstract discussion above. In the first, the hero, Dangerfield, is in a shop buying cigarettes. The pickup attempt fails.

"A fine day, sir."

"Aye."

"Forgive the impertinence, sir, but are you the new gentleman living up on the rock?"

"O aye."

"I thought so, sir. And is it to your liking?"

"Splendid."

"That's fine, sir."

"Bye, bye now."[5]

In the second, a few lines later, Dangerfield is outside walking. The pickup attempt succeeds.

A girl approached.

"Mister, could I have a light?"

"Certainly."

Dangerfield striking a match, holding it to her cigarette.

"Thank you very much."

"You're welcome on a lovely evening like this."

"Yes, it is lovely."

"Quite breathtaking."

"Yes, it is breathtaking."

"Are you out for a walk?"

"Yes, my girl friend and I are walking."

"Around the head?"

"Yes, we like it. We've come out from Dublin."

"What do you do for a living?"

"Well, I guess I work."

"At what?"

"My girl friend and I work in Jacob's."

"Biscuit factory?"

"We label tins."

"You like it?"

"It's all right. Gets boring."

"Walk along with me."

"All right. I'll get my girl friend."[6]

Notice that in the first attempted pickup, Dangerfield's single-word replies to his accoster's questions and his refusal to aid the accoster's search for integrating topics indicates his wish to terminate the encounter; in the second, his more-than-necessary elaborations of his answers and his own exploratory questions indicate his wish to continue the encounter. Observe, too, that in the second pickup, he takes advantage of the other's request for a service to effect a topic transformation, first to the weather, then to the other's present activity, and finally to her occupation—all the while apparently calculating whether a pickup is possible, before ultimately deciding to petition overtly to prolong their encounter.

6. The last task a person must accomplish before he can consider his pickup of a stranger completely successful is to set up a *second encounter* or, at least, the opportunity for one. He must first obtain the other's name, for in giving his name the other gives symbolic consent to being open for future encounters. If their first meeting has gone extremely well, he may arrange for a second one on the spot ("How would you like to have dinner with me on Friday?"). Or he may obtain the other's telephone number or address in order to arrange for a specific meeting later. Or he may merely inquire about the other's routine ("Do you come here often?") and leave their next meeting to chance ("So do I. I'll look for you"). His chance of seeing and talking with the other again is augmented by the fact that from now on he can pick the other out of the passing crowd. Moreover, the integrating topics discovered in their first encounter provide good openings for their next encounter ("Hello. I've been thinking about what you said and it occurred to me that . . . ").

FACILITATORS

One stranger who wants to meet another usually need not create his pickup *ex nihil*, however. He will usually find their first encounter facilitated by a number of factors that supply qualifiers, clearances, openers, and integrating topics, as well as the means to induce the person he accosts to want to meet him.

The first of these facilitators consists of any *visible peculiarity* the person he hopes to meet happens to have. Thus, he may more easily pick up someone who has an extraordinary appearance. Unusual features are usually positive, as when a girl has flaming-red hair, although they may be negative if they are neither repulsive nor permanent, as when a man has a broken arm in a cast. He may also more easily pick up someone who carries or is accompanied by an extraordinary accouterment—unusual pieces of clothing, equipment, or accessories make pickups easier. A woman may walk a pink poodle on a leash as bait to ensnarl potential accosters, whom she can then reel in. Helen Gurley Brown suggests in *Sex and the Single Girl* that one good way for a girl to expedite getting herself picked up is to carry a controversial book:

> There are perfectly good ways of making it easy for a man to talk to *you*.... The thing to do is to give him something to start a conversation *about*.
>
> Carry a controversial book at all times—like Karl Marx's *Das Kapital* or *Lady Chatterley's Lover*. It's a perfectly simple way of saying, "I'm open to conversation," without having to start one.[7]

(Needless to say, a book that would inspire the most male pickup attempts would be *Sex and the Single Girl* itself.) Sometimes, extraordinary accouterments are even sold as such, advertised less for their intrinsic utility than for their extrinsic value of expediting pickups ("You meet the nicest people on a Honda" reads the copy on a billboard sign). Finally, he may more easily pick up someone who is engaged in an extraordinary activity. These often consist of usual activities done out of their usual contexts, as when someone is sketching the other customers in a public restaurant, or those done by a social category other than that which usually does them, as when adults fly kites.

The visible peculiarity of the person approached may serve as the qualifier that helps the approacher decide to initiate an encounter. It may serve this function especially if it is esoteric rather than merely extraordinary. If an *extraordinary* appearance, accouterment, or activity is one possessed or done by a few and recognized as such by many, then an *esoteric* appearance, accouterment, or activity is one possessed or done by a few and recognized as such by only a few. A person carrying Ouspensky's *In Search of the Miraculous*, for instance, is a person carrying an esoteric accouterment. Since only a few like-minded readers would carry so occult a work, anyone who knows about it is likely to consider anyone who displays it a candidate for a close relationship.

The visible peculiarity of the person approached may also help the approacher to determine whether the other is cleared for an encounter with him. Anyone who is building a boat in the front yard rather than in the back is simply begging to be approached and asked about it.

Furthermore, the visible peculiarity of the person accosted may serve as that *hook* the accoster can tie his opener onto. A person is usually preoccupied with his peculiarity. Thus, if the accoster comments on the clouds in the landscape a stranger is sketching ("Looks like they're about to produce rain"), he is likely to get an extensive reply ("You get that effect by juxtaposing light patches with dark ones"); whereas if the accoster comments on the clouds overhead ("Looks like it's about to rain"), he is likely to find that the other has not completely taken in what he has said ("Huh?"), forcing him to say again that which hardly merits being said once. Since these visible peculiarities are personal, they are also better openings than services or weather because they may themselves be integrating topics ("I've got one of those cycles too. Do you have any trouble with the generator? Mine keeps shorting out"), or they may lead into them easily ("How did you get that broken leg?" "Skiing." "Oh, I'm a ski bug, too. Where do you go?"). A common way an accoster uses the visible peculiarity as an opener is to remark that it is one of the best of its type ("That's a beautiful dress you're wearing"). This technique effects an early transition to possible integrating topics ("Where did you ever get it? I've been looking all over town for a dress like that"). And it serves to compliment and disarm the person whose visible peculiarity it is by implying that he or she must be one of the best, too, in order to have one. (No one, of course, ever opens to a stranger with: "My, what an ugly dress you're wearing. Tell me where you got it so I will never ever shop there.")

Finally, the accoster may utilize the accostee's visible peculiarity as a means to predispose the latter to want the encounter to continue. It may provide the accoster with just the opportunity he needs to appear agreeable and intelligent by allowing him to display his opinions and exhibit his expertise ("That's a great book you're reading. Did you see George Lichtheim's review of it in *Commentary?*")

The second facilitator for pickups is the *prior knowledge* an accoster has of the person he wants to accost. One way he may have acquired previous information is if the accostee is someone he has "seen around." Those with whom he has had prior visual contact are usually coinhabitants of adjacent territories (e.g., neighbors), work-place associates (e.g., colleagues), or service personnel (e.g., the waitress at the restaurant where he breakfasts). Countless studies have confirmed the common-sense observation that those who get married usually had lived in residential propinquity with one another.[8] "Prior knowledge" seems to be the intervening variable. Residential propinquity leads to many chance visual contacts that create the prior knowledge that facilitates the future pickup. The recent growth of "singles apartments," in which a building or an entire development is reserved for the unmarried in order to expedite their acquaintance under natural conditions, exploits the fact that propinquity breeds pickups.[9]

An accoster can decide whether it is desirable to initiate an encounter with someone he has seen around because he has already seen a sample of the latter's behavior. Moreover, if he knows the other has also seen him around, he will feel the pickup has an even greater chance of success because the latter will not be afraid of him and will be inclined to be nice to him since they are likely to see each other again. Also, he can more easily find an opener because he already knows something of the other's interests. In fact, he may even be able to open with an integrating topic ("How's your garden? I saw you working on it yesterday. What kind of fertilizer do you use? I can't seem to get anything to grow in mine").

An encounter between two strangers is especially expedited when those who have seen each other recurrently in one physical context see each other out of it. The context in which their previous repeated sightings have occurred now becomes a bond between them, and the fact that they are now out of it provides a natural opener and integrating topic ("What are you doing here? Who's minding your store?"). The more distant their new context is from their old, the more likely they will want to meet each other. Should unacquainted fellow college students chance to meet in a nearby city, they will often stop and talk with each other; should they chance to meet in Europe, they will often spend the day or more together.

Another way a person may have acquired previous information about someone he has never met is if the latter is someone he has "heard of."[10] Knowing another's reputation expedites a pickup in several ways. What an accoster knows about the other helps him to decide whether he would like to meet the latter, whether the latter would like to meet him, and what come-on self is likely to be most successful. Moreover, the accoster can open by showing he has possession of the other's name and thus is concerned with him in his personal particularity and not in one of his possible social categories, such as customer or victim ("Pardon me, but aren't you..?"). And should he know the other's interests, too, he will know where integrating topics are likely to be found.

This reputational form of prior knowledge has also been institutionalized recently. Computer dating services capitalize on the fact that they facilitate pickups by providing strangers with prior knowledge of each other. These services allow each stranger to assume that the other is open for an encounter because each bothered to apply to the service, provide each stranger with an opener by reference to the name of the service, and suggest to each stranger where to look for integrating topics insofar as both matched applicants are supposed to have similar interests. Furthermore, these dating services assure the strangers that they will like each other (except, of course, for the nagging doubt each may entertain that anyone who needs a dating service cannot be all that good).

Still another way he may have acquired previous information about the person he wants to accost is if they both visibly belong to the same social category. What he knows about himself insofar as he is a member of this category is also likely to hold true for other members. The most common visible criteria sorting individuals into social categories are age, sex, class, race, and size. Occasionally, religion (e.g., Amish), residence (e.g., Southerner), nationality (e.g., Scandinavian), sexual orientation (e.g., homosexual), and an increasingly important new classification that might be called "counterculturism" or "norm-averseness" (e.g., hippies) can also be visibly distinguished. Those belonging to the same social category are more likely than those belonging to different ones to have the same interests and problems and, therefore, integrating topics and desire to meet one another. Men and women, of course, are a special case. (Some people, though, who seek higher status or who, because they have not been properly socialized,[11] seek lower status seem to feel that social categories other than their own are much greener pastures in which to graze for intimates. Thus, some whites are drawn exclusively to blacks and vice versa, some Christians exclusively to Jews and vice versa, and so on.) However, since most of the above categories are so broad that intracategory variation is almost as great as intercategory variation, the meeting of two members of the same category is not facilitated very much by that fact alone, unless their particular common category happens to be a minority one relative to the social context in which they find themselves. In fact, not only does the context highlight one of the social categories of which an individual is a member, but as the context shifts, his dominant social category also shifts. In other words, the context determines how relevant common membership in a particular social category will be in motivating two individuals to initiate interaction. For example, though two teenage strangers are more likely to pick up each other in a high school than either is to pick up a strange adult there, they are much more likely to meet each other if they are the only two adolescents at a summer resort for adults. So, too, in the 1960s, strange hippies were less likely to greet each other in New York's East Village than in Dekalb, Illinois, but they were more likely to acknowledge each other than they were straight strangers in both places. Members of extremely small social categories, such as midgets, meet each other extremely easily because they are almost always likely to be in a minority, relative to their social context.

The third facilitator of pickups is the *setting* in which they occur. The surroundings in which someone sees a stranger may provide the clue to his character that seems to qualify him as a potential intimate. If someone has enough interest in experimental films or experimental food to go to an underground film festival or a macrobiotic restaurant, he is likely to have enough else in common with many of the other people he sees there to make a close relationship with them both desirable and possible.

Openings, too, may be provided by the setting, especially if some spectacle is occurring, such as a flaming public building or a urinating public drunk. Moreover, however much modern technology alienates man from man, its constant minor breakdowns provide excellent opportunities for pickups. Complaining about the automatic elevator's refusal to arrive just when the button is pushed or about the automatic soft-drink machine's failure to produce when the lever is pulled are excellent means of gaining the attention of anyone else waiting to avail himself of these fruits of civilization. In a similar but more extreme vein, the same major catastrophes that inconvenience or even destroy the lives of many persons expedite the personal relations of many others. For instance, the night the electricity failed in the Northeast is said to have turned on countless close relationships. In his study of disasters, Tamotsu Shibutaini found that

> people who undergo together a derangement of their way of life are drawn together.... Conventional barriers to social intercourse disappear, and new communication channels develop spontaneously. Strangers talk freely to one another, and everyone joins in a common spirit of camaraderie."¹²

This camaraderie can occur because the common desire of the victims for information about the genesis, extent, and termination of the disaster provides them with openers' and integrating topics, while their common social category of "human being" suddenly overrides their disjunctive ones.

Necessity is the mother of intimacy in other ways as well. People immobilized together at too close a distance for too long a time may find it uncomfortable to remain silent (since, as we shall see in Chapter 3, only the very intimate can tolerate silence under these conditions). In fact, Georg Simmel points out that it is only relatively recently that strangers have been forced to spend long periods near each other in silence: "Before the appearance of omnibuses, railroads, and street cars in the nineteenth century, men were not in a situation where for periods of minutes or hours they could or must look at each other without talking to one another."[13] Strangers are lightly anchored near each other when they are sitting in a lounge, on a park bench, or in a cafeteria, or when they are standing on a long line. Strangers are heavily anchored near each other by accident, as in a stuck elevator or a stalled subway, or by design, as in a prison or a mental hospital. But however their proximate anchoring occurs, they are "all in the same boat" and hence have little to lose and much to gain by meeting their shipmates.

Furthermore, the setting in which someone sees a stranger he wants to meet may help the former determine whether the latter is available to meet him. Some ecological areas are literally known as "pickup places." Anyone found in certain bars, cafeterias, parks, beaches, or swimming pools is automatically cleared as a potential pickup. Some total environments, like ships and country hotels, and some temporary environments, like rock concerts and be-ins, oblige their inhabitants to be open to meet anyone who wants to meet them. Since settings that require those in them to lower their usual reserve about meeting others so facilitate pickups by giving potential accosters more courage to accost, they have been institutionaliized in parties, in college mixers, and, recently, in "singles clubs":

> Singles clubs fall very roughly into two categories. The first is a slightly more sophisticated version of the college mixer. These clubs primarily provide a place for singles to

meet, in a social, party-like atmosphere. The second kind
of club attempts to involve singles in group activities—
from discussions to outings—and let "mixing" develop
naturally.[14]

In other words, the first of these clubs clears everyone for interaction, whereas the second also provides everyone with integrating
topics.

Fourth, the meeting of strangers is facilitated if both of them
belong to the same institution or association and encounter each
other within it. The fact that they share common interests and
problems is both a cause and effect of their belonging to the same
organization. These common interests and problems enhance the
probability that they will want to meet each other and enhance
their ability to do so by providing natural openers and integrating
topics ("Did you go to English class today? I couldn't make it.
Did I miss anything important?"). Since strangers who belong to
the same institution or association are often expected or even required to meet each other, their first encounter is not looked upon
as a pickup at all, though I can find no other term in English that
is applied to it ("I don't know how we first met. He was always
around when I was. I just 'met' him, that's all").

Finally, it is also not called a pickup when a third person helps
two strangers to meet; a pickup, it seems, is essentially a do-it-yourself proposition. But in this case the term "introduction" is commonly applied and contrasted with "pickup." The *catalytic person,*
who brings two strangers together and holds them together in
interaction with each other until they can sustain it by themselves,
facilitates their potential relationship in several ways. He helps
each stranger determine whether he wants to meet the other because he usually introduces only those he feels will like each
other; his knowledge of their backgrounds implies, at the very
least, that each is a safe person with whom to be acquainted. Continuing her advice on how to meet men, Helen Gurley Brown
suggests:

> Getting a shiny gift-wrapped male from a friend is a
> relatively painless way to meet him. It's super-respectable,

even innocent. It was their idea you go together, wasn't it? You can even convince yourself that you are doing them a favor.

Also a friend-sponsored man spares you those painful mid-romance discoveries. If a find is represented as a single, practicing architect, he has usually put up a few buildings and files a separate tax return. Contrast him with the fascinating real estate magnate you meet on the plane who, it turns out, actually manages a six-unit motel with his wife. (It can take *weeks* to unscramble a pack of lies like his.)[15]

The catalytic person also provides the strangers with an opener, for his introduction of one to the other is itself usually enough to get the latter's attention (it's embarrassing if it does not). His résumé of both of their backgrounds may lead to integrating topics ("Oh, so you went to the University of Chicago. Did you ever take a class from...?"). And since the catalytic person knows both strangers, he has some idea what interests they have in common, and can throw out one of these as a possible integrating topic. Even if one of the strangers fails to pick up on his offering, however, he can still keep the ball rolling by continually tossing out other topics he feels are likely to interest them.

The catalytic person, in fact, need not be physically present at the introduction. As a synthesizing agent, he has the power to unite strangers at a distance by writing one of them a letter of introduction to the other, or by telling one to look up the other. In both of these cases, he provides some likelihood that both strangers will want to get to know each other, an opener ("Pardon me. You're X, aren't you? Your friend Y told me to look you up when I got to town"), and an integrating topic ("Just how is old Y? I haven't seen him in years").

Nearly everyone who has been settled in a place for a time can function as a catalytic person. If a newly arrived stranger can manage to meet just one resident on his own, he can easily and rapidly increase the number of people he knows, for the person he has met will introduce him to his own intimates, such as his wife or girl friend, his friends, his roommates, and his relatives.

Some catalytic people, though, can expand a stranger's social horizons far more widely than others. So-called "friendly people" are especially useful for a stranger to meet, for they are gatekeepers to large herds of acquaintances. And besides these semiprofessional catalytic people, there are true professional ones, like matchmakers and those who run introduction services.[16]

A qualification: I have considered these facilitators predominantly from the point of view of the passive person for whom they are already in place. However, those skilled at being picked up and those skilled at picking up can create the opportunities that must be handed to those less adept. One man's given is another man's taken. For instance, since certain settings have the reputation of being pickup places, individuals often go to these places precisely to pick up or be picked up. And since institutions and associations expedite the meetings of their members, individuals often join them expressly to meet others. Helen Gurley Brown has already provided some examples of how a girl can actively encourage others to pick her up. A *New York Times* article on bicycling in Central Park suggests others:

> "Bicycling's a much nicer way to find men than hanging around the 'in' East Side bars like Maxwell's Plum or Friday's," said Judy Bell, a blond secretary. "There's something innocent about riding a bike that seems to appeal to men."
>
> To help attract men, some girls let air out of their tires or fall off their bicycles.
>
> "I 'fell' off my bike in front of Lincoln Center," 23-year-old Nancy Bayley said. "I ruined my stockings, but five men asked me out. One was a cellist. How else could I have met a cellist?"[17]

Conversely, it is not hard to come up with many examples of how a male Casanova can actively seduce a pretty stranger into her fatal first hello. He can always carry matches in order to be able to offer to light the cigarette of any girl in his vicinity who takes one out. He can make up an unusual but apparently harmless service he needs from a girl that requires a protracted encounter to perform ("Excuse me. I'm a graduate student in sociology writing my dissertation on how women meet men. I wonder if I could take some of your time to interview you about your pickup experiences"). He can create in her a need for a service he can then perform, as when he pickpockets the handkerchief out of her purse in order to be able to return it. He can pretend each has prior knowledge of the other ("Haven't we met somewhere before?"). He can get himself properly introduced by first picking up one of her less intimidating friends. And, if he is sufficiently determined, he can set off a disaster (like capsizing her canoe) in order to have the opportunity of rescuing her.

COMPLICATIONS

Just as there are characteristics of a stranger that may qualify him for a potential intimacy, so there are those, like low status or ugliness, that may disqualify him. *Disqualifiers* are extremely important at the beginning of a potentially intimate relationship in determining its future course. Since intimacy entails a merger of selves (see Chapter 6), a person may fear that his own essential being would become contaminated if he were to become intimate with someone he feels to be unqualified—something loneliness might nevertheless drive him to consider.

Analogously with qualifiers, disqualifiers, may be manifest or latent, universally repulsive or particularly repulsive for those with specific distastes. An extreme, universally repulsive, manifest disqualifier is called a *stigma*, which may be defined as a visible peculiarity of an individual that makes it harder for him to meet, or be met by, the average person as a potential personal relation. A paraplegic girl, for instance, is not likely to have as much social success as her normal sisters in getting herself picked up. Another interesting kind of disqualifier is the *pair stigma*, which may be defined as a visible defect that is not inherent in either individual himself but would be inherent in their potential intimate relation. Pairs of people who differ extremely on any social-sort ing criterion are usually stigmatized as a couple. Neither a boy who is 5'5" nor a girl who is 5'11" is stigmatized in themselves, but they usually cannot be seen together without drawing amused stares. Similarly, neither a 28-year-old man nor a 12-year-old girl is stigmatized for that reason alone, but they usually cannot carry on their affair in public.[18]

One stranger who is about to approach another may discover that the latter is accompanied by a disqualifying accouterment that indicates him to be the sort of person with whom the former would not get on. The life-long Democrat is not likely to strike up a conversation with the person sitting next to him who is wearing a Republican campaign button. Accouterments may also function as "occupied signs," telling others that the person who flashes them has been "taken" and is not cleared at the moment for new intimate relations—regardless of how qualified he may appear. A male college student is not likely to try to pick up the pretty coed sitting next to him in class if he sees a wedding ring on her finger. Moreover, one stranger who is about to approach another may discover that the latter is engaged in an activity that requires his total concentration and hence signifies that at the moment he does not want to be disturbed. If a man who is about to speak to the pretty girl ahead of him in line at the bank discovers that she has a gun on the teller whom she is quietly robbing, he is likely to have second thoughts as to whether this is the appropriate time to attempt to pick her up—or whether he wants to pick her up at all.

His prior knowledge of the other might suggest that the other is not for him. He may have seen the other behaving in a way that disgusted him; he may have seen the other harshly reject someone who had attempted a pickup. He may have heard that the other has a bad reputation for the way he conducts his personal relations: that he flirts, that he kisses and runs, that he exploits his mistresses, that he is untrustworthy, or that he has had several marriages. He may expect that a relationship with a member of the other's social category would not work out. They may have nothing in common, consequently, no integrating topics.[19] Or he may feel that a member of that social category would not particularly want to meet him. The reticent middle-aged homosexual who would like to meet the muscular members of a local motorcycle gang is likely to content himself with only a sigh. ("My type doesn't like me.") Even if two strangers belong to the same social category, they may not want to meet if they do not like the part of their identity given by this common category membership. For instance, blacks who are trying to pass as whites, Jews who have converted, and those who are social climbers prefer not to associate with their own kind.

The setting itself may make it difficult to meet. Although an interesting spectacle to which the strangers are oriented will facilitate their meeting, as we have seen, an extremely engrossing spectacle, such as a concert or a baseball game, will not—at least during the intervals when involvement is at a high pitch. It is not a good idea to try to pick up a stranger in the middle of a triple concerto or a triple play, although these do provide excellent openers and integrating topics after they are over. The setting, moreover, may limit the amount of time the strangers can spend together, making it too brief an interval for them to bother to pick up one another. It is hardly worth opening with the stranger who is on the down escalator while you are passing him on the up.

Furthermore, large parties and other institutionalized social gatherings often so overwhelm their participants with encounters with strangers that they seem to hinder the search for intimates more than they help. As the partygoers are expected to take on all comers in interaction, a particular kind of come-on self—an impervious, having-a-good-time, party personality—often grows over their essential nature. Perhaps the psyche, drawing upon the biological roots of its wisdom, in self-defense tends to callous the part of itself that is being rubbed raw. Whatever the cause, since this come-on self is likely to bear little relationship to one's total self, it not only allows no lead-in to one's total self, but it also makes the evaluation of potential intimates more difficult.

The institutions of which an individual is a member may hinder his meeting potential intimates by limiting their availability. Institutions are considered "ingrown"—no longer breeding grounds for personal relations—when all of their members have used up one another's intimacy potential and can find no new recruits for possible personal relations. The office secretary may bemoan the fact that she does not like any of the eligible men in her department and that those she does like are married. Members of ingrown institutions seem to languish because they have only pseudointimate associations with those for whom they are less than suited. In other words, their relationships consist solely of the outer physical behavior of intimates without any inner psychological correlative. One of the main sources of stress for someone incarcerated in a total institution is the limitation on the number of potential intimates available. An inmate will find it as easy to exhaust everyone inside as he will find it difficult to meet anyone outside.

Finally, the catalytic people a stranger has met may turn out to be *dead ends*. Having been introduced to everyone they know, he may still find himself without potential intimates and be back where he started, having to seek them again on his own. On the other side, the attractive power of a potential pickup might be neutralized by any *anticatalytic people* in the vicinity. Helen Gurley Brown cautions a woman that those who accompany her may make it harder for her to get picked up:

> Don't always move in a safe, sane little band of girls. One girl alone on a beach towel is a man attracter.... Four girls together are a stop signal to flirtation. Eight girls together murder it unless a roving volleyball team comes along looking for a game.[20]

The companions of the person who is picked up may feel envious that they themselves were not thought attractive enough to be picked up; accordingly, they may demand their share of the accoster's attention. Thus, the unattractive friend of a pretty girl may make pointed comments to the male accoster who obviously prefers the pretty girl to her. These companions may feel that the picked-up person is their property, and keep reminding him of his obligations. Thus, the unattractive friend may keep reminding the pretty girl who is talking enthusiastically to the handsome stranger that it is late and that they have to go.[21]

A person can actively use these disfacilitators to avoid being picked up in the same way that he can actively use facilitators to encourage an accost. On-duty waitresses often wear wedding rings in order to keep from having to repel the advances of customers; off-duty professors often attempt to look busy when they are approached for friendship by forward students.

All the above items either disqualify an individual from being a potential intimate or hinder his being picked up, just as all the items listed in the preceding section either qualify him as a potential intimate or facilitate his being picked up. Since a failed pickup is likely to be a traumatic event for all concerned, a potential accoster who notices a feature of the situation that might make his pickup more difficult is not likely to begin what he expects is likely to fail.

A pickup fails when the accoster can find no integrating topics to interest the person he approaches and finds it degrading to continue to search for them. Pickup failure occurs almost always because the person accosted does not encourage or actually discourages the accoster. In this case, the accoster has been rejected or "shot down." But if he must break off the encounter because he cannot get it moving, he is admitting that he has failed to prove himself to be a person worth knowing. And since the other knows him only by the come-on self he has shown, the other will extrapolate his failure in initial interaction to his inadequacy in total personality. The stranger whose first attempt to meet another miscarries has likely spoiled himself forever as a potential intimate for the other; in any event he has made any future attempt on his part to pick up the other much more difficult.

Those who need their self-esteem constantly reaffirmed by others will transform their failure in the other's eyes into a failure in their own. They will attribute the fact that they have flunked a specific interaction test to a general flaw in their own essential being, and thus suffer for it more than the intrinsic nature of the case would seem to merit. The *shy* are those who are afraid that their first encounter with a stranger will be a fiasco; consequently, it often is, for their integrating topics are contrived and forced, as they are less concerned with the topic than with its coming off. The shy are to be contrasted with the *friendly*, who do not consider the possibility that their first encounter may end badly; consequently, it less often does, for they can come up with integrating topics more easily. And even if their pickup fails, the fact that they are damaged in another's eyes does not bother them as much, since they seem to be able to sustain their self-esteem without outside support.

Since the shy fear their pickups will fail, they go to great lengths to convince themselves that they do not want to attempt to pick up a stranger. Rather than make a faulty first impression, they would make no first impression at all. They look for what could possibly go wrong with the pickup, and then withdraw at the first disfacilitator they see or imagine. Conversely, since the friendly feel their pickups will succeed, they try to convince themselves that there is opportunity for a pickup whenever they see a stranger. They look for what could possibly go right with the pickup, and advance at the first facilitator they see or imagine. Coming upon an attractive person who is an apparently well-qualified candidate for intimacy, the immediate reaction of a friendly person is likely to be, "There's no harm in trying, and even if that person is already going with someone, it might be interesting for us to talk"; whereas the immediate reaction of a shy person is likely to be, "If a person that good-looking isn't already going with someone, there must be something wrong. Besides, it's late. I think I'll go home."

(Let me note here parenthetically that the success of a pickup is facilitated or hindered by many of the same characteristics of the person accosting as those of the person accosted. Symbols of high status or handsomeness may qualify a person as an acceptable accoster for a large number of accostees; symbols of low status or ugliness may disqualify him as an acceptable accoster for a large number of accostees; his accouterments or his reputation might also qualify or disqualify him, etc.)

For his part, the person accosted is likely to be aware that the failure of the person accosting to pick him up may damage the latter's self-esteem. Depending on the accostee's own character,

momentary mood, and immediate impression of the accoster, he
will attempt either to intensify or to diminish the damage. The
accostee can take a hard line with his accoster and put him down
when he tries to pick him up. Thus, an accostee who is an interpersonal "hawk" may be rude: he may ignore his accoster's opening, give short, sharp replies to his accoster's questions, or even
tell the accoster that he is disgusting and should go away and
stop bothering him. The accostee may also take a soft line with
his accoster, in order to cushion his collapse when he discovers
that he cannot pick him up. Thus, an accostee who is an interpersonal "dove" may be polite: he may respond neither too much nor
too little to the other's openers and integrating topics, or he may
even bring up a few integrating topics on his own, hinting at the
same time that he does not want the encounter, and especially the
relationship, to continue. For instance, he may look at his watch,
say he is late for an appointment, and leave, leaving his accoster
wondering whether there really was an appointment or if it was
merely a polite way of nipping any blooming relationship in the
bud. The very ambiguity of the terms in which the accostee casts
his rejection helps the accoster salvage his self-esteem; by coating
his thorn of rebuff with the puff of politeness, the accostee signifies that he still respects the accoster as person even while refusing him as an intimate. But should the accostee's cues be too
subtle, his accoster may not get the hint and take his politeness
for encouragement, forcing the accostee to repel his accoster more
blatantly.

On the other side, the accoster can "come on strong," pointedly
ignoring the accostee's polite attempts to dissuade him from the
pickup, and then attempting to override the rude ones to which
the accostee is eventually forced to resort. Or he can "come on
weak," backing away at the first bat of an eye ("You wouldn't
want to talk to a lonely old man like me, would you?"). How one
comes on to a stranger and how a stranger turns oncomers off is
correlated with the class, ethnicity, or race of each stranger and
the combination of both. It is often enthralling to observe, from
the sociological perspective at least, lower class black men, who

usually come on strong, attempt to pickup liberal middle class white women, who usually are only capable of putting off such accosters politely.

It is harder to succeed in pickups of potential love relations than in first encounters of potential friendships for three reasons.

First, love relations tend to be based on both the manifest qualifiers of appearance and the latent qualifiers of personality, whereas friendships tend to be based solely on the latent qualifiers of personality. Consequently, potential lovers are more likely than potential friends to be upset when manifest qualifiers turn out to be antithetical to latent ones. Those who are attractive on the surface often turn out to be repulsive underneath; conversely, those who repel at first appearance often turn out to have a magnetic personality. Unfortunately, this inconsistency of the exteriors with the interiors of pickups for potential love affairs sometimes results, on the one hand, in our getting stuck in encounters and relationships with those we do not like and, on the other hand, in our passing by encounters and relationships with those we might like. In general, some of the greatest tragedies in love relations stem from the fact that the same person can possess both extreme qualifiers *and* extreme disqualifiers.

Second, each party may presume a different potential for their association. The boy may wish to become a lover; the girl may wish to have a friend. Cross-sex first encounters are less likely to be spontaneous and more likely to be awkward than same-sex first encounters, because each party is less certain of the other party's intentions for their potential relationship. Moreover, cross-sex first encounters are more likely to be unsuccessful than same-sex first encounters because love relations are *univalent* (unlike friendships, which are *multivalent*), and either party may announce that his one opening is closed. A girl might inform the boy who would like to become her lover that her slot for lovers is filled, though she still has some vacancies left for friends. Although one party can bring up a *disintegrating topic* ("My boyfriend says...") anytime during the course of the first encounter, thus destroying the potential of the relationship for the other party, the party of the first part will usually indicate lack of clearance for a relationship when the party of the second part attempts to arrange a second encounter ("I'm sorry. I can't go out with you. I already have a boy friend").[22]

Finally, as we shall see further in Chapter 6, intimate relations may reach the level of *exclusiveness* in which both intimates are cut off from large segments of their present social network and from future potentially intimate relationships with others. An outcome of such exclusiveness is much more common in cross-sex than in same-sex relations. When one sperm reaches an egg and fertilizes it, a membrane immediately forms around the egg, blocking the entrance of any other sperm. Perhaps this biological analogy of social processes is more than a mere analogy; perhaps not. In any event, it is this anticipated constriction of one's social circle, social contacts, and, ultimately (as we shall see), social self that often makes the first encounters of potential love relationships so uneasy and anxious an experience.

In this chapter, the *probability* dimension of an intimate relation has been considered and the first major force uncovered that transforms isolated individuals into interlinked intimates: *their potential (or high probability) to form a closer association.* The precise referent of this potential varies with the stage of the relationship. The potential of strangers to become acquainted, immediately manifested in their personal and situational aspects, draws them into seeking their first encounter. The potential of acquaintances to become intimate, latently discovered in their integrating topics during their initial meeting(s), draws them into seeking further encounters and conjunctive forces. And the potential of intimates to remain intimates, revealed as their relation evolves, draws them into seeking to sustain the higher-order forces that hold them together.

CHAPTER 2

Let's Get Together

STRANGERS, having met, become acquaintances. Acquaintances who feel they might become intimates must meet again. They must establish their continued encounters on a regular basis. In modern society these future meetings may not be assumed, they must be arranged. Over 350 years ago, Francis Bacon observed, "*Magna civitas, magna solitudo* [A great town is a great solitude]: because in a great town friends are scattered; so that there is not that fellowship, for the most part, which is in less neighbourhoods."[1] The dispersal of potential intimates in advanced societies has made it a relatively difficult conscious accomplishment for those who wish to congregate to contrive their corporeal copresence.

There are two aspects of corporeal copresence: a *kinematic* component, consisting of coming together physically, and a *phenomenological* component, consisting of coming together perceptually. The latter includes each individual's orientation to the other's physical location both when they are apart and when they are together.

In this chapter, I will consider the whole cycle of "being together" and "being apart" that acquaintances who are becoming intimates set up. Specifically, I will treat the impulses that push an individual to seek out others (including the techniques by which he actually arranges his meetings with them), the ways he merges into an encounter with them when he meets them, and the impulses that eventually pressure him to part from them again. I will show how increasing intimacy facilitates every stage of this process of coming together and going apart. Finally, in the Complications section, I will consider how this cycle of copresence intimates construct can be broken up by forces beyond their control.

COMING TOGETHER

Why do individuals want to be together? The answer to this seemingly simple question is not so obvious as it appears. I will not presume to enumerate all of the reasons that impel one person to seek out others, but will consider here only four: the impulse to receive stimulation; the impulse to express experiences; the impulse to assert self; and the impulse to enhance the enjoyment of certain activities. (In the following chapters, I will implicitly be considering in addition to these mundane causes more important reasons why individuals want to come together, such as the need for favors and the urge for union.) As acquaintances become more intimate, they can better enable each other to act on these impulses.

One reason an individual is impelled to seek out others is based on the fact that he sometimes finds he needs a certain amount of external stimulation and will want to move toward whatever source will provide it. Humans are *stimulotropic* in the same way that some plants are heliotropic: they continually orient themselves toward a source of stimulation in the same way certain plants continually orient themselves toward the sun. A person may wish to seek out those who will serve him as alternative transmitters of the stimulation he cannot find in his immediate environment. His immediate spatial surroundings may not be able to stimulate him because he is overly familiar with them or because they themselves are overly repetitive. He may also move through periods of time in which the volume of external stimulation is decreased. When much of the mass media shuts down— after midnight and Sundays and summers—or when there are breaks in his work—cigarette, coffee, lunch, an hour between classes—there come into his hands fragments of time that are too small to use for many activities. He may wish to transform his acquaintances into intimates who will become for him portable generators of stimuli, ready to be turned on at almost any time in almost any place.

Conversely, it is an essential characteristic of *loneliness* that an individual is unable to pass the time by himself and has no intimate available to help him do so.

Another reason an individual is impelled to seek out others is based on the fact that he needs a receptacle into which to spill the surplus emotional residue of private experience that has accumulated in him. He may wish to transform his acquaintances into intimates who will help him to drain off these excess emotions. Bacon puts it this way:

> A principal fruit of friendship is the ease and discharge of the fullness and swellings of the heart, which passions of all kinds do cause and induce ... but no receipt openeth the heart, but a true friend; to whom you may impart griefs, joys, fears, hopes, suspicions, counsels, and whatsoever lieth upon the heart to oppress it, in a kind of civil shrift or confession.[2]

Since private experiences are often either pleasurable or painful, an individual will desire to seek out someone who can increase his enjoyment of the former and decrease his discomfort from the latter. Bacon continues:

> This communicating of a man's self to his friends works two contrary effects; for it redoubleth joys, and cutteth griefs in halfs. For there is no man that imparteth his joys to his friend, but he joyeth the more; and no man that imparteth his griefs to his friend, but he grieveth the less.[3]

On the one hand, an intimate can not only heighten an individual's pleasure but also extend his ephemeral enjoyment beyond the natural mortality point of its usual arc. Thus the Englishman William Cowper's satiric refutation of the Frenchman La Bruyère's aphoristic affirmation of solitude:

> I praise the Frenchman, his remark was shrewd—
> "How sweet, how passing sweet is solitude!"
> But grant me still a friend in my retreat
> Whom I may whisper—Solitude is sweet.

On the other hand, an intimate can not only moderate an individual's pain, he can also end it sooner. Thus, the reader of this book, coming upon a passage that displeases him, may seek out his intimates in order to vent his annoyance by reciting to them the offending passage together with his criticism of it. By telling the anecdotes that crystallize his private experiences, an individual is charging his intimate with stimulation at the same time that he is discharging his own excitement.

Conversely, it is another essential characteristic of *loneliness* that an individual is unable to sustain his private pleasures or to relieve his private pains by himself, and is unable to find an intimate who is willing to help him do so.

(Holidays, especially Thanksgiving and Christmas, are particularly bleak days for the solitary individual. He is supposed to be full of cheer at the same time that he is actually empty of those alternative sources of stimulation that make life tolerable for the lonely—e.g., most public places close down. The constant reminders that they are such joyous occasions for those who are with their intimates makes them into such miserable occasions for those who have no intimates to be with. It is hard to be festive alone.)

A third reason an individual is impelled to seek out others is that the human self must continually prove itself against something. The self is maintained by withstanding or overcoming opposition, especially the opposition of other selves.[4] Just as the body can maintain its physical tone only through constant exercise against the resistant natural environment, so the self can maintain its psychological tone only through constant interaction with the resistant social environment. A person does not feel he is in complete control of his self unless he can maintain himself not merely in a contest in his imagination, but in a workout against the real social world. Only by asserting and defending one's particular self-embodiments against the armor and assaults of others—arguing ideas, exhibiting clothing and possessions, etc.—can one feel self-possessed. An individual may wish to transform his acquaintances into intimates who will stand against him this way whenever he asserts his self.

Conversely, it is an essential characteristic of *loneliness* that the self begins to deteriorate when it can find no intimate against which to exercise and must make do with such autodialectical activities as talking to oneself, admiring oneself in the mirror, etc. Too many rounds of solitary shadowboxing will eventually incapacitate the self as well as the body for interaction with others when one gets into the ring of an actual encounter with them at long last.

These three impulses provide the reasons individuals want to seek each other out for what I will call a *pure encounter*,[5] in which they are oriented predominantly to each other, as they are when they are only talking. It is useful to distinguish a pure encounter from a *common activity*, in which they are oriented predominantly to something outside their mutual interaction, as they are when they go bowling together. (Of course, they may also pursue intermediate activities, such as driving in the country, in which they shift back and forth from internal to external orientations.)

A fourth reason an individual is impelled to seek out others is based on the fact that he would like to participate in certain activities that are both more feasible and more enjoyable when undertaken with others. He may wish to transform his acquaintances into intimates who will engage in these common activities with him. Aristotle thought it was worth noting that:

> Every man wishes to share with his friends that occupation, whatever it may be, which forms for him the essence and aim of his existence. So we find friends who drink together, and others who dice together, while yet others go in together for physical training, hunting or

> philosophy. Each set spend their time in one another's company following the pursuit which makes the great pleasure of their lives. And their wish is to be always with their friends, they do what these do and take part with them in those pursuits to the best of their ability.[6]

There are some activities, such as tennis or bridge, that an individual may personally enjoy but that cannot be done alone. Although he may find acquaintances and strangers to help him enjoy himself while he engages in these activities ("Tennis anyone?" "Anyone want to be a fourth for bridge?"), he is likely to conceive of his set of intimates as stocking a *game preserve* of partners who are almost always available. There are other activities, such as going to a movie or a play, in which an individual can participate alone, but which are much more enjoyable when he engages in them in conjunction with his intimates, who can enhance the pleasure of common activities by being there as they can extend the pleasure of single activities by listening to a description of them. In front of any common source of satisfaction— the cosmic or the comic, the Grand Canyon or Lenny Bruce—the smile on the face of each intimate as he turns toward the other provides positive feedback for the beatitude of both. Consequently, whenever an individual has an opportunity to engage in activities that are likely to be pleasurable, such as going to entertainments or traveling, he will usually wish to seek out his intimates to accompany him.

Conversely, it is a fourth essential characteristic of *loneliness* that an individual is unable to engage in or to enjoy certain activities on his own or to find an intimate who is willing to help him do so:

> The lack a single person feels most acutely is when he leaves his group to go off somewhere on a trip.... It can occur in front of a castle, on the quiet deck of a boat going up the Rhine, or on any overlook anywhere, looking at a sunset. Faced with such a sight, the natural tendency is to want to turn to someone to say, "Isn't that beautiful!" and to enjoy it together. And when you turn, there isn't anyone there.[7]

Having decided to meet each other for the foregoing reasons, individuals must *make arrangements* to alter their movements in order to come to occupy the same space at the same time. As they become more intimate, such arrangements become easier.

I will use the term *date* to refer to those meetings with each other that both plan. To make a date with another is to negotiate a time to meet that both can mesh with their individual schedules with a minimum of modification ("Pick you up at seven?" "Too early. I couldn't be ready by then. Eight?" "Seven-thirty." "OK"). They usually choose a time when their meeting will be separated temporally from their meetings with others. Dates with acquaintances and intimates, however, differ from appointments with role-relations. Though both usually involve temporal segregation from others, the former are usually relatively open-ended in regard to their duration, whereas the latter are usually temporally bounded, often by another appointment.

Individuals who anticipate that they will want to see each other again after an interval of time, during which they expect those psychological pressures that cause them to want to meet each other again to reaccumulate, often make a date for their next encounter during a phase of their last—usually, just before the final phase in which they terminate their meeting. Increasing intimacy facilitates date-making insofar as each becomes more certain the other wants to make one. Consequently, he can be more specific about when he would like their next meeting to take place (Compare "I'll meet you for lunch on Thursday" with "I'll be around Thursday—maybe I'll see you then" with "See you around").

Those who cannot pinpoint their next reunion during their last union may later arrange it by telephone. Telephones have become so indispensable a way of setting up rendezvous in modern society that one wonders how copresence was arranged before they were invented. Letters, obviously, played a more important role in setting up encounters in the past than they do today,[8] though letters require a relatively large time interval between the plan to meet and its execution. Presumably, members of the lower classes who desired to meet were reduced either to making arrangements during their last encounter or to living within shouting distance from one another ("Yoo-hoo, Mrs. Bloom . . . "). The upper classes could send servants back and forth carrying messages—what would Shakespeare have done without these human telephones who often garbled their transmissions?—and, after the late eighteenth century, visiting cards.[9]

When both do not make mutual plans to meet, one may still make plans to meet the other. On the one hand, he can attempt to arrange an encounter actively by looking for the other. To look for someone is to insert oneself behind his possible course of movements and then to travel ahead on this course faster than he does, thus overtaking him ("He just left. You'll find him at . . . "). As each acquaintance becomes more familiar with the other's routine movements, the more he knows where there is a good chance the other may be found.

On the other hand, he can attempt to arrange an encounter passively by making himself available to the other. To make oneself available to another is to insert oneself ahead of his possible course of movements and then to wait until he catches up. An individual often prefers to make himself available to another rather than to look for him in order not to disturb him if he is busy, and to let him be the one to decide whether or not to initiate the encounter. This technique is particularly preferred by those who are not yet certain of the possibility of increasing intimacy with a particular acquaintance, for an individual indicates his interest in intimacy with another whenever he goes *out of his way* to initiate interaction with him. Someone who does not yet want to indicate this interest will prefer not to appear to be seeking out the other intentionally, but merely to appear to be running into the other by chance. In this way, he forces the Fates to bear the onus of his own initiative.

The usual meeting places of individuals have alternated between public and private. From the fifteenth century through the seventeenth, they met in what Philippe Ariès calls "big houses"— the semipublic places in which everyone lived. In seventeenth-century France, however, the individual began to promenade on certain public streets and squares at certain times in order to maximize the likelihood of encountering his acquaintances and intimates.[10] (Although dying out in its original form, this practice continues today in small towns in Europe and in the Sunday-afternoon strolls through the local greenery and squares that townspeople in this country often take. In a somewhat altered form, promenading is flourishing among the young today. College students and counterculture types often parade back and forth along streets "where the action is," in hopes of running into their acquaintances and intimates. High school students seem to do their promenading in automobiles as they drive back and forth along the "main drag.") In early eighteenth-century England, individuals met in the more than 2,000 public coffee houses of London; in late eighteenth-century France, they met in private salons. At the end of the eighteenth century, a person also had "at-home days," times at which he announced he would receive callers in private. (At-home days seem to have been to intimates then what office hours are to role-relations now.) By the nineteenth century, individuals again began to frequent public places—or, as we say today, to "hang out." Unlike the promenaders, who move about, the habitués fix themselves in one locale and wait for their acquaintances and intimates, who also frequent the same locale, to join them. In Romance-language countries, the outdoor café maximizes the likelihood that those who promenade and those who habituate will run into each other.[11] In English-speaking countries, pubs or bars or lounges are customary places for adults to frequent. Recently, in America, those who are old enough to drive but not old enough to drink seem to make themselves available to those who promenade in cars by hanging out at, appropriately enough, drive-in restaurants.

A person often develops a habitual pattern of movement from place to place called a *routine*. He is kept on his recurrent course by a kind of social inertia, insofar as it would take more effort for him to leave his customary path than to stay on it. As their relationship progresses, acquaintances who are becoming intimates may decide to divert their customary course of movement in such a way as to come together periodically. By expending the relatively small amount of energy this "course correction" takes, they can avoid expending the ultimately greater amount of energy that continued planning of each one of their meetings would take. Acquaintances who are becoming intimates, then, set up *intersecting routines.*

One way they make their routines intersect is to join the same institution or association, whose rhythms will periodically sweep their bodies together. Suburban women may join the Tuesday Afternoon Sewing Circle: whenever it meets, they meet. Some institutions allow leeway to intersect. In the academic world, those who wish to come together may intentionally take some of the same classes. They may also take advantage of the free time that many institutions permit in order to spend it together. Two secretaries who work in different buildings may try to schedule their lunch breaks so that they may eat in the same place at the same time. Finally, outside of institutional vortices, they may set up a little circulating routine of their own in which meetings are not specifically planned but are "understood" ("On Wednesdays, we always meet for tea at three"). Whenever these recurrent meetings of intimates occur, it appears, phenomenologically, to them as a *warm time* in the temporal flow of their day or week, and is eagerly anticipated.

Another aspect of *loneliness* is to have no warm time to look forward to.

The extreme form of intersecting routine, which intimates may set up in order to maximize their amount of copresence while minimizing the technical problems in arranging it, is known as "living together." Celia, in Shakespeare's *As You Like It,* tells how living with her cousin Rosalind allowed them to participate in a large number of common activities:

> . . . we still have slept together,
> Rose at an instant, learn'd, play'd, eat together,
> And wheresoe'er we went, like Juno's swans,
> Still we went coupled and inseparable.[12]

In our society, during weekdays, adults who sleep and eat (usually breakfast and dinner) in the same place at the same time usually manage to ensure a maximum of about fifteen hours of copresence a day (including about eight hours of sleep), even though the

work institutions to which one or both belong keep them apart
for the other nine.

Having decided to meet each other, individuals must choose not
only a time but also a place. The three most important criteria
they use to determine where to meet are: the purpose of their
meeting; the availability of public or private places;[13] and the
stage of their relationship.

When they plan to meet for small talk, they usually prefer to
hold their encounters in a public place. The essential feature of
a public place is that it is a reservoir of stimulation for any encounter immersed in it. Not only do public places provide diversions external to the interaction, such as landscape and people-
scape, they also provide diversions internal to the interaction, such
as food and drink. Although light conversation can be engrossing,
it is generally not so engrossing that small talkers do not appreciate the secondary diversions that abound in public places and
help to keep them from being oriented to each other too exclusively.

Those who arrange to meet often distinguish among public
places according to the degree of external diversions they provide,
ranging from empty rooms to strobelighted discothèques;[14] according to the degree they were designed to be intimate meeting
places, ranging from comfortless street corners to comfortable lob-
bies and lounges; and according to the degree they will deplete
the intimates' resources, ranging from parks, which are free, to
eating and drinking establishments, which are expensive.[15]

When individuals plan to meet for serious talk and other activities, such as sex, in which they expect to be oriented to each
other completely, they usually prefer to hold their encounters in a
private place. These screen out many of the stimuli that swarm
around public places and pull the blinds on many of the outside
observers who loiter in public. Those who expect their heavy
conversations or other activities to be totally engrossing do not
want their attention diverted by happenings outside the oval of
their interaction and do not want to have to keep up their ap-
pearances vis-à-vis outsiders. In other words, they hold their encounters in private places whenever they wish to segregate themselves spatially from other events, which might distract them, and

from other people, who might observe them. A man may not wish to propose marriage to a girl in an outdoor café where passing handsome strangers keep catching her eye and where customers sitting nearby might hear her laughingly reject him ("Marry you! You must be joking!").

Homes are usually most convenient for encounters in which total mutual involvement is expected. Homes are especially good for marathon conversations and activities because they are free and contain creature comforts not found in other private places: soft chairs, temperature control, bathrooms, beds, etc. Domiciliary copresence management—visiting—varies with the level of the relationship. Acquaintances must request permission to visit ("May I stop over?") or to be invited. Intimates may visit each other much more freely and easily, for they may arrive without permission or invitation. "We need never to stand on ceremony with [our Friend] with regard to his visits," mused Thoreau in one of his retreats. "Wait not till I invite thee, but observe that I am glad to see thee when thou comest. It would be paying too dear for thy visit to ask for it."[16] Acquaintances, moreover, must warn of their arrival (e.g., by calling first) to give each other time to prepare the appropriate "face" (e.g., by making it up) and "front" (e.g., by cleaning up the house). Since (as we shall see further in Chapter 4) intimates need not hide from each other their undressed bodies and undusted households, they may arrive unannounced. Intimates are those who say to each other, "My house is yours," or "You are always welcome here." In the extreme, they may mean what they say enough to give each other the keys to their homes.

(Certain public places also attempt to emulate homes by being "intimate settings." Thus, some liquor lounges and restaurants provide soft lights, comfortable chairs, background music, discreet waiters, and even alcoves to separate those who wish to be away from other customers.)

When the home is not available, those who wish to meet for nonpublic activities must find some other private place. The problem of finding a suitable trysting place is especially acute for lovers, who would usually be hounded out of their homes by such housemates as parents, husbands, wives, housemothers, and dormitory counselors. In romantic literature, boundary spaces, like walls, as in *A Midsummer Night's Dream,* and balconies, as in *Romeo and Juliet,* have proved to be popular places where lovers can meet secretly. Today, neutral spaces, like hotel rooms, have become fashionable places to rendezvous, as in the movie *The Graduate.* Woods and country meadows are perennial favorites. The automobile has increased the ability of lovers to reach secluded spots (as well as providing them with such creature comforts necessary for sustained intimate activities as heaters, radios, and back seats). The need for extradomicilic places for the private meetings of lovers has been socially recognized insofar as certain areas have been semiofficially reserved for them. Just as in the past every town had its "behind the old sawmill," so today every city has its "lovers' lane" within a short drive from the city proper.

Acquaintances, whose encounters flow less spontaneously than do those of intimates, usually prefer to meet in public rather than private places, for the former's relative abundance of secondary diversions provides them with enough time to consider what they will say next, whereas the latter's relative scarcity of secondary diversions forces them to be more oriented to each other than the conversation can perhaps bear. Those who are becoming intimate generally prefer to retire to private places, where their heavy conversations and activities can take place undisturbed and unobserved. Those who have become intimate often reemerge to some degree into public places in hope that the stimulation found in these places will prove to be a nutritious supplement to their steady diet of each other.

The point of transition between public places and private places is a crucial one in heterosexual affairs. Cross-sex acquaintances who want to increase the intensity level of their relationship will eventually reach the point at which they must shift the dominant activities from those acceptable in public to those only possible in private. Thus, "Would you like to come up?" at the end of an early date represents a critical attempt to escalate intimacy. Since sex is likely to be waiting at the top of the stairwell, whoever invites the other to come up or whoever agrees to come up knows that this invitation or this acceptance indicates a wish or willingness to intensify the relationship. Usually, the inviter does not mention this intention directly, but substitutes some more acceptable surrogate ("... for some coffee" or "... for a drink") in order to blur over the fact that he was actually attempting to raise the level of the relationship, should this offer be rejected. There will be more on ambiguous attempts to intensify intimacy in the next chapter.

Phenomenologically, wherever a person customarily meets his intimate becomes a *warm spot* in his environment. The Dutch proverb "The road to a friend's house is never long" testifies to the fact that it often seems to a person that his environment "slopes downward" to these warm spots. Moreover, the scattering of his intimates over a city, a country, and the world affects a person's perception of these spatial units. Thoreau's aphorism is apt: "Nothing makes the earth seem so spacious as to have friends at a distance: they make the latitudes and longitudes."

Another essential chracteristic of *loneliness* is that an individual feels he is lost insofar as he must wander about his environment with no warm spots to provide him with spatial orientation.

Each potential intimate can use the above modes of coming together as *diagnostic aids* to indicate the intensity level of the relationship—on a scale between mere acquaintances and full intimates—the other would like to have their association attain and maintain. Specifically, each can estimate the other's desire to intensify their intimacy by the degree the other seems to be going out of his way both to look for him and to be available to him, as well as by how often and where the other arranges his next encounter with him.

THE ENCOUNTER

When one person finally manages to get into the actual presence of another, he must merge with him into an encounter. As acquaintances develop into intimates, they find such mergers easier because the temporal and spatial boundaries of their encounters become more permeable.

As the intensity of their intimacy increases, individuals can move more rapidly through the beginning phase of their planned encounters in order to get to the purpose for which they were planned. The *warm-up* or greeting phase of an encounter ("Hello. How are you? What have you been doing?") functions to affirm the diffuse totality of the relationship, i.e., each shows the other that he relates to him as a whole person and considers him an end in himself. In the *pitch* or point phase for which one planned the encounter ("Could you lend me five dollars?"), he relates to the other in only one of his specialized aspects (e.g., as an economic reserve) and treats him as a means. Since each acquaintance must show what each intimate can assume (namely, that he considers the other to be an end), the more intimate they are, the less they need indulge in lengthy preliminaries before staging their main event. Sometimes an intimate can even omit his warm-up and deliver his pitch directly (contrast the breathless "Could you lend me five dollars?" of intimates with the more leisurely and seemingly more casual conversation of acquaintances: "Hello. . . . How are you? . . . What have you been doing? . . . By the way, I'm a little short of cash at the moment. Could you lend me five dollars until Tuesday?").

Even when they come upon each other by chance, intimates may merge into an encounter more easily than acquaintances. When acquaintances run into each other on the street, each assumes the other's greeting is a terminal hello unless the latter forcefully indicates his inclination to prolong their interaction ("What are you doing now? Come get some coffee with me"). When intimates run into each other in the street, however, they need not make open requests to continue their interaction past the greeting phase; in fact, they must supply overt excuses to discontinue it at this point. Each intimate assumes the other will want to sustain a chance encounter unless he gives evidence that he does not ("I have to go. I'm in a hurrry"). A slightly different exchange takes place when one individual comes upon another who is seated, since encounters are expected to last longer when individuals are sitting with each other than when they are standing. If they are acquaintances, the individual who is sitting generally has the prerogative to decide whether the encounter will be transformed into one of relatively long duration in which both individuals are seated. Either the stander requests permission to sit down ("May I join you?") or the sitter invites him ("Why don't you sit down?"). (That the stander has no authority in this situation can be seen by trying to imagine his saying to the sitter, "Why don't you stand up?") But if they are intimates, the stander is expected to sit down with the sitter automatically or give an excuse for not doing so. If the sitter seems to be preoccupied with a book or with other people, however, intimates use the same polite interaction format as acquaintances: the stander asks permission to join ("Are you busy?") or the sitter invites him ("Pull up a chair").

At the other end of their encounters, individuals also find their partings to be easier to manage as their intimacy increases. Since most intimates have intersecting routines, they are assured of seeing each other again. Each can break off without exhausting his supply of ideas on any particular integrating topic, for he expects to get another chance to finish the exposition of his views. But since acquaintances are not so certain they will ever see each other again, each often feels he must protract the encounter until he asserts or qualifies everything he wants to say, for he may not get another chance. Furthermore, each intimate need not bother to reaffirm the value of their encounter because he knows the other assumes it; each acquaintance must manifest this value because he knows the other will not take it for granted ("It's been nice talking with you"). Finally, each intimate may presume the other wants to meet him again and therefore need concern himself only with the technical problems of where and when; acquaintances can presume no such thing, and so must take into account that the more specifically he attempts to arrange their next meeting, the more he reveals an interest in the other that may not be reciprocated.

One of the learned rules of interaction requires both interactants in every pure encounter always to be oriented to each other, mentally and physically. As their relationship evolves, however, they become freer to break out of the spatial confinements in which this rule locks them and follow their fancy to wander away from the other in mind and body.

Intimates may withdraw their orientation from each other in order to engage in some inward or individual pursuit. While in each other's presence, they may each be silent, read, sew, doze, or daydream. But acquaintances may do none of these things. While in each other's presence, they must continue to spin out to each other an unbroken thread of talk, for their whole relationship is supported only by a thin tightrope of conversation that each must sometimes go to great lengths to sustain.

Intimates may also withdraw all or part of their orientation from each other in order to concern themselves with events occurring beyond the boundaries of their encounter. While maintaining their conversation, they may look, not at each other, but outward into the encounter's environment. If they are sitting, one may suddenly and without warning get up and go to the other side of the room (e.g., to mix drinks), forcing the other to talk more loudly. If they are standing, one intimate may suddenly and without warning start to walk away (e.g., to go to a water fountain), forcing the other to begin to walk with him (when the other notices his partner's stretching the encounter boundaries). And if they are walking, one intimate can suddenly and without warning stop (e.g., to look in a shop window), forcing the other to stop with him (when the other notices his partner's absence). The overall relation between the intimates supports and smooths over these particular interruptions. Acquaintances, however, can extrude out their encounters in none of these ways without making an open request or an elaborate signal. Otherwise each indicates to the other either that something extremely important is happening outside of their encounter—in which case the other should turn around and look or move, too—or that he is of that class of individuals who have not read their Emily Post—lower class? foreigners? immigrants?—or that he is deliberately trying to insult the other—because he is bored by him? because he is unable to stand the sight of him?—or that he should be incarcerated in a mental hospital—has been? is about to be?

In general, pure encounters become less tense and, accordingly, more enjoyable as intimacy increases: whereas acquaintances are more constrained from orienting themselves elsewhere but have more need to do so, intimates are less constrained from orienting themselves elsewhere but have less need to do so.

Common activities are also undertaken more easily as the relationship develops. Acquaintances assume all their pursuits will be separate ones. Consequently, when they want to engage in a common activity, each must either invite the other to join ("I'm going to the movies. Want to come?") or request permission to come along ("I heard that was a good picture. I'd like to see it, too. Mind if I join you?"). Intimates, especially those who live together, assume all of their pursuits that possibly can be common ones actually will be. Consequently, when one of them suggests an activity ("I feel like a movie"), he does not need to invite the other nor does the other need to ask permission to come along ("Well, what shall we see?").

GOING APART

"You may like a man's company," observes Aristotle, "without wishing to have it all the time."[17] But what precisely are the factors that impel those who are together to wish to be apart? Whatever these factors are, they seem to act more slowly as acquaintances become more intimate.

One individual may find that the other has exhausted his supply of stories, and consequently has nothing further with which to stimulate him. He will want to leave the other, whom he now finds "boring," in order to seek stimulation in someone else or in solitary pursuits. Conversely, he may have spent his own emotional charge, the one that prompted him to seek out the other in the first place. His tale is told. His tears are dried. His laughter run down. He feels "flat" and "stale." He feels the other is getting bored with him. He would like to be alone in order to have those inputs of private experience that will recharge the supply of anecdotes he uses to spark his conversations with others. As that expert on solitude, Thoreau, tells us:

> There are times when we have had enough even of our Friends, when we begin inevitably to profane one another, and must withdraw religiously into solitude and silence, the better to prepare ourselves for a loftier intimacy. Silence is the ambrosial night in the intercourse

of Friends, in which their sincerity is recruited and takes deeper root.[18]

Since others are a source of stimulation, they are also a source of distraction. When an individual wants to devote his undivided attention to some activity, he will often want to get away from others in order to do so. Thus, he may want to be alone in order to contemplate nature, or art, or himself, or in order to accomplish that "work" by which he maintains or enhances his own relationship to his environment. He will begin to find others irritating insofar as he wants to be totally oriented elsewhere while they continue to demand some of his attention.[19]

Perhaps the most interesting reason why an individual wants to get away from others is to "relax," or, more precisely, to relax that self he presents to them. It would take us too far afield of our present topic to discuss the nature of the self at any length. Suffice to assert here the First Law of Psychodynamics: The more distant the self a person presents to another is from the "idling" or "disengaged" self he presents to himself when he is alone, the more psychological energy he must use up in order to sustain it.[20]

In order to relax and regenerate the psychological energy he expends in sustaining the self he presents, an individual will want to get away from others. He must seclude himself, to catch his breath, as it were, in order to be able to face them in the future. As the relationship becomes more intense, the closer the self he presents to his intimate comes to the self he presents to himself (i.e., the more "spontaneously" he can behave), and the longer he can maintain it easily. In other words, interactions between acquaintances are more tiring psychologically than interactions between intimates (except when the latter are engaged in the exhausting activity of resolving the problems of their relationship itself). Acquaintances, then, feel the need to part from each other more quickly than intimates. For instance, since an individual with stomach gas will try harder to keep from breaking wind in front of an acquaintance than in front of his wife, he will be in more of a hurry to flee the former than the latter. But there are some releases he cannot have even in the presence of his intimates. In order to rid himself of the residual aspects of his personality that will begin to clog and poison his psychological system, he must be alone. John Barth presents an excellent example of a person's need for solitude, his need to relax that self he presents to an intimate while expressing other of his psychological potentialities, in the famous passage in *End of the Road* where Jacob Horner has just convinced Rennie Morgan to peep through the window with him at her husband Joe:

> It is indeed the grossest of injustices to observe a person who believes himself to be alone. Joe Morgan, back from his Boy Scout meeting, had evidently intended to do some reading, for there were books lying open on the writing table and on the floor beside the bookcase. But Joe wasn't reading. He was standing in the exact center of the bare room, fully dressed, smartly executing military commands. About FACE! right DRESS! 'Ten SHUN! Parade REST! He saluted briskly, his cheeks blown out and his tongue extended, and then proceeded to cavort about the room—spinning, pirouetting, bowing, leaping, kicking. I watched entranced by his performance, for I cannot say that in my strangest moments (and a bachelor has strange ones) I have surpassed him. Rennie trembled from head to foot.
>
> Ah! Passing a little mirror on the wall, Joe caught his own eye. What? What? Ahoy there! He stepped close, curtsied to himself, and thrust his face to within two inches of the glass. Mr. Morgan, is it? Howdy do, Mr. Morgan. Blah bloo blah. Oo-o-o-o blubble thlwurp. He mugged antic faces at himself, sklurching up his eye corners, zbloogling his mouth about, glubbling his cheeks. Mither Morgle. Nyoing nyang nyumpie. Vglibble vglobble vglup. Vgyliggy-BLOO! Thlucky thlucky, thir.
>
> He snapped out of it, jabbed his spectacles back on his nose. Had he heard some sound? No. He went back to the writing table and apparently resumed his reading, his back turned to us. He turned slightly, and we could see: his tongue gripped purposefully between his lips at the side of his mouth, Joe was masturbating and picking his

nose at the same time. I believe he also hummed a
sprightly tune in rhythm with his work.
Rennie was destroyed.... [21]

Once intimates establish a copresence cycle, they view the temporal interval between their get-togethers as normal or abnormal
according to whether the spatial interval they are apart is such
that they can maintain their meetings on a regular basis. A *normal
separation* is one in which they are close enough spatially to be
easily accessible to each other should one want to see the other.
Obviously, such accessibility is a product of cost and convenience
and varies by class. Normal spatial separations for intimates of the
jet set are much wider than normal spatial separations for intimates of the subway set.

An *abnormal separation* occurs whenever intimates break the
rhythm of their regular encounters. An individual who goes on
a trip is not easily accessible to his intimates. Whenever a person
leaves town, then, he must inform all his intimates that their
copresence cycle will be broken for a long but definite period of
time. Conversely, an individual knows who his intimates are, in
part, by who tells him they are leaving town.

We have considered here the oscillation of inclination between
"being together" and "being apart" that is at the heart of personal
relations. As acquaintances become intimates, the pulsating nature
of this pattern becomes more pronounced. When intimates are
apart, their need to receive stimulation from each other and express their excitement to each other increases, while their need to
relax their presented self and fulfill their other personal and social
obligations decreases. When they are together, their ability to
provide stimulation and their desire to express their excitement
to each other decreases, while their need to relax their presented
self and fulfill their other personal and social obligations increases.
In general, when they are alone, pressure for them to come together rises while pressure for them to remain alone subsides,
until their impulses are tipped in favor of seeking sociability;
when they are together, pressure for them to remain together subsides while pressure for them to go apart rises, until their impulses
are tipped in favor of seeking solitude. This rhythmic cycle of

impulses for contraction and expansion of interaction distance constitutes the *systole* and *diastole* of personal relations.[22]

COMPLICATIONS

It is one of the agonies of the human condition that intimates cannot always pendulate externally in interaction to the same rhythm they pulsate internally in inclination. The actual flow and ebb of intimates together and apart is likely to be controlled less by the floodgates of their own desires than by the influence of their physical and social circumstances and by the practical problems involved in arranging their conflux and disflux.

The physical and social circumstances in which the intimates find themselves may expedite their being apart and hinder their coming together, or vice versa. In either case, these circumstances are likely to ignore their personal rhythms, their proclivities for conjunction and disjunction. On the one hand, they may feel bored because they cannot receive stimulation from each other and frustrated because they cannot express themselves to each other; on the other hand, they may feel irritated because they are receiving too much distraction from each other and flat because they have nothing more to say to each other. Some instances of these disruptive circumstances are as follows:

Intimates who can spend only a brief time together before or between long abnormal periods of separation usually try to squeeze all the intimacy they can out of their encounter, as though intimacy were some kind of juice which they can suck in more of through concentration and effort. Summer lovers who must separate in the fall to go off to colleges in different cities often attempt to spend all of their time together when they return for their winter vacations in order to make up for lost time. And those who attend noncoed colleges often feel they must put in an entire weekend with their friend of the opposite sex in order to make up for the five days they have been separated. But personal rhythms cannot be adjusted so easily, and the lovers may be as dissatisfied with spending all of their time together during vacations and weekends as they are dissatisfied with spending none of their time together during school terms and weekdays.

The relentless beat of the institutions to which intimates belong may drown out their personal rhythms by periodically dislodging one intimate from the other and carting him away, whether he wants to leave or not. Thus, every weekday morning for forty years, the husband's job drags him unwilling from the bed of his wife. Their continual absences from each other leave husband and wife with a positive charge of attraction to each other, which they feel as a constant desire to be together. But, in retirement, they may suddenly find that their continual copresence leaves them with a negative charge of repulsion from each other, which they feel as a constant desire to be apart. With the husband constantly around the house, they may quickly begin to get on each other's nerves.

Total institutions can impose an even more rigid grid on the intimates' oscillating impulses to be with each other and to be away from each other. Friends who are put in different cellblocks in prisons and concentration camps may have nonintersecting routines and seldom get a chance to be with each other, whereas friends who are put in the same cell may have totally overlapping routines and seldom get a chance to be away from each other. This ability of total institutions to savagely override personal rhythms is one of the main punishments endured by those imprisoned in them. Hell, to paraphrase Sartre, is not being able to get away from other people.

Along with these circumstantial obstacles to unions and separations, there are practical problems in arranging to come together and to go apart. On the one hand, each intimate can have difficulty in finding a place to be alone. Those who live in isolated country houses and small boats and, to a somewhat lesser extent, those who reside in country sanatoriums and small provincial colleges may have nowhere to go to get away from each other.[23] On the other hand, both intimates can have difficulty in finding a place where they can be together. Those who belong to discriminated against social groups, like adolescents, are especially afflicted with a dearth of rallying points. They cannot avail themselves of public accommodations, for these are often reserved for older groups, and they cannot avail themselves of each other's homes, for these are often under parental surveillance. Those who belong to antagonistic social groups, like the Capulets and the Montagues, also have difficulty in finding places to be together. They cannot be seen together in public, and they cannot be caught separately in each other's domiciles.

Finally, intimates can have difficulty in finding time to be together. An individual may discover that the increase in his work load has cut down the amount of free time that he can spend with his intimate. Beyond this, any schedule that takes into account the time each intimate must spend with his other intimates cuts down still further the amount of "coincident" free time they have to spend with each other.

External circumstances and technical problems are not the only factors that hinder the intimates' easy-come, easy-go existence. We have already seen that there gradually accumulate within intimates pressures that cause them to want to be together when they are apart and to be apart when they are together. Unfortunately, these pressures do not necessarily build up in each intimate at the same rate. Each intimate may at times find his desire to seek or to avoid copresence to be out of phase with the other's.

Intimates, especially those who live together, can assume they will be together in the immediate future, thus making their common activities easy to arrange but their individual pursuits difficult to work out. Intimates lose their freedom to engage in private pursuits without taking special steps. Each must provide the other with an excuse or a justification[24] for engaging in a particular pursuit alone. One can excuse himself from joint participation by claiming that he is forced by circumstances outside of his control to undertake the activity at a time when the other intimate has something else to do (as when a husband who wants to go to a play—or to a tryst—alone tells his wife, "They only have tickets available for Thursday night. That's when your bridge club meets, isn't it?"). Or he can justify his undertaking the activity alone by pointing out that his difference from the other makes the pursuit more appropriate for him than for the other (as when a husband who wants to go to a movie—or to a tryst—alone tells his wife, "You wouldn't like it. It's a man's picture"). In general, acquaintances find their individual pursuits ready-made, but must manufacture their common ones out of invitations and permissions, whereas intimates find their common activities prefabricated, but must fabricate their individual ones out of excuses and justifications.

Once the cyclical pattern of coming together and going apart is set, it develops a life of its own insofar as both intimates feel obligated to maintain it. There are times when each intimate may not want to be with the other, because the pressures that caused him to part from the other have not yet fully subsided or because he has something more important to do. In spite of his desires, he may still feel that it is his duty to seek out the other and to be available to him.

Intimates usually take turns originating their get-togethers (or, more precisely, each tries to maintain the proportion of their total number of encounters in which he had sought out the other at around 50 percent). Consequently, if either intimate falls too far below his share of initiating interaction, he may feel that he owes the other a visit. Similarly, when the other wants to see him and he does not feel like seeing the other, he may feel obliged to meet with him anyway.

However, he can also try to use the alternative technique of avoiding a specific meeting with the other while maintaining his availability for such meetings in the future. Since his intimate has a claim on his availability only if he can find him, an individual can keep from having to refuse a request for an encounter if he can keep from receiving it. When he does not want to see his intimate, he may not answer his phone or his doorbell or keep away from those places where his intimate is likely to come upon him. For instance, he can have a serious talk with someone in those public places where their encounter is surrounded by strangers who have no claim on his availability, but not in those public places where his intimates congregate, for they have such a claim and may attempt to intrude, forcing him to reveal his lack of availability and hence the limits of their relationship ("May I join you?" "I'm sorry, we're having a private conversation"). (Another problem with going to those public places where one's intimates gather is that one is often forced to proclaim publicly the relative rating of his relationships with each of them. If he goes to a cafeteria and discovers that two individuals who are intimate

with him but not with each other are sitting at different tables, he must snub the one to satisfy the other, for he cannot join both at the same time.)

An individual who must openly decline to meet with his intimate can maintain his availability by excusing his refusal with the claim that forces beyond his control prevent him from holding an encounter at the time his intimate wants to arrange it. In disclaiming responsibility for his refusal, he shows that he still wants to be considered available for future meetings and is trying to keep up his relationship obligations. He can enhance the legitimacy of his excuse if he suggests that their encounter be postponed rather than canceled and specifies the time when he will next be free to meet.

For their part, the intimates of an individual can help to keep his potential availability intact by not attempting to intiate encounters with him when he looks busy or by accepting his excuses when he claims to be. Of course, an individual cannot remove himself too often, give too many excuses, or put off too many meetings without wearing thin his cloak of innocence.

In this chapter, the *congregation* dimension of an intimate relation has been considered and a second major force uncovered that transforms isolated individuals into interlocked intimates—*the routinization of their cycle of coming togethers and going aparts.* Intimates increase the binding power of this force insofar as they intersect, or even overlap, their customary routines of movement and insofar as they puncture the pellicle of privacy that causes the unacquainted and, to a lesser extent, the merely acquainted to bounce off each other whenever they run into each other by chance.

CHAPTER 3

Tell Me You Love Me

As INDIVIDUALS left the community, in which the higher orders of interpersonal relations were relatively well defined, to wander about in society, in which the higher orders of interpersonal relations were relatively ill defined, it became more important for them to indicate to one another precisely what their relationship was. In this chapter, I will consider how individuals communicate the level of their relationship to each other through certain aspects of the structure of their language—taking language in a broad sense to include both verbal (linguistic) and nonverbal (kinesic) behavior, but restricting the discussion to Indo-European languages. (This is not to say that individuals do not also communicate the level of their relationship through the other dimensions of personal relations discussed elsewhere in this book, such as the frequency with which they initiate interaction.) Specifically, they indicate the level of their relationship through various sets of distinct linguistic and kinesic signals. One signal in each set is used only by those who consider themselves acquaintances; another is used only by those who consider themselves intimates; the rest are used only by those who consider themselves somewhere in between. Structural linguistics contains the notion of distinguishable communication units: "phonemes" for sound units, "morphemes" for meaning units. I propose the term *phileme* (from the Greek word "philia" meaning intense positive relationship—

see Introduction, footnote 1) for the smallest distinguishable unit of a person's behavior that indicates his level of intimacy with whomever he is interacting. There are as many philemes as there are behaviors that indicate intimacy, level. I propose the term *phileme family* for a set of related philemes, one of which a person must use at a particular interaction junction to signal his specific level of intimacy with whomever he is interacting. The philemes of the same family are related insofar as they are similar (but distinguishable) forms of behavior that serve different communicative functions (specifically, communicate different levels of intimacy) at the same interaction point. This chapter is a monograph in the science of *philemics*: the study of those elemental behavioral units (philemes) through which interacting individuals communicate the intimacy level of their relationship. (In a larger sense, however, this whole book is a treatise in the more encompassing science of PHILEMICS: the study of all the behaviors through which interacting individuals construct as well as communicate their relationship.)

To clarify the terms "phileme" and "phileme family," the reader might imagine two individuals who are each sitting in front of separate boards on which there are rows of switches (i.e., phileme families). When they are mere acquaintances, each individual has all the switches on his board in the down position (i.e., he is communicating through the acquaintance phileme in each family). Over the course of their association, each individual throws more and more of his switches to the up position until they are all up (i.e., he is communicating through the intimate phileme in each family). When all of the switches on both boards are up, both individuals consider themselves full intimates. Personal relations differ in quality insofar as each relationship stabilizes with the switches in different phileme families not completely up. Personal relations are complicated by the fact that both individuals do not necessarily move up equivalent switches at the same time (i.e., they do not necessarily communicate their intimacy level through the same phileme family).

I will begin this chapter by describing various phileme families, move on to a discussion of the effects of simultaneously indicating different intimacy levels in various phileme families, turn to an analysis of the process of progression within each phileme family and through all phileme families, and end by pointing out some of the problems involved whenever interacting individuals attempt to communicate the intimacy level of their relationship.

COMMUNICATION ELEMENTS

I do not assert that the following list of linguistic and kinesic phileme families is complete. In fact, it is likely that the more subtle signals by which we imply and infer our precise degree of closeness to others are yet to be discovered. Nor do I assert that the following analysis of phileme families fully reflects contemporary usage, for the present inflation of the signals that indicate relationship level is causing acquaintance philemes to fall into disuse while the intimate end of the spectrum is becoming increasingly popular. (Where only the intimate phileme in a given family is noted, the acquaintance phileme in this family is taken to be merely the nonuse of the intimate phileme.)

First, speakers of most European languages, unlike speakers of English, must indicate their degree of association whenever they refer to each other by the second-person-singular pronoun. Anglo-Americans have only one choice for this pronoun, "you"; as Roger Brown, a social psychologist, points out, Europeans, have two:

> The European development of two singular pronouns of address begins with the Latin 'tu' and 'vos.' In Italian they become 'tu' and 'voi' (with 'Lei' eventually largely displacing 'voi'); in French 'tu' and 'vous'; in Spanish 'tu' and 'vos,' later 'usted'). In German the distinction began with 'du' and 'Ihr' but 'Ihr' gave way to 'er' and later to 'Sie.' English speakers first used 'thou' and 'ye' and later replaced 'ye' with 'you.' As a convenience we propose to use the symbols 'T' and 'V' (from the Latin 'tu' and 'vos') as generic designators for a familiar and a polite pronoun in any language.[1]

Speakers of Russian also must choose between two similar forms of this pronoun, *Vy* and *Ty*.[2] In general, European acquaintances address each other with the *V* form of the pronoun; European intimates address each other with the *T* form. Brown goes on to note that individuals use the 'T' form to subordinates and dependents as well as to intimates,[3] implying that intimates consider themselves to be mutually subordinate and dependent.

Second, although speakers of English are not so aware as their European counterparts of what it means to be forced to indicate the level of a relationship whenever they address one another by pronoun, they are equally aware of what it means to be forced to indicate it whenever they address one another by name. Generally, acquaintances call each other only by last name and title ("Mr. Jones"); intimates call each other only by first name ("John"). Pierre Choderlos de Laclos, in *Dangerous Liaisons*, has Marquise de Merteuil write to her friend Vicomte de Valmont, commenting on the progress of his attempted seduction of a young woman relative to the progress of his rival, Chevalier Danceny:

> Notice that when she writes about you it is always 'Monsieur de Valmont,' that all her ideas, even those you have engendered in her, invariably lead her to Danceny, and that she never calls him 'Monsieur,' but simply 'Danceny.' In that way she distinguishes him from all others; even though she gives herself to you, she speaks familiarly only of him.[4]

Sometimes strangers who have just met will attempt to put their association on the same first-name basis that intimates are on in the hope of making their relationship as informal as their names ("Franz Kafka is the name. But you can call me Franz. All my friends do"). Or one will request permission to call the other by his first name, as Comte de Passavant asks Olivier Molinier in Andre Gide's *The Counterfeiters*:

> Well, allow me to say, Olivier... you don't mind my calling you Olivier, do you? I really can't say Monsieur; you're too young, and I'm too intimate with your brother Vincent to call you Molinier.[5]

One intimate often marks the times he feels extremely close to
the other by directly addressing the other by the other's first name
("What should I do? I love you, Judy! What should I do?"). On
the other hand, since only acquaintances and role-relations use
last names, one intimate can decrease the usual closeness between
himself and the other by directly addressing the other by the
other's last name. Thus, a boy who momentarily becomes irritated
with his girl friend may indicate the extent of his annoyance with
her by pulling down to acquaintance his switch on this phileme
family ("Look here, Miss Smith, I want you to stop it!"). Conversely, since only intimates use first names, one acquaintance or
role-relation can decrease the usual distance between himself and
the other by directly addressing the other by first name. Thus, a
faculty member who must criticize a graduate student's dissertation may try to decrease the distance between himself and the student, which his censure has suddenly expanded, by pulling up to
intimate his switch on this phileme family ("Come now, Murray,
surely you can give a better interpretation of this process than
that!").

Third, acquaintances who become intimates come to address
each other with certain nouns that, at least etymologically, name
situations of close physical and, consequently, psychological relationship. "Comrade" and "chum" originally referred to those who
slept in the same room. "Companion" and "mate" originally referred to those who ate together. But by far the most important
source of names for close relationships is the family. "Buddy" is
believed to stem from baby talk for brother. "Partner" is believed
to stem from the word for joint heir. Paul Friedrich, a linguist,
describes some of the kinship terms found in Russian, many of
which are similar to those found in English:

> In Russian, numerous kinship terms of address and
> many other quasi-kinship terms such as 'Kum,' 'ritual
> co-parent,' were frequent in conversation, particularly
> among the peasants. All classes of Russians interjected
> kinship terms such as 'brother' or 'little mother' . . . when
> consciously or subconsciously trying to create an informal,
> congenial atmosphere with non-relatives. And there were

numerous combinations of proper names, ranging from nicknames, to diminutives, to the first name alone, to the first name plus a fixed epithet ('Mikhail the Wolf'), to the first name plus an informal or formal patronymic ('Ivanych' as against 'Ivanovich').[6]

Note that intimates often call each other by those kinship terms used to subordinate and dependent members of the family,[7] just as they call each other by that pronoun form used to all subordinates and dependents, further supporting the implication that intimates consider themselves to be mutually subordinate and dependent.

Related to the above modes of address (usually used by friends), which name situations of close relationships, are those "endearments" (usually used by lovers) that name those positively valued categories the beloved is supposed to belong to or that name those positively valued attributes the beloved is supposed to possess. These endearments fall into definite groups:

1 Those in which the beloved is considered to be higher than human in the sense of sacred ("Angel," "Divine")
2 Those in which the beloved is considered to be lower than human in the sense of innocent: either as a small animal ("Chick," "Lambkins," "Pet") or as a small child ("Baby," "Honey Child")
3 Those in which the beloved is considered to be like a pleasurable taste sensation ("Sweets," "Honey," "Sugar")

Fourth, individuals feel they are united whenever they refer to one of the groups of which they are both members ("Jews are ..."). They feel even more united whenever this common group consists of only the two of them, as it does when they use the plural form of the first-person pronoun ("We must ... " " ... to us"). An individual who says "we" or "us" expands his self-boundaries to include the other, hence transforming their separate identities into a common one ("What shall we do tonight?" "Let's talk about us"). They feel most united whenever they set their common unit off against a third person ("We think you should ... "),

against a group ("We always..., but they never..."), or against
everybody else ("It seems like we're the only ones in the world
who..."). In his novella *The Kreutzer Sonata,* Leo Tolstoy portrays a situation in which a husband is disturbed over the intimacy
implied by his wife's choice of the plural form of the first-person
pronoun. The husband has just entered the room where his wife
and her would-be lover were practicing a concert piece together:

> "'How glad I am that you have come: we have not
> decided what to play on Sunday,' she said in a tone she
> would not have used to me had we been alone. This
> and her using the word 'we' of herself and him, filled me
> with indignation. I greeted him silently."[8]

Mere acquaintances would never say "we." (In writing, "we"
functions in a similar fashion. We can easily understand why an
author would be tempted to use it in order to appear to be merely
stating a point of agreement between himself and his reader, with
whom he seems to share a common perspective, whenever he
wants to make an assertion that is not completely clear or con-
vincing.)

Fifth, individuals indicate to each other the level of relationship
they have through the level of etiquette or "register" of the language they use. Bilingual acquaintances usually address each
other in their acquired language if it is of higher status; bilingual
intimates normally address each other in their original language.
Thus in Latin America acquaintances speak in Spanish or Por-
tugese, intimates in their native Indian tongue; in eastern Canada
acquaintances speak in English, intimates in French; and in Israel
acquaintances speak in Hebrew, intimates in Yiddish. As uni-
lingual acquaintances become more intimate, they spice their
speech with more "slang," "jargon," or other parochial forms of
language. In this way, each intimate indicates to the other that
he considers him a member of that small elite group that knows
the meaning of these esoteric words—a group that is set off against
all those who do not know these semisecret meanings.[9]

Sixth, whereas acquaintances must dilute a minimum of information into a maximum of words, intimates can concentrate a

maximum of information into a minimum of words. Thus, intimates are likely to omit certain weak words ("... coffee's cold") or even leave out the information conveyed by grammar entirely, relying on single words ("cold") or on intonation ("engh").[10] Basil Bernstein, a linguist, provides further instances of how economically intimates use language:

> ... the speech of intimates is played out against a backdrop of assumptions common to the speakers, against a set of closely shared interests and identifications, against a system of shared expectations; in short, it presupposes a "local cultural identity" which reduces the need for the speakers to elaborate their intent verbally and to make it explicit. In one sentence, the [greater] extent to which the intent of the other person may be taken for granted, the more likely the structure of the speech will be simplified and the vocabulary drawn from a narrow range.... The observer ... eavesdropping on inclusive relationships ... might have difficulty at first in following the speech as it would tend to be fast, fluent, relatively unpaused, and so the articulatory clues would be reduced.... If intent does not have to be verbalized and made explicit, if much can be assumed and taken for granted, there is no need to use a level of verbal planning which requires careful selection and fine discriminations. Consequently, he could expect that there would be a reduction in the number of qualifiers, a simple verbal stem limited to the active voice.[11]

Alternatively, by using this abridged form of communication, intimates indicate to each other that they have such a "local cultural identity." (I would suggest, however, that the speech of intimates is inexplicit only when they are talking about matters that do not concern their relationship itself. When they are talking about their relationship itself—in what I call in Chapter 7 a *metaintimate conversation*—they attempt to make their speech as well-defined as possible; here, above all, they do not want to risk being misunderstood. Hence, the structure of their speech becomes more complex; their tempo decreases as they think before they speak; their vocabulary increases as they search for the right word; their articularly clues and qualifiers abound as they try to convey the precise nuance of their meaning.) In general, since acquaintances do not know the extent of each other's background knowledge about any particular topic, they cannot easily determine how much more information to supply in order to make themselves understood. On the one hand, they often provide too little information and, consequently, misunderstand each other. On the other hand, they often provide too much information and, consequently, bore each other while insulting each other's intelligence ("I know." "I see"). But as they become more intimate, they come to know how much background knowledge each other possesses about a particular topic and, consequently, can supply exactly the right amount of additional information to get their point across ("You know." "You see").

Seventh, as acquaintances develop into intimates, they begin to use certain verbal expressions to indicate that their emotions are oriented to each other and are positively valenced, such as "I like you" or "I'm fond of you" or, most positively valenced, "I love you." When one intimate uses any of these expressions, the other will usually reecho the sentiment ("I like you, too").

Eighth, the speech of acquaintances who are becoming intimates becomes "warmer" in quality or tone. Specifically, it becomes softer, demanding more active participation and identification to be understood, and it becomes fuller of overtones and reverberations, perhaps indicating the complexity and richness of the relationship. (It has been suggested that the speech of lovers has a "nasal touch" because sexual impulses swell the membranes of the nose, which, in turn, affects the tone of voice.)[12]

Finally, although intimates can communicate to each other their degree of association through the various forms of speech that we have seen, they can also do so eloquently through silence. In fact, when they engage in certain activities, such as making love, they actually create a distance between themselves as soon as they utter the merest word.[13] Only intimates and strangers can comfortably remain in each other's presence without speaking, for mutual silence seems to denote either a very close or very distant relationship. Consequently, acquaintances who are in each other's presence usually feel compelled to keep talking in order to avoid either raising or lowering the level of their relationship. The silence of intimates differs from the silence of strangers in that speechless intimates are usually continuing their conversation with each other quite loquaciously through the various kinesic forms of communication to which we now turn.

Kinesics is the study of nonverbal communication, especially the language of body movements and gestures. The kinesic communications of intimates fall into two groups: (1) *topological modalities*, involving such spatial relations as side-by-side and matching, and (2) *organ modalities*, involving such spatial distancing as eye contact, space contact, and physical contact. Most Westerners, especially American men, seem to be so afraid of being considered homosexual if they communicate nonverbally to intimates of their own sex that they have become "kinesically mute." For this reason, I will restrict the following discussion of the kinesic communication of those who are becoming intimates to cross-sex pairs. Although most Western same-sex intimates select only sporadically from among the possibilities listed below, some, such as European women (if the Czech film *Daisies* (Chytilova, 1967) is portraying them at all accurately), seem to fear being considered homosexual so little that they can engage in almost as much kinesic communication as cross-sex intimates can.

Only intimates choose to sit or stand in the topological relationship of side-by-side. Shoulder to shoulder they are united by the fact that, together, they are confronting a common environment, task, or person, while continually coordinating their responses to whatever is external to their relationship.[14] Saint-Exupéry somewhere expressed this topological relationship of intimates when he said, "Love does not consist of gazing at each other but in looking together in the same direction." Since only those who actually are intimates can choose to be side-by-side, those who would like to appear to be intimates sometimes adopt this position, regardless of how uncomfortable it is, in order to indicate to each other that they really are already intimates. When a couple goes to a restaurant, they are likely to sit face-to-face during the early phase of their relationship, switch to side-by-side during the middle phase in order to attack their dinner together and confront the other customers as a pair, and finally, during the late phase, when they are so certain of their relationship that they need not communicate it so uncomfortably, switch back again to face-to-face in order to eat and talk more easily.

Intimates communicate through a second topological modality when they pattern themselves or their embodiments in a manner that is similar or symmetrical. Albert Schefflin, a psychiatrist, has found that intimates sometimes position their limbs in a similar or symmetrical fashion:

> Old friends or colleagues who have long-term ties sometimes shift into postural congruence [i.e., each holds his own head or limbs in a way that is identical with, or the mirror image of, the other's] at times when they are temporarily arguing or taking opposing sides, as if to indicate the ultimate continuity of their relationship.[15]

Intimates may also wear clothing or ornaments that are matching (i.e., similar or symmetrical), to indicate that each is more like the other than he is like those who dress differently. There are such matching clothing of lovers and spouses as "his & her" shirts and blouses, coats, sweatshirts, and bathing suits, and such matching ornaments as rings and sunglasses—the list could be extended almost indefinitely. In fact, Life magazine suggests that the trend for intimates of different sexes to wear matching clothing is increasing:

> This is the year that what's his is hers and what's hers is his—in a word, unisex. In Europe and in the U.S., with-it young couples, no longer inhibited by what looks masculine and what looks feminine, are finding that looking alike is good fashion as well as good fun.[16]

More and more today, it seems, men and women intimates want to cloak their sexual differences in sartorial similarities.

Individuals communicate through the organ modalities by touching or not touching each other—if we take "touching" in a broad enough sense to include contacts that are other than merely physical. In this broad sense, then, they touch each other whenever they cast their eyes on each other. Focusing on the eye more closely, we see that it contains two distinct phileme families, in each of which intimates and acquaintances make different choices.

First, although all interacting individuals can close one eye momentarily while looking at each other, only intimates may "wink" at each other in this way. When acquaintances wink at each other, they feel they have become more than acquaintances, temporarily at least. The very brevity of the wink makes it ideal for collusive communication. Thus, two intimates who are watching a third individual violate various norms of personal propriety may wink at each other to indicate a common amusement. Since the two are, in part, watching each other's reaction to the scene of the third, they can catch the optical flicker that would be missed by the third, who is too involved in making a fool out of himself to be aware of how powerfully he has united his audience against him.

Second, although all individuals can look at various of each other's features for various lengths of time, only intimates may "stare" at those of each other's features, like legs and breasts, that are "off limits" to the merely acquainted. When acquaintances want to look at these forbidden zones, they are permitted only to glance at them briefly. But it is when intimates look each other in the eye that their mutual involvement is communicated at peak intensity. Georg Simmel has observed:

> The mutual glance between persons, in distinction from the simple sight or observation of the other, signifies a wholly new and unique union between them. . . . By the glance which reveals the other, one discloses himself. By the same act in which the observer seeks to know the observed, he surrenders himself to be understood by the observed. The eye cannot take unless at the same time it gives. The eye of a person discloses his own soul when he seeks to uncover that of another. What occurs in this direct mutual glance represents the most perfect reciprocity in the entire field of human relationships.[17]

It is well known that lovers spend a great deal of time gazing longingly and wistfully at each other's communication apparatus, particularly the eyes. In the autobiography of his Harlem boyhood, *Manchild in the Promised Land,* Claude Brown provides an illustration:

> For the next two years whenever I was in the city, Sugar and I never had to say anything to each other. We came out of that room with a whole lot of understanding. Sugar could look at me and make me smile or even laugh, and it wasn't because she looked funny either; it was just that sometimes when she looked at me, I felt so good I just had to laugh or at least smile. And I could look at her and make her whole face light up.[18]

The upper classes provide another illustration of the ocular communication of intimates. From *Dangerous Liaisons:*

> ...those gentle eyes were staring at me! They were immediately lowered again; but, wishing to favor their return, I looked away. Then there was established between us that tacit agreement, the first treaty of timid love, which, to satisfy the need to see each other, allows looks to follow one another until it is time for them to mingle.
>
> Convinced that she was completely absorbed in this new pleasure, I took it upon myself to watch over our common safety; but after ascertaining that a rather lively conversation was saving us from being noticed by the rest of the company, I tried to make her eyes speak their language openly. For this purpose I first surprised a few looks, but with so much reserve that her modesty could not be alarmed; and to put my timid beauty more at ease, I appeared to be as embarassed as she was. Little by little, our eyes grew accustomed to meeting, then remained together for a long time; finally they stopped turning away altogether and I saw in hers that soft languor which is the happy signal of love and desire.[19]

Such intense mutual involvement communicated by those who look "eye to eye" would prove too much for acquaintances who, unless they are trying to become intimates, need but catch each other's eye to blush and look away. (Conversely, since winks and stares are communicative behavior reserved for intimates, strangers who "make eyes at" each other by winking or staring indicate they might like to become intimates and encourage each other to initiate a pickup.)

Edward Hall, an anthropologist, has pointed out that a person does not end with his body, but rather is surrounded by an invisible penumbra of "personal space."[20] In other words, a person is not sharply cut off from his physical environment, but tapers off into it gradually. Consequently, a person can use his zone of personal space as an organ that contacts others and is contacted by others. Strangers and acquaintances, however, try to avoid overlapping their personal spaces and apologize if they must, as when one has to lean across another to reach something. But as acquaintances become intimates, they tend to intrude more and more into each other's personal space by standing and sitting closer and closer to one another.[21] Intimates are those who go, so to speak, "space in space" together.

Intimates have always used their physical interval to indicate their psychological "closeness" in the same way that enemies have always used theirs to indicate their psychological "distance." At least as long ago as the Babylonian Talmud, it was said: "When our love was strong, we slept on the breadth of a sword; but now that our love is weak, a bed of sixty cubits is not wide enough." And at least as recently as the opening of the American West, it was said: "This town ain't big enough for both of us."

What is it about the physical interval between two individuals that allows them to use it to indicate their psychological interval? Hall gives this description of the way individuals who are physically close to each other affect each other:

Intimate Distance

At intimate distance, the presence of the other person is unmistakable and may at times be overwhelming because of the greatly stepped-up sensory inputs. Sight (often distorted), olfaction, heat from the person's body, sound, smell, and the feel of the breath all combine to signal unmistakable involvement with another body.

Intimate Distance—Close Phase:
This is the distance of love-making and wrestling, comforting and protecting. Physical contact or the high possibility of physical involvement is uppermost in the awareness of both persons. The use of their distance receptors is greatly reduced except for olfaction and sensation of radiant heat, both of which are stepped up. . . .

Intimate Distance—Far Phase (6–18 inches):
Heads, thighs, and pelvis are not easily brought into contact, but hands can reach and grasp extremities. The head is seen as enlarged in size, and its features are distorted. . . . At the point where sharp focus is lost, one feels the uncomfortable muscular sensation of being cross-eyed from looking at something too close.[22]

In short, as the physical interval between people decreases, it seems that each loses his own visual orientation while he gains the other's sensory stimulation. Perhaps the willingness, and even wish, to do so physically symbolizes each person's trust that the other will provide him with a sufficient substitute for his lost ability to orient himself on his own, as well as his acceptance of all of the other's effusions, whatever they may be.

Finally, as acquaintances develop into intimates, they obtain (implicit) permission to touch or, in the extreme, press and compress each other physically. Touched or pressed or compressed aspects of an individual that communicate an intimate relationship level include both those connected and those unconnected with his body. Unlike acquaintances, intimates may help each other adjust their clothing and groom one another. And each may fondle the other's permanent possessions, like books, and temporary possessions—those he acquired by virtue of the fact that they happen to be inside his zone of personal space—like the back of one's chair.

Intimates usually use hands, lips, and genitals as *contacting organs* and hands, arms, shoulders, lips, body, breasts, and genitals as *contacted organs.* Even though they may make use of various combinations of contacting and contacted organs (except for certain prohibited permutations), they often use the same organ to give and receive contact. Thus, they may touch *hands*, and are often seen "hand in hand." They may touch *feet*, though "playing footsie" is usually only a humorous parody of the other modes of kinesic discourse. They may touch *heads*; in fact, girls may use their *long hair* not only as a contacted organ that is stroked but also as a contacting organ that is drawn across a boy friend. They may touch *arms*, either by going "arm in arm" to indicate that their selves are as intertwined as their arms, or by "embracing" to indicate that their selves encompass each other as much as their arms do. They may touch *lips*, in what most people call "kissing." And they may touch *sexual organs*, in what sociologists call "engaging in genital-to-genital communication."

In addition to the above linguistic and kinesic phileme families, acquaintances who are evolving into intimates also develop a "private language" consisting of words and gestures that have lost the old meanings which everyone recognizes and have acquired new meanings to which only the intimates themselves respond.[23] The language of intimates becomes filled out with private symbols both because they undergo common experiences that create them and because they tend to pick up each other's linguistic and kinesic habits.[24] The fact that married couples and other long-term intimates often develop like patterns of talking and acting accounts for the fact that, to outsiders, they often seem so similar. Intimates have difficulty in communicating with outsiders in proportion to the number of private symbols that begin to pervade their linguistic and kinesic vocabularies.

(Let me note parenthetically that since many of these private symbols are nonverbal, intimates who have come to rely on them encounter difficulties when they attempt to communicate in ways other than face-to-face.[25] Intimates who talk over the telephone find each other less than all there, for each does not receive the information the other normally sends over visual channels, such as gestures and facial expressions. It is hard to have an I-Thou relationship over the telephone. Letter correspondence cuts out even more information, such as that supplied by voice tone and emphasis, and the slower feedback hinders the immediate correction and qualification of statements that are being misunderstood. However, written language does contain some substitutes for the lost linguistic *articulators* (!), and the very slowness of transmission usually allows a letter writer enough time to compose his intended effect in as clear a way as he can, thus using his restricted resources with optimal efficiency.)

Each intimate may read the momentary fluctuations of the other's fondness for him in the shifting ratio of acquaintance signals to intimate signals that the latter chooses to broadcast. After an argument, for instance, a girl knows her boy friend remains close to her as long as he tries to take her hand, while her boy friend knows she remains distant from him as long as she tries to avoid his touch.

For those who are in love, the interpretation of intimate communication assumes a special place. The lover so consecrates all of his beloved's behavior that her every word and gesture compose for him a holy book, one he feels compelled to read over and over again in memory in order to diagnose the precise degree of her devotion to him and, hence, the precise gradation of his state of grace. Thus, the lover overinterprets the love letters his loved one sends him, biting his lip when he discovers that her first "I love you." merits a mere period instead of an exclamation point, smiling ecstatically when he discovers that her second "I love you!" is underlined three times. (In point of fact, he cannot accurately discover the extent of intimacy signified by her communications to him until he has the baseline of her communications to acquaintances against which to compare them. Some beloveds are given to exclaiming their ardor; others are not.) But if love is prone to read affection into actions in which it is not intended, jealousy is prone to read disaffection into actions in which it is not intended, and the slightest slight to oneself or smile to someone else portends the end of the affair.

COMMUNICATION PROCESSES

Two topics will be considered in this section: (1) the simultaneous combination of philemes from different families, and (2) the sequential progression of philemes within each family and through all of them.

1. It may have occurred to the reader during the above discussion that intimates communicate about the level of their relationship in a manner that differs only slightly from the way enemies communicate about theirs. A few instances: since an individual can use the 'T' form of the second-person-singular pronoun to a subordinate as well as to an intimate, he can use it to insult an enemy as well as to indulge a friend. Similarly, he can use a kin term or a diminutive as much to affront ("Look here, sonny...") as to endear ("Look over here, baby..."). He need modulate his tone only a bit to transform his effect from barely controlled love to barely controlled hate. His silence can declaim either speechless affection (a tacit understanding) or speechless disaffection (the silent treatment). He can confront another eyeball to eyball as well as see eye to eye with him. He can transform his loving gaze into a hating glare merely by tightening the muscles around his eyes a barely perceptible degree.[26] He can overlap another's personal space with his own to signal either that both share a common territory or that the latter cannot defend his individual territory from an intruder. He can close to contact distance to make love or to fight. He can fondle another's possessions gently; he can handle them roughly. His friendly poke can become an unfriendly punch; his endearing caress, a painful squeeze; his kiss, a bite; his intercourse, rape.

How, then, does someone who receives one of these signals from another distinguish whether the other is indicating he is a friend or an enemy? We cannot always discover his criterion by looking for it in the signal itself—as we have just seen, the difference between a friend's signal and an enemy's signal is often only marginal. We must sometimes seek it in the combination of all the signals used in the total communication. Whether a person intends a particular signal to signify closeness or distance may depend on whether the other signals he is sending simultaneously are those used by intimates or enemies.[27] If one individual says to another, "You motherfucker!" while smiling and taking his arm, he means it as a term of flattery, not of effrontery.[28] Or if "her lips say 'no,' but her eyes say 'yes,'" she means that her seducer should continue. Note that the total communication is a product not only of the linguistic and kinesic signals mentioned above, but also of such contextual features as the surrounding situation, the history of the relationship, and the communication immediately preceding the one at issue. In general, we may consider the surrounding signals to constitute the *key signature* by which the composer of the total communication designates how he wants the *note* of a particular signal to be interpreted.

I must add that the above musical model is not completely adequate to handle the complexities of actual human communication, in which it is often difficult to distinguish the notes from the key signature. While his smile and touch indicate that the person who calls another a "motherfucker" feels close to him in general, his word choice indicates that he feels distant from him in some particular way. And while the eyes of the seduced give the seducer a green light to proceed, the "no" from her lips gives him a yellow light to proceed with caution, for her total communication indicates that she feels ambivalent about her seduction. In brief, then, although interacting individuals may indicate the level of their relationship in a straightforward manner by sending only intimate signals, they often indicate the precise degree of their sentiment by combining into a total communication the philemes of intimates with the *phobemes* of enemies.

But even this analysis does not satisfactorily describe the subtlety of the way intimates communicate, for their complex, qualified communications may actually indicate a more intense relationship than their simple, unqualified ones. Since the difference between the signals of intimates and the signals of enemies is often small, a person who sends intimate signals implies that he is capable of sending enemy signals as well. Consequently, his overt expression of how much he likes the other and feels benevolent toward him may carry an undertone: "Look at the potential I have to hate and to harm you." However, the very fact that he was careful to send intimate, not enemy, signals in his overt statement seems to add: "But, of course, I don't hate you and wouldn't harm you." Conversely, intimates can often make their relationship seem even more intense by explicitly expressing how much each can potentially dislike and damage the other ("You prick! I could kill you for that!"), while implicitly denying that he does or would want to do so (e.g., by taking his arm and smiling), than they can by explicitly expressing merely how much each actually likes the other and feels benevolent toward him ("You prince! I could kiss you for that!"). Intimates who communicate through these double negatives feel intensely close insofar as they make each other aware of how strong their relationship must be in order to withstand such potential hostility. Therefore, intimates, especially those who are adolescent or lower class, often signify their friendship by hitting each other and insulting each other. For example, they usually indicate that their relationship is more intense when they refer to each other as "a real motherfucker" than when they refer to each other as "a real nice guy."

Similarly, intimates who are certain about the level of their relationship occasionally may even communicate the way acquaintances do. Each may call the other by his last name or switch to more formal speech or begin to sit far from the other on a sofa. By jokingly threatening to roll back the clock on their relationship to the time when they made the acquaintance choice in a phileme family, each reminds himself and the other how far their intimacy has progressed.

Banter or kidding around, then, may be seen as a communication mode in which intimates combine those communicative choices in various phileme and phobeme families that simultaneously signal different levels of intimacy and enmity in order that their total communication indicates the momentary state of their whole relationship in all its ambivalent complexity.[29]

2. Acquaintances who are trying to become intimates find that phileme families differ in the number and kind of choices they offer to communicate the level of the relationship. Some phileme families offer only two choices, like a two-position switch—one phileme that indicates acquaintance and one phileme that indicates intimacy. Instances of these *binary* phileme families include the choice between 'T' and 'V' forms of the second-person-singular pronoun and the choice between not touching and touching. Other phileme families offer a range of choices between acquaint-

ance and intimacy that are separated from one another by quantum jumps, like a multiposition switch that clicks into each place. Instances of these *discrete* phileme families include the choice among last name, first name, nickname, or diminutive, and the choice among touching various parts of an individual. Still other phileme families offer a range of choices that shade gradually from acquaintance to intimacy, like a switch that can be moved from one position to the other by infinite degrees. Instances of these *continuous* phileme families include the tone of talk and the interval of interpersonal distance.

Acquaintances who are trying to become intimates also find that phileme families differ in regard to how much they must adhere to the intimate choice, once they have made it, when they communicate through that phileme family again. In some phileme families, once individuals make the intimate choice, they usually continue to make it thereafter, in the same way that a springless switch set to a certain position stays in that position. For instance, after one person has called another by his first name for the first time, he tends to continue to call him by his first name whenever he adresses him by name again. In other phileme families, once individuals have made the intimate choice, they need not always make it thereafter, but they now have the potential to make it again easily, in the same way that a springed switch, once moved to a certain position, may go back to its original place while retaining its newly acquired elasticity. For instance, lovers need not continually hold hands after they have done so for the first time, but they are now able to do so again whenever they please. Thus, the intimate choice in many phileme families operates in terms of a potential that is often not realized. The communications between two individuals, therefore, often reveal to an observer only the lower limits of their relationship and tell him nothing about its upper limits. Although he can surmise that the couple he sees holding hands are more than mere acquaintances, he cannot guess whether they are also sleeping together.

We have now come far enough to be able to understand the mechanism of transition between the acquaintance phileme and the intimate phileme in each family. I propose the term *allophiles* (paralleling "allophones" and "allomorphs" in linguistics) for those philemes in different families that signal approximately the same intensity level for the relationship. For example, since a couple who stare deeply into each other's eyes could communicate nearly the same intensity level for their relationship by kissing, the mutual glance and the kiss would be allophiles. When interacting individuals choose a more-than-acquaintance phileme in one family for the first time, they may now assume, through a kind of "halo effect," that they are also free to choose its allophiles in other phileme families. Thus, those who look deeply into each other's eyes for the first time expect henceforth to be permitted to kiss each other as well. In terms of our switchboard model, as soon as both individuals have raised one pair of switches to a certain height, they expect to be permitted to raise other pairs of switches to a similar height. (Sometimes, however, such *lubricators* as alcohol, marijuana, etc., may be needed to loosen sticky switches.)

One would-be intimate begins the process of increasing the intimacy level of a relationship by *testing* whether or not the other actually wants their relationship moved to a higher level. He usually conducts this test by means of those continuous phileme families in which the signal level is easily raised to the precise degree of intensity he wishes to communicate and easily lowered again should the other show signs of not wanting a relationship of that intensity at the moment. He gradually increases his signal strength in these continuous phileme families until he is indicating approximately the same intensity level for the relationship as if he signaled the more intimate phileme in certain binary or discrete phileme families. For example, he may slowly warm the tone of his voice or slowly decrease his distance from the other until he reaches the same intensity level for the relationship he would be indicating if he took the other's hand or said, "I love you." At this point, he suddenly crosses over to the allophile in the correlated binary phileme family (to take the clearest case) and signals its more intimate phileme. So the boy sits closer and closer to the girl on the sofa until he is convinced that she would not mind if he puts his arm around her. After their relationship has entered a new phase, would-be intimates may try to *lock* it into this higher level by using a binary (or discrete) phileme family that, once tripped over to the more intimate phileme, stays put in its new position. So the lovers seal their newfound affair with a kiss. The interplay among continuous, discrete, and binary phileme families accounts for the feeling, common to those whose intimacy is developing, that the intensity level of their relationship is increasing unevenly—sometimes slowly, sometimes rapidly.

In general, those who are becoming intimates proceed through the various phileme families in the following sequence: the non-mutually oriented silence of strangers; the linguistic forms of acquaintances; the linguistic forms of intimates; the mutually oriented silence of intimates; reciprocal looking; reciprocal closing; and reciprocal touching. Within the phileme family of physical contact, they use hands, lips, and genitals as contacting organs, in that order, and hands, arms, shoulders, lips, body, breasts, and genitals, in that order, as contacted organs. This order seems to follow the progression through which individuals embody aspects of their selves that are more and more important to them. (It is interesting to note in this connection Denis de Rougemont's discovery, as reported in *Love in the Western World*, that a mystical Buddhist cult in India and a romantic Christian cult in Europe during the late Middle Ages both ritualized a similar sequence of phileme families—gazing, speaking, touching, kissing, and intercourse—in order to symbolize the stage through which a soul progresses to God.)[30]

I must stress, however, that many individuals (particularly those belonging to certain class and ethnic subgroups) do not follow the general sequence of phileme families described above. Some attach much less importance to certain phileme families than their place in this series would normally indicate; others attach much more importance than normal to these same phileme families. One man might put his hands all over those with whom he still uses only the acquaintance phileme in all the other families; another man might avoid the slightest physical contact even with those with whom he has already used the intimate phileme in all the other families. Were both of these men to interact, they would each interpret the same communicative behavior differently and, consequently, misunderstand each other's statement about the degree of their association.[31]

Love scenes in movies provide excellent illustration and summation of how individuals escalate the level of their relationship through the philemes and their families. These scenes illuminate both *points of crossover*, at which individuals cross from communicating through one phileme family to communicating through another, and *trip mechanisms*, by which they abruptly raise the intensity level of their relationship by suddenly switching from an acquaintance phileme to an intimate phileme. On the screen, a man and woman who are about to become lovers often follow this scenario: (1) They are talking to each other about matters external to their relationship; (2) they suddenly catch and hold each other's glance; (3) their involvement drains from their talk; (4) one says something like, "I think I'm in love with you," though this step may be omitted; (5) they lapse into silence; (6) while their eye-to-eye contact continues, they gradually move closer together; (7) they touch, embrace, and kiss (while turning off eye contact by closing their eyes in order to sharpen their reception of close—more intimate—communication by tuning out distant distractions). The scene dissolves, though in recent films it continues somewhat longer while the couple rotate to a horizontal position in which they carry on their kinesic conversation somewhat further. In either case, the audience is expected to assume that, in the infinitesimal interval before the next scene, their relationship has spurted to a higher level, for we next see them engaging in such hard-core intimate communication as holding hands during a romp through the woods.

COMPLICATIONS

The ascent of acquaintances toward intimacy is, alas, not often so idyllic a journey as that described above. Jack may not be certain Jill wants to go with him all the way up that hill. And Jill may not be certain she even wants to take that first big step. When one acquaintance communicates an intimate phileme for the first time, and the other acquaintance allows it to stand, the latter commits himself to being open in the future to receive further intimate communications not only of this same phileme, but also of all its allophiles. The woman who permits a man to kiss her once not only grants him the potential to kiss her again whenever he pleases, but to take her hand as well. Although it is possible for one individual to disengage himself after he has allowed the initial step, he will find it much more difficult than before, for every time he cooperates with the other's attempt to increase the communication level of the relationship, he induces the other to have "rising expectations" concerning its ultimate outcome. Hence, one of the most critical periods in personal relations occurs when an acquaintance makes an intimate choice in a crucial phileme family for the first time.

Crucial phileme families are those that, once tripped to intimate, almost immediately set off a chain reaction in which many other phileme families are switched over to the intimate position as well. In cross-sex personal relations today, first touch (e.g., taking the other's hand), first "I love you," and first sexual intercourse are the most difficult transitions to make. It is not easy to receive, for the first time in a relationship, an intimate choice in one of these crucial phileme families, for the recipient who accepts it without protest commits himself to tolerating a torrent of further intimate communications. A Frenchwoman who allows a man to sleep with her today should expect him to attempt to "tutoyer" her tomorrow.

It is even more difficult to initiate the intimate choice in one of these crucial phileme families, as every reader of romantic novels knows (see the Stendhal quotation below). If the other person decides to reject his intimate communication, he will experience a sudden blow to his self-esteem, for it will call into question his power to attract others. The hand that gently turns aside his attempted kiss ("No, please don't") will strike him like a slap in the face. In order to save face,[32] a person is usually careful not to attempt to move up to intimate those communication switches he expects the other to throw back to acquaintance. As we have seen, one person often first tests the other's reaction to a slight increase in a continuous phileme family before attempting to discover the other's reaction to a large increase in a binary phileme family. The boy who wants to kiss the girl sitting next to him on a park bench, where they had stopped to look at the moon after their first date at the movies, is likely to proceed first by resting his arm behind her on the bench back, then by bringing it around her shoulders very slowly in order to see whether she will remain seated or whether she will put him off, saying, "Um... I'm very tired.... I think you'd better take me home... so I can get some sleep." Since the boy has not fully committed his self-esteem to this exploratory probe (here: his arm-shoulder contact), he dreads its rejection less than he would the rejection of a serious "advance" (here: his kiss) to which he has fully committed his self-esteem.

The success of an individual's attempt to effect a major increase in the communication level of his relationship with another depends, in part, on his timing. If he moves too rapidly while giving the other too little warning about his intentions, the other might reject him out of surprise and indecision; if he moves too slowly while giving the other too many tentative tests, the other might reject him out of boredom and disgust. In fact, the testing procedures that he uses to discover the other's attitude toward him as a potential intimate actually help to determine this very attitude, for the kind and extent of testing to which he resorts reveal to the other his character and courage.

If one person's tests of the other's attitude toward him as a potential intimate produce ambiguous results, he may still decide he wants to attempt to up the intimacy ante of the relationship, come what may. But, in order to do so, he must adopt strategies to handle the other's possible rejection of his attempt to raise the stakes. These strategies can be either aggressive or defensive.

One kind of aggressive strategy consists of techniques to coerce the other to match his raise. He may courageously plunge ahead with an act of faith in his ability to overpower the other's resistance, a technique Stendhal amply illustrates in *The Red and the Black*:

> One evening [Julien] was speaking with animation, enjoying the pleasure of expressing himself well to young women; as he gesticulated, he happened to touch Madame de Rênal's hand, which was resting on the back of one of those painted wooden chairs that are placed in gardens.

The hand was instantly withdrawn, but Julien decided it was his *duty* to make Madame de Rênal leave it in place when he touched it. . . .

[The next day] the ruthless struggle between his sense of duty and his timidity was so painful that he was in no condition to observe anything outside himself. The clock of the château had just struck a quarter to ten, and still he had not dared to attempt anything. Indignant at his own cowardice, he said to himself, "At exactly ten o'clock I will either do what I promised myself all day long I would do tonight, or go up to my room and shoot myself. . . ."

Finally, while the echoes of the last stroke of ten were still hanging in the air, he put out his hand and took Madame de Rênal's; she withdrew it immediately. Julien, not too clearly aware of what he was doing, seized it again. Although he himself was deeply moved, he was struck by the icy coldness of the hand he was holding. He squeezed it with convulsive force; she made a final effort to draw it away from him, but finally it remained in his grasp.

His heart was flooded with joy, not because he was in love with Madame de Rênal, but because a terrible ordeal had just come to an end.[33]

Another kind of aggressive strategy consists of techniques to persuade the other to match his raise. He may promise great gains if the other accedes to his demands, and/or he may threaten dire losses should the other still refuse. In other words, he may promise to make his potential intimate's future better than it would otherwise be and/or threaten to make it worse. Promises include material rewards, such as merchandise or money, and relationship rewards, such as eternal love or marriage. Threats include material punishments, such as rape or murder, and relationship punishments, such as going away ("You'll never see me again") or suicide.

Defensive strategies are those to *save face* and/or to *save the relationship* should the other refuse to match his raise. One kind of defensive strategy consists of techniques to deny to himself that he actually wanted to become more intimate with the other. An individual who tells himself that he was not fully committed to becoming the other's initimate will feel that he should not take the other' rejection as a blow to his self-esteem. Thus, he will try to convince himself that the other "just wasn't worth it," or was "not for him," and that, in any case, his attempt to become intimate with the other was only halfhearted; in fact, his indifferent approach to this endeavor actually constituted his prior rejection of the other.

Another kind of defensive strategy consists of techniques to deny to the other that he actually intended to become more intimate with him. Since he is innocent of intent, regardless of what the other might have misunderstood him to mean, the latter should neither change his attitude toward him nor destroy what relationship they have. He can use the defensive technique of *retreat through clarification* by communicating his purpose in so ambiguous a way that he can claim that he meant something other than the intimate interpretation the other rejected. A homosexual who hints to his straight friend that he would like to increase his intimacy with him, only to find that his friend is shocked and offended at the suggestion, can attempt to save the relationship by saying something like, "No, no. I didn't mean it that way. I only meant that..." (A person may find it hard, however, to come up with an initial communication that both gets his message across and allows easily of another meaning. If the communication is too ambiguous, he might not be able to make the other understand its intimate intent; if it is not ambiguous enough, he might not be able to retreat to an alternative interpretation.) He can also use the defensive technique of *retreat through persiflage* by communicating his purpose so offhandedly that he can claim that he did not intend it to be taken as seriously as the other, who rejected it, took it. In one of his short stories, Vladimir Nabokov provides an excellent illustration of this technique to save the relationship:

> Nina, who stood on higher ground, put a hand on my shoulder and smiled, and carefully, so as not to crumple

her smile, kissed me. With an unbearable force, I re-
lived (or so it now seems to me) all that had ever passed
between us beginning with a similar kiss; and said
(substituting for our cheap, formal ['vous'] that strangely
full and expressive ['tu'] to which the circumnavigator,
enriched all around, returns), "Look here—what if I love
you?" Nina glanced at me, I repeated those words, I
wanted to add... but something like a bat passed swiftly
across her face, a quick queer, almost ugly expression,
and she, who would utter coarse words with perfect simplicity, became embarrassed; I also felt awkward...
"Never mind, I was only joking," I hastened to say,
lightly encircling her waist.[34]

We have looked at the rejection of the attempt to raise an acquaintance phileme to an intimate phileme from the point of view
of the person whose intimate communication is turned (back)
down. Let us now examine this rejection from the point of view
of the person who wants to turn it—and hence him—down.
Although he may not care what happens to their relationship
after he has blocked that switch, he usually wishes to preserve
what degree of association they have. In heterosexual relations,
rejections are particularly hard to manage when one tries to move
from the status of friend to the status of boy friend or girl friend,
while the other wants neither the gain of a lover nor the loss of
a friend. A rejector will find it difficult to maintain the equilibrium of his relationship with the rejectee insofar as his rejection
has destroyed one of the forces holding the other to him, namely,
the *potential* they had to become intimates "all the way." Consequently, he may try to keep their relationship intact by "tem-
porizing," i.e., by putting off a final yes or no ("Don't be in such
a hurry. Let's see how things go between us"). By repulsing all
tentative advances during the trial period, he may be able to convince the other to make no further serious ones, or he may only
be putting off the inevitable showdown that will occur should the
other—heedless of his hints not to try again—commit himself to
another serious attempt to make their relationship more intimate.
If a person decides he must go through with his rejection, how-

ever, he can still attempt to save the relationship by helping the one he rejects to save face. Indeed, unless he does so, the rejected is likely to become so humiliated that, out of shame, he will lower the level of relationship that, out of merit, he failed to raise. One way the rejector can help the rejectee to save face is to avoid articulating his rebuff. The rejector can collude with the rejectee by pretending that the latter never attempted to make their relationship more intimate. A girl whose hand has just been taken by an unwanted suitor while sitting by a lake may not withdraw it immediately but rather disengage it after a few minutes in order to point at a splashing fish. By this technique, she takes the onus upon herself to initiate the next intimate communication by retaking the boy's hand. If she does, she signals that she concurs with the switch to the intimate phileme and hence stabilizes the transformation. If she does not, the boy knows where he stands in her regard without her ever having to verbalize it. In this way, they may remain acquaintances or friends without ever discussing so potentially painful an incident. Of course, the boy may not get the point and try again, forcing the girl to spell out to him more clearly the cold fact of his failure.

Another way a rejector can help the person he rejects to save face is to acknowledge the latter's attempt to become his intimate while shifting the blame for its lack of success from the rejectee's unworthiness to carry on such a relationship to the rejector's own inability to do so. A girl who wants to turn down a boy who has just confessed his love for her may phrase her rejection in such a way as to blame her past ("I haven't recovered from Clive yet, and it will be a long time before I want to take on anyone else"), her present situation ("I'm too busy with SDS work to want to get involved with anyone at the moment"), her other social ties ("Teddy will be back from England in a few months, and I want to remain faithful to him"), her higher values ("I love you too, but I love God more"), her psychological problems ("It's not just you. I can't seem to love anyone"), or her sociological prejudices ("You're not my type"). In this way, the rejector allows the person rejected to retain his confidence in his attractive power; unless, of course, the latter reflects too long on the fact that if he were attractive, the former would not have considered these obstacles too difficult to surmount.

An individual must worry not only about how to raise his communications to the intimate level with the right people at the right time, but also about how to avoid raising them with the right people at the wrong time and with the wrong people at any time.

When an individual who wants to become an intimate of another is not yet certain that the other wants such a relationship, he often finds himself caught in the no-man's land between the philemes of a family. This is especially true in a binary phileme family. On the one hand, he may feel that the acquaintance phileme conveys too great a distance, which may encourage the other to think him formal and, consequently, keep back himself. On the other hand, he may feel that the intimate phileme conveys too close a distance, which may encourage the other to think him forward and, consequently, keep back himself. For instance, acquaintances who are becoming intimate often pass through a phase in which they are undecided about what formality of name to use to refer to each other ("Mister President?" "Richard?" "Dickie?"). Usually they avoid the dilemma by avoiding the phileme family. Thus, they may refer to each other by a pronoun instead of by name ("Hey... ah... you"). Europeans are deprived even of this escape; as we have seen, their second-person pronouns are as much a phileme family as their proper names. Consequently, they must go through far more complex maneuvers to evade this problem. In *The Counterfeiters*, Andre Gide provides an illustration of the extremes of circumlocution to which Olivier and Edouard must resort in order to hide from each other their love for each other:

> Olivier shrugged his shoulders. "One never knows. If one doesn't happen to be in good form on the day..."
> ...He was embarrassed, too, because he wanted and yet was afraid to say ["tu"] to Edouard. He contented himself by giving his sentences an impersonal turn, so as to avoid at any rate saying ["Vous"]; and by so doing,

> he deprived Edouard of the opportunity of begging him
> to say ["tu"].[35]

When one individual does not want to become an intimate of
another, but is forced, by circumstances beyond his control, to
make a communication to this person of the sort made by those
who are or who want to become intimate, he must try to cancel
out the intimate implication of his communication by sending
further signals. Accidents that imply what must then be denied
commonly occur at many of the above-mentioned kinesic phileme
families. If an individual discovers that he happens to be walking
side-by-side with a stranger, he will have to speed up, slow down,
or stop in order to make it appear the chance event it actually
was. (The reader can satisfy himself that this is indeed what will
occur by attempting to walk next to a stranger for a while and
watching what he does.) If an individual who is staring at a
stranger discovers that his stare is being returned, he will have to
shift his eyes in order to make his stare appear only the frozen
instant of a scan. Similarly, if one who blinks because of something in his eye discovers that the stranger in front of him has
noticed it, he will have to rub his eye in order to make his eye
movement appear the blink it actually was, and not the wink it
might have been taken for. If an individual is forced to overlap a
stranger's personal space with his own for some time, as in an
elevator, he will have to appear preoccupied with himself or with
the changing floor numbers in order to ignore the intimate relation implied by the distance they are apart. Similarly, if he is
forced to touch a stranger in crowded public transportation at
rush hour, he will have to stiffen his muscles in the area touched[36]
in order to make his touch seem as unavoidable and unpleasant to
him as it must be to the other. In these last two cases, the context
in which the accidental communication occurs helps its embarrassed sender to dampen its intimate interpretation, for these contexts are commonly recognized as circumstances in which intimate
messages are often misfired.

As an instance of attempts to deny that a relationship is as intimate as its communicative behavior implies, prostitution is the
most interesting because it is the most extreme. Since, in Western

society at least, sexual intercourse communicates more psychological closeness than nearly any other act, those who prostitute themselves often engage in further behavior that communicates great psychological distance. In order to contradict the implication of indiscriminant intimacy that they are communicating genitally, some prostitutes will appear self-preoccupied, unresponsive, and bored with what they are doing. They will make their activities seem merely to be "work"—a job like any other—by appearing to be concerned only with the money they receive and the time it takes to earn it. In other words, prostitutes try to make their relationships with their customers as formal as possible by offsetting the very high intimacy they are communicating in one phileme family with the low intimacy they are communicating in all other phileme families—an imbalance of intimate communications that often generates much tension.

Certain people seem to enjoy the process of becoming intimates more than the state of being intimates. These individuals, called flirts or coquettes, are usually (though not always!) women; their victims are usually (though not always!) men.[37] Georg Simmel defines coquetry as consisting of "allusive promises and allusive withdrawals—to attract the male but always to stop short of a decision, and to reject him but never to deprive him of all hope."[38] In terms of the communication model developed here, to flirt is to keep all the acquaintance philemes from being changed to intimate ones while still maintaining their potential to be so switched. A flirt tries to get a man to switch to an intimate phileme either without her making the switch herself or with her switching back down immediately to the acquaintance phileme the communication that she had only momentarily switched up to the intimate. Helen Gurley Brown gives her students the following example of how to flirt:

> Select a man at a nearby restaurant table.... Spotted him? Look straight into his eyes, deep and searchingly, then lower your gaze. Go back to your companions or magazine. Now look at him again in the same way... steadfastly, questioningly. Then drop your eyes. Do it three times and you're a flirt!

> Want to flirt some more?
> A man is talking to you, nothing very personal. Look
> into his eyes as though tomorrow's daily double winners
> were there.... Never let your eyes leave his.... Looked
> at so, a man usually stops whatever he is saying and
> kisses the girl![39]

("Why, Mr. Brown! How could you do such a thing?") Here,
the man, caught with his flag of intimacy up, is left to dangle it
alone. By pretending that she will reciprocate, the woman gets the
man to commit himself to an intimate phileme before she does.
By so doing, she becomes the center of power in the relationship
because it is now up to her to decide whether or not to ratify the
request to become her intimate, which she has tricked him into
making. She retains her power as long as she can keep him off
balance and from knowing "where he stands" in her regard.

A woman cannot continue to flirt with a man once she has
been caught at it, for then he will no longer trust any more of her
intimate communications, he will see there is no potential in their
relationship, and, consequently, he will no longer respond by
sending intimate philemes himself. In order to keep his hope alive
enough for him to continue to play her game, the flirt must not
acknowledge that she was merely flirting. Since, as we have seen,
certain communications intimates make intentionally (like looking
each other in the eye) may be made by nonintimates accidentally,
a flirt will try to make her intimate communication look like an
accident. Whether a particular communication is merely an accident often depends on the temporal interval it is sustained: a long
time signifies intention; a short time signifies accident. Flirts send
out their deceptive semaphores in that ambiguous temporal interval
between the long and the short. (Flirts also communicate through
an ambiguous spatial interval—for instance, sitting at middle distance from men on sofas or in cars.) Whatever interpretation,
and consequent response, a man makes of her meaning, the flirt
has the power to show that she intended the other one.[40]

Flirting, then, in this respect is the opposite of banter. Whereas
those who banter signal that their relationship is lower than it

actually is, those who flirt signal that their relationship is higher that it actually is.

Flirting would not be nearly so effective were it not similar to what I will call the *holding pattern*. An individual will put a relationship into a holding pattern when he honestly wants intimacy with the other but is too shy to commit himself to initiating it or when he honestly feels uncertain about its desirability. In the holding pattern, he will send the other ambiguous single signals or many mixed signals (some indicating a desire to become his intimate, others indicating a desire to remain his acquaintance —either simultaneously or alternatively). An individual may put his relationship with a potential intimate into this phase for a while in order to gain time to decide whether he wants to intensify the intimacy or to diminish it. When a relationship is in a holding pattern, should the other try to raise its intensity level, he will lower it, and should the other try to lower its intensity level, he will raise it. The holding pattern, however, cannot be held too long without subjecting the other (who finds his every move—whether up or down—blocked) to excessive stress and making the other aware of the interactional frustrations involved in becoming the intimate of so indecisive a person. For instance, a boy who procrastinates in his attempt to intensify intimacy with a girl, for fear of being rejected and losing what relationship with her he has, may eventually convince her that an affair with him would be too disconcerting. When he eventually gets up the courage to try to request such an affair, she will have to turn him down.

Since those who dishonestly wish to flirt and those who honestly are merely insecure or indecisive transmit the same equivocal signals, a person confronted with these ambiguous broadcasts will have difficulty deciding which is which. The fear of deceit has poisoned many a potential personal relation, especially for those who have been beguiled too often in the past, by making each party so suspicious of the other's intimate communications that he will not respond in kind without taking inordinate precautions.[41]

Finally, it should be noted that even after intimates are certain of the level of their relationship, they are not free from problems in communicating it. Like the other aspects of intimacy, the intensity levels of their association that each wishes to communicate to the other may get out of phase. One may want to tell the other how close to him he feels, while the other, momentarily at least, does not feel like reciprocating. Nevertheless, the latter will usually feel obligated to respond in kind, for he knows that, if he does not, he will destroy for the future the intimacy that exists in the present only insofar as the intimates continue to tell each other it does. Should the other kiss him, hug him, or tell him, "I love you," he must kiss or hug the other back or reply "I love you, too" with as much enthusiasm as he can muster, whether he feels like it or not, in order to keep the other from complaining, "What's wrong with you today? You're so cold to me."

In this chapter, the *communication* dimension of an intimate relation has been considered and a third major force uncovered that transforms isolated individuals into interlinked intimates: *the continual verbal and nonverbal statements they make to each other that they are intimates.* Sometimes these statements are made singularly; sometimes opposing ones are mixed together. Sometimes they are made aloud or made visible; sometimes they exist only as a potential based on the memory that, having been made at least once previously, they can be made again. In any case, as acquaintances become intimates, they become able to make more and more of these statements to each other and they receive more and more of these statements from each other.

CHAPTER 4

Getting To Know You

Besides, Sir, as you and I are in a manner perfect strangers to each other, it would not have been proper to have let you into too many circumstances relating to myself all at once.... As you proceed further with me, the slight acquaintance which is now beginning betwixt us, will grow into familiarity; and that, unless one of us is in fault, will terminate in friendship... then nothing which has touched me will be thought trifling in its nature, or tedious in its telling.[1]

Near the beginning of the labyrinthian life he is about to unfold, Tristram Shandy announces in this way that he and his reader are going to conduct their relationship according to the formal rules by which such relationships are properly conducted. His comment is appropriate to the eighteenth century in which it was written, for it was during this period, especially in England, that communal life began to be transformed into social life at an accelerating rate, and the new rules of etiquette for interpersonal manners in a mass and mobile society began to be established more formally. Shandy's remark would have had little meaning to a person living in a gemeinschaft, in which the same people encountered one another throughout their lifetimes, and in which everyone knew almost everything there was to know about one another from the time they were children. His remark, however, was quite meaningful to those living in a gesellschaft, in which many strangers encountered one another for the first time, and in which they often had to learn what there was to know about one another, starting from scratch.[2]

Members of society have a harder time learning about one another than their communal counterparts had for three reasons. First, they have more to learn. Since the life activities and experiences of social man are more differentiated from one another than those of communal man, the former can less easily assume that what is true about himself holds true about others. Second, this same social differentiation allows each person to acquire more control over the distribution of information about his own unique activities and experiences. Third, he is more likely to desire to keep some of his individuating characteristics "secret" from other people both because they conflict with the characteristics he shares with others and because he identifies more with his unshared characteristics than with his shared ones.[3] "The secret," said Georg Simmel, "is a first-rate element of individualization. It is this in a dual role: social conditions of strong personal differentiation permit and require secrecy in a high degree; and, conversely, the secret embodies and intensifies such differentiation."[4] In sum, since a person feels he is what he hides, and since what he hides always contradicts what he seems, he will be extremely careful to allow a complete picture of himself (i.e., one including both his secret and his surface characteristics) to be obtained only by those who he comes to feel will neither mind this discrepancy nor harm him through it.[5]

Because of this greater behavioral differentiation, information control, and concealment concern, each member of a society has to manage both the input of information about others and the output of information about himself more consciously than any member of a community ever had to do. Accordingly, those in society whose acquaintance is more than passing present to each other, phenomenologically, a chiaroscuro facade, as in a Rembrandt portrait—a foreground of light promontories (what is shown) and shadowy crevices (what is concealed) standing out against a background of obscure and murky features (what is not yet discovered).

The first section of this chapter will consider *familiarity*, or the public knowledge of each other that acquaintances acquire merely by associating with each other over a long period of time. Intimates, too, are familiar with each other in this sense, but they know more than each other's public parts. The second section will consider *confidentiality*, or the secret knowledge of each other that intimates alone acquire and that is concealed from mere acquaintances, however long term. Finally, the complications section will consider how both kinds of knowledge, especially the latter, can be falsified, forced, blocked, and betrayed.

FAMILIARITY

When acquaintances associate with each other over a long period of time, regardless of whether they remain acquaintances or turn into intimates, they become "familiar" with each other. Each gradually constructs a picture of the other toward which he orients himself. This picture is never finished but is continually subject to supplementations,[6] though the number and extent of these modifications decrease rapidly as the relationship goes on. The palette from which they paint their portraits of each other consists of five main classes of items. Roughly in the order discerned, they delineate physical, behavioral, social, psychological, and temporal dimensions. Of course, some items from the later classes may become apparent before some items from the early classes. (For convenience, I will begin by referring only to acquaintances, though my description of their five-dimensional construction is intended to apply to that of intimates as well, insofar as they are also acquaintances.)

Physical

Since the physical appearance of an individual is his most apparent aspect, it is usually the first thing acquaintances learn about each other. Appearance is the product of anatomical characteristics, clothing, and kinesics (i.e., manner of holding and moving body and limbs). To those who know him, a person's physical appearance not only implies his other aspects, such as his social class, it also constitutes the axis around which they organize these other aspects.[7] Even though each of his acquaintances may wish to relate to different of his aspects—one may like his wisdom, another his warmth, for instance—all of them can get at the aspect they want only through the medium of his physical appearance. In order to be able to find this desired aspect in the future, each must be able to recognize its container and its label: his face.

Behavioral

Acquaintances become familiar with each other's manner of behavior. They learn such general behavioral features as, for instance, each other's self-saving techniques (how he defends himself when someone disagrees with him or when he makes a mistake), other-saving techniques (how he supports the selves of others), other-attacking techniques (how he assaults the selves of others), interaction competence (whether he always has a ready reply to raillery or suffers it in embarrassed silence), and interaction commitment (proportion of playful behaviors to serious behaviors). Eventually, each might get a chance to see how the other behaves in extreme situations and crises (e.g., from blown-out fuses to blown-up buildings). From observations of the other's behavior, each acquaintance comes to be able to predict, with more and more accuracy, how the other would behave in circumstances besides those in which he has specifically observed him ("It's just like him to do something like that").

Sociological

Acquaintances learn each other's social attributes. Generally, they attempt to learn the same things about each other that sociologists and those who make up most application forms do: present address, birth place, ethnicity, socioeconomic class, age, place and kind of employment, education, and marital status. In other words, they will try to locate each other on various geographic, social, stratifying, economic, cultural, and interpersonal coordinates. If they are members of overlapping groups, they can learn each other's group status or reputation. Besides these attributes, certain social categories may consider other ones relevant to know. Thus, college students usually ask each other what school they go to, what year in school they are, and what their major is. Servicemen out of uniform usually try to ascertain each other's rank, outfit, specialty, and base. And religious Catholics inquire about diocese, parish, and priest.

Psychological

Acquaintances gain knowledge of the cognitive and cathectic aspects of each other's psyche. The former includes general knowledge, ideas, attitudes, beliefs, opinions, tastes, interests, values, and goals. The latter includes the range of emotions, the particular ways each emotion is expressed in behavior, the *charged symbols* that set them off (e.g., the Vietnam war or long hair), and the frequency of bad or good moods (i.e., heightened or lowered degrees of irritability or disagreeability, which are passing). Each acquaintance wishes to discover the other's psychological aspects not only in general, but in particular those he is oriented to and those that are oriented to him. Thus, each may be especially interested in learning whether the other possesses the psychic elements he has found to be important in his past relationships (e.g., a sense of humor) and what the other thinks, feels, likes, and dislikes about him.

Temporal

Acquaintances learn each other's biographies, which show how their present behavioral, sociological, and psychological elements have accumulated and developed. It generally takes acquaintances longest to learn the temporal sequence of each other's past (and projected) life because a person seldom pours out his whole life story in one sitting, usually dribbling it out in anecdotes that are both discrete and disordered. An autobiographer usually feels dissatisfied when he is interrupted before he completely finishes telling an anecdote about himself, implying that these stories are self-contained atoms. An auditor of these *autobiography atoms* usually feels confused when he tries to arrange them in a temporal sequence, implying that they are retold in an order other than that in which they occurred ("Why don't you begin at the beginning?" "Oh, I see. First you ..., and then you ...").

Although acquaintances seem to learn about these aspects of each other over the course of their association, precisely how they do so is unclear. Somehow the simple techniques they use provide them with knowledge of each other adequate to their purposes— despite the complex philosophic problems concerning the way these techniques actually work. One philosophic problem involves the question of how one person can know anything at all (e.g., the other's physical appearance). A second philosophic problem involves the question of how one person can know things that have no immediate empirical reference (e.g., the other's social attributes and biography). A third philosophic problem involves the question of how one person can know what is going on in another's mind (e.g., the other's psychological propensities). It would be too difficult to discuss these questions here. They have constituted some of the central epistemological problems of philosophy, at least since the time of Descartes. And, in the past hundred years, social theorists have also produced an extensive, though far from definitive, body of work on these topics.[8]

In passing, I will merely note that acquaintances employ the following concrete techniques to become informed about each other: the minor indirect mode of talking to mutual acquaintances or reading documents (such as newspaper articles on each other or book-jacket biographies); the major direct mode, which includes both passively observing each other (including his possessions and the company he keeps) and listening to each other (including his talk about third persons and about himself), as well as actively questioning each other (obtaining information not only through his actual answers but also through his manner of giving them). Acquaintances also employ the following concrete techniques (similiar to those used by social scientists)[9] to check the "reliability" and "validity" of the knowledge they acquire about each other.

Acquaintances will consider their picture of each other to be a *reliable indicator* of each other's features only if it is *not* derived from behaviors that result from passing moods or particular circumstances. The only way for those who have just met to refine each other's essential and continuing aspects from each other's contingent and transient ones is to meet each other again at a later time in different circumstances. *Second meetings* thus constitute an important stage in personal relations. The later time at which it occurs allows them to separate out the effects of the first mood, while the different place allows them to separate out the effects of the first circumstance. Still later meetings in still different circumstances allow them to sharpen their picture of each other's core behavior and personality. They can also use this same procedure to determine what their future relationship is likely to be. Although they can dismiss one occurrence of a certain mode of interaction as a fluke, the second augurs a lifetime of repetitions.

Constructing a reliable picture is complicated because two tasks must be attempted simultaneously, though the accomplishment of one depends on the prior accomplishment of the other. On the one hand, each acquaintance must first typify[10] the range of behaviors associated with the other's moodless and circumstance-free personality, in order to determine whether a particular behavior resulted merely from his mood or circumstance. On the other hand, each acquaintance must first determine whether a particular behavior resulted merely from the other's mood or circumstance, in order to typify the range of behaviors associated with his moodless and circumstance-free personality. Presumably, it is the frequency and consistency of a particular behavior, relative to all of a person's other behaviors, that determines whether the behavior in question is essential or merely contingent. (Hence, it would be imprecise to say that a person is "always in a bad mood," for such irritability is comparative, either to the baseline of his previous state—"He's been in a bad mood lately"—or to the baseline of other people—"He's an irritable person.")

One acquaintance will often help the other construct a reliable picture of himself by telling him when (he feels) his actions are merely contingent and therefore should not be added to the other's image of his essence ("Don't mind me. I'm not myself today"). When one acquaintance decides that some of the other's actions result merely from the latter's mood or circumstance, he does not use these actions to modify his conception of the other further, except insofar as he now sees the other as moody or easily moved. However, he may alter his momentary response to the other ("I'd better go now. I can see you're in a bad mood").

Acquaintances will consider their picture of each other to be a *valid indicator* of each other's actual features only if they can work out the inconsistencies of this picture. These inconsistencies usually result from the fact that acquaintances obtain information about each other from semi-independent sources. They must correlate: (1) what he says about himself now with what he said about himself before; (2) what he says about himself with what can be observed about him; and (3) what he says about himself with what others say about him. Because everyone holds stereotypes about the ways the elements of a person are supposed to correlate with one another, the dialectic between the stereotype and an individual's particular combination of elements may throw both into question. When we learn that the bearded hippie we have met has just returned from a Young Republican convention, we may disregard our stereotype of bearded hippies or of Young Republicans, or more likely we will keep our stereotypes and conclude that there is "something fishy" about him.

Why do acquaintances want to become familiar with each other? Actually, each may not especially care to learn about the other, but does so involuntarily simply because his characteristics are revealed over the course of a long acquaintance. It is more likely, though, that each will want to learn about the other. There are several positive reasons for this inquisitiveness. He may be generally curious about life and see the other as an interesting instance of it. He may want to fill in the other's blanks in order to facilitate their interaction. (If he can discover what the other finds tantalizing or taboo, he can bring up the former while playing down the latter.) Finally, and most importantly, he may want to learn enough about the other to decide whether it would be worthwhile to attempt to raise their relationship from acquaintance to initimate.

Conversely, why do acquaintances want each other to become familiar with themselves? Again, each may not especially care whether the other learns about some of his elements enough to take the precautions that may at times be necessary to conceal them. Here too, however, there are likely to be several positive reasons that will motivate him to reveal some of his characteristics. He may think the other needs to know certain things in order to understand and appreciate some of the motives behind his apparently peculiar behavior. (For example, if he is reading *The New York Times* in a college classroom and suddenly utters a "Wow!" he may have to explain to the acquaintance sitting next to him that he used to go with the girl who is described in the article as having been arrested at a political rally for biting a police dog.) He himself may want the other to learn enough about him, especially his likes and dislikes, to make their interaction easier. Finally, he may reveal himself in order to stimulate the other to do the same. (Although each acquaintance can increase the amount of self-information the other volunteers by providing him with information about himself in general,[11] he can acquire the particular information about the other he wants by providing information about himself in the same area: "I'm in sociology." "Well, isn't that interesting. I'm in English, myself.")

At this point, it is necessary to distinguish intimates from acquaintances in regard to the mental *magnitude* of the components they use to construct their pictures of each other. Acquaintances compose theirs solely out of middle-size pieces (such as major social statuses and general psychological features), whereas intimates compose theirs not only out of these middle-size pieces, but also out of both large, important chunks (such as crucial secrets, which will be taken up in the next section) and small, trivial particles (such as the mundane past and present events of each other's lives and the exhaustive elaboration of each other's psychological elements: interests, goals, tastes, opinions, etc.). Each acquaintance intends for the other to learn only matters of middling moment, because the latter is not trusted to receive more significant segments and not interested in receiving less significant ones. But each intimate intends for the other to learn his most and least salient items as well, because the latter has convinced him that he can be trusted and that he is interested.

A related difference between acquaintances and intimates is that, whenever a change occurs in any of their public portions, acquaintances wait for chance to reveal it, whereas intimates desire to disclose and discover it as soon after it occurs as possible. This desire of intimates to keep their picture of each other up-to-date is usually strong enough to last long after they have been abnormally separated. Should they be suddenly reunited, they seem to spend the first part of their reunion asking about each other ("What have you been doing with yourself?") and the second part asking about mutual friends ("Have you heard from Douglas? The last I heard he was . . ."). Each intimate wants to keep track of the other after they have been abnormally separated in order to determine whether any of the other's identity components has changed. Identity components especially susceptible to change—and hence usually asked about—include employment change ("What's he doing now?"), status change ("How's he doing?"), interpersonal change ("Is he married yet?"), and body-image change ("How's he look?"). It is important for someone who has not received information about his intimate for some time to learn about these transformations in his intimate's identity —not only to ascertain whether his intimate has altered too much for them to revive their old relationship ("Why, you haven't changed a bit in all these years!"), but also to evaluate his own features and fortunes by the evolving yardstick of his old point of reference ("Well, guess what: Westinghouse just made me New York sales manager. How are you coming along at G.E.?" "All right, I suppose. They recently appointed me a vice-president." "Oh").

Since intimates like to meditate on each other's minutiae, they are usually only too happy to give these details to each other, for each can better clarify to himself what he communicates to another.[12] Although each intimate can passively help the other to articulate himself merely by being his sounding board, he can actively help him to conceptualize himself still further by responding in certain ways. He may indicate that he does not understand what the other is talking about, forcing him to rephrase his self-characterizations in words ever new and precise ("What I'm trying to say is that I'm..."). He may provide the other with a phrase or formula that describes the latter's aspects more appropriately than any the latter could have thought of by himself ("In other words, you mean you're..."). He may insist that the other obtain a firm grasp on areas of life besides those in which the latter already has one (e.g., political), forcing him to clarify his conception of himself in relation to these new areas[13] ("Well, I hadn't thought of it before, but I suppose I'm..."). He may disagree with or disapprove of what the other has told about himself, forcing the latter to find new arguments to justify, and hence delineate, himself more sharply ("Look here. I'm this way also because..."). He may help the other to attain a consistent self-conception by forcing him to reconcile the various aspects of himself that the latter has revealed ("But you just said you are ..."). And, finally, he may help the other to attain a continuous self-conception by forcing him to reconcile what he said about himself in the past with what he says about himself in the present ("But yesterday you said you were...").

Moreover, each intimate may wish the other to become thoroughly familiar with him in order to feel freer to pretend he is what he is not. (*Pretense down* should be distinguished from *pretense up*. Each intimate is pleased the other knows him insofar as he can now pose as being worse than he is; each is displeased the other knows him insofar as he cannot now pose as being better than he is.) It is only when he is certain the other has already formed a relatively stable picture that he can engage in actions he does not want added to this picture. When he is certain the other knows who he is, he can safely play at being someone else without worrying that he will be presumed actually to have the inferior qualities he is merely pretending to possess. Only then can he safely perform the little vignettes (Yiddish: *shticklach*) in which he mimics anyone from the President on down without fear of being taken for what he is merely making fun of. (The better actor a person is, the less intrinsic cues he gives that he is acting, and the more his audience must rely on their previous knowledge of him to know when he is merely posing.)

In addition, once each intimate is certain that the other knows his general intellectual outlook, he can experimentally defend various intellectual positions that are at variance with local norms (e.g., that Negroes were better off under slavery than today) without being presumed to possess the other attributes that locals believe are possessed by those who usually defend such positions (e.g., dumb, close-minded, fascist, racist).

Since an individual's theatrical portrayals or experimental positions are often fed by psychological fuels of which he is scarcely aware, he often becomes more involved in these portrayals or positions than his audience. When they tire of his dissimulating before he does—as is often the case—they make known their wish that he stop pretending to be someone they know he is not or stop defending the position they know he does not actually believe ("Come on" or "Come off it").[14] Only intimates dare use these phrases to each other, not only because only intimates know each other's true selves and beliefs, but also because only intimates can take the insult insinuated in their implication that each is not infinitely interesting or persuasive no matter what part he performs or premise he defends.

CONFIDENTIALITY

To be *familiars* is one thing; to be *confidants* is another. Like acquaintances, intimates are familiar with the public aspects of each other; unlike acquaintances, they are also privy to the private. It has already been noted that an individual in gesellschaft identifies his essence more closely with the qualities he hides than with the qualities he displays. Consequently, when he finally allows his intimate to see behind the mask he presents to the world, he feels he is allowing the other to see him as he really is. Indeed, the word "intimate" itself is derived from two Latin words meaning "to make known" and "innermost." Recently, too, a friend has been defined as "a person with whom you dare to be yourself." Whether a person really is what he thinks he is when he is with his intimates, however, is a question beyond the scope of this book.[15]

What an individual hides behind the mask he presents to the world, what he attempts to keep secret from everyone except his intimates, are his *weaknesses*, i.e., his inability to withstand certain pressures from his environment. (Even such latent strengths as the miser's buried gold become overt weaknesses whenever they are concealed.) He wants to conceal his points of vulnerability from those who, should they discover them, would (he feels) attack him at those very points. We are all Achilles with our tender heels to hide.

Every person is dialectical in the sense that his arms of steel rest upon feet of clay. Intimates come to learn that each other's surface strengths are only the hard crusts over their subterranean soft spots ("I didn't like him at first. He was loud and obnoxious. But once I got to know him I could tell that he wasn't really like that inside"). In a 1960s *New Yorker* cartoon, one member of a rather hip-looking couple is saying to the other: "Just think. When we first met, I didn't know your hang-ups and you didn't know my hang-ups."

The mutual portraits of each other that acquaintances draw are flat, hollow, and indistinct—mere silhouettes—because they are filled in only with the monochrome of each other's public particles.[16] But the mutual portraits of each other that intimates paint have more depth, density, and definition—high relief—because they are filled in with the polychrome of each other's private particles as well. Every dimension of which a person is composed may include items that he would prefer to conceal from everyone except his intimate.[17]

Physical

He may wish to conceal some extreme or slight anatomical stigma (e.g., his general psoriasis or the small size of his penis), or some physiological stigma (e.g., heroin addiction or colostomization), or the general appearance of his body and the steps he must take to girdle it into an acceptable shape. For these reasons, he will try to keep others from seeing him while he is dressing or undressing or performing his unsavory physiological functions (e.g., "shooting up" or emptying his colostomy pouch).

Psychological

He may wish to conceal his tastes (e.g., perverse), his opinions (e.g., that blacks are dumber or smarter than whites), his goals (e.g., to become a famous writer),[18] his ideas (e.g., half-thought-out ones), his ignorance (e.g., of the books that he, as an intellectual, ought to have read), his emotions (e.g., fear or love), and his frustrations (e.g., those that result from his failures).[19] Although others may wonder why anyone would want to hide some of these psychological aspects, such as goals or opinions, he may be so identified with them while being so uncertain of their actual worth that he would suffer intensely were they merely mocked.

Sociological

He may wish to conceal his ethnicity (e.g., Jewish), or race (e.g., Negro), or class of origin (e.g., lower-middle) if he is attempting to pass as a member of a social group (e.g., Wasp upper-middle-class) different from the one to which he actually belongs. He may also wish to conceal his financial affairs if he fears that others would behave differently toward him (e.g., stop or start offering to buy his lunch) should they discover he were richer or poorer than he claimed to be.

Behavioral

He may wish to conceal his behavior during the times (e.g., when he is drunk, high, or acting childish) it differs greatly from his normal standards of conduct (e.g., when he is crawling around on the floor, pretending he is a cat).

Temporal

He may wish to conceal the fact that he has not always possessed the sociological qualifications he now claims to have. For example, he may claim to be an average, normal person, one of the main criteria for which is always having been one; whereas in fact he had once been a convict or a Communist.[20] He may also wish to hide the past incidents of his life in which he did not live up to his present standards of conduct, such as the times he behaved cruelly or cowardly. And he may further wish to keep secret what the future has in store for him (e.g., he is dying of cancer and has six months to live) or what he has in store for the future (e.g., his plan to assassinate the President).

Only to his intimates will he feel safe confiding any of these items.

It should be stressed that every culture, historical period, and social group makes its own division of all possible particulars that compose a person between those that are considered critical weaknesses, to be kept secret from everyone except their intimates, and those that are not. In our society, a person can achieve the status of mental patient either by casually telling a mere acquaintance what would generally be considered his most intimate aspects or by arduously telling his closest friend what would generally be considered his least intimate aspects. Thus, he could get himself committed to a mental hospital either by matter-of-factly describing to an acquaintance his disgusting anatomical details ("I have a terrible case of hemorrhoids. Let me show them to you") or by agonizingly confessing to his friend, after months of hinting that he would like to reveal to him his essential secret, something he has never told anyone before, that, more than anything else in the world, he hates the color blue ("It's everywhere! I can't stand it! I see it wherever I go!").

Perhaps the most important kind of knowledge (at least in Judeo-Christian societies) that is considered intimate (in the sense that it should be distributed only to a select few) is sexual knowledge. The interconnection between sex and knowledge has been recognized since biblical times:

> The association of eros and knowledge is made in the Bible in at least three ways. First, the Bible indicates that

the response of Adam and Eve to the eating of the tree
"to make one wise" (Genesis 3:6) was to make aprons out
of fig leaves. Thus, the first act informed by knowledge is
depicted as somehow involving the genitalia. Second, the
Bible uses the word "yada" which means "know" to denote sexual intercourse. Third, the Bible uses the expression "uncover the nakedness of" in injunctions against
illicit sexuality, as, for example, "None of you shall approach to any that is near of kin to him, to uncover their
nakedness."[21]

The Freudians have suggested that all nonsexual aspects of
intimate relations are merely sublimations of sexual ones.[22] But
having found the Freudians with their genitals where their heads
should be, I feel it is necessary for us to invert them. The sex act
itself is not the prototype of intimate knowledge but merely the
particularization, for copulation actually consists of the penetration and revelation of an essential secret. A woman's vagina, and
especially her virginity, is her secret essence insofar as it is the last
aspect of herself she will yield to a man and, in so doing, consider
herself to be totally "possessed" by him. Conversely, a man usually
wants to make love to a particular woman, especially for the first
time with her, less to sate his senses than to seize her soul.[23] Or
so it was until recently.

It was the very *modesty* with which a woman covered up her
"privates" that transformed her genitals into her quintessence. It
was her very reticence in revealing her erotic areas that transub-
stantiated her sex into a secret and enhanced its value far beyond
what a mere few inches of flesh would seem to merit in itself.
"Modesty," says Stendhal, "is very flattering to a lover's pleasures;
it makes him feel how many laws are being broken for him."[24]
This thought is expanded by Ortega y Gasset:

> The thing that is repugnant and monstrous about the
> prostitute is her contradiction of feminine nature, by vir-
> tue of which she offers the anonymous man, the public,
> that hidden personality which ought to be revealed only

to the chosen one.... On the other hand, the "classic" example of feminine matters, Don Juan, is preferably attracted by the most modest woman, the one who hides herself most completely from the public, who, in feminine morphology, represents the opposite pole from the prostitute. Don Juan, in fact, falls in love with the nun.[25]

With the recent decline in feminine modesty, however, her spirit has departed from her sex, and copulation has consequently become more an act of physical gratification than of psychical satisfaction.

Men, but more especially women, may go to great lengths to keep everyone but their intimates from becoming informed of their sexual sector. They may feel that the most important sort of secret knowledge others can acquire from them is "carnal knowledge." It pervades their every dimension.

Physical

A person may wish to conceal the fact that the physical appearance of his genitals is almost the total opposite of the rest of his physical appearance in shape, color, texture, liquidity, odor, pilosity, and neatness. With the rise of civilization, he may come to consider his genitals to be a wild and uncivilized growth, a hangover from the primitive past, discrediting his claim to civility.

Psychological

A person may wish to conceal his sexual preferences, which may be not only quite bizarre in their own right but quite at variance with the staid image of himself he usually wishes to convey. Moreover, he may wish to conceal his sexual problems, which also may be not only embarrassing in themselves but contrary to his desire to be seen as generally competent in all his interactions.

Sociological

In Judeo-Christian societies, a person may wish to conceal the fact that he is violating a social taboo, for all forms of unmarried sex, and even some forms of married sex, are officially prohibited.

Behavioral

A person may wish to conceal the uninhibited habits that overcome him when he is sexually aroused, for they too are often at
odds with the image implied by his more controlled behaviors.
When he is in the "wild abandon" of orgasm and its preliminaries, he will often find it hard to keep up his usual personal
proprieties, such as his rule never to drool.

Temporal

A person may wish to conceal his past or projected sexual affairs; specifically, the information with whom, doing what, and
how often.

Since a man, but more especially a woman, is likely to consider
much of the sexual information on these five dimensions to include points where he or she is pregnable, he or she is likely to
be concerned with concealing it from all but a trusted intimate.

(The relatively strict rules in our society governing the access
of others to the sexual aspects of a person's life allow him relatively great control over the distribution of knowledge about his
sex life, especially its physical dimension. Our *erogenous zoning
code* not only localizes what we consider to be the erotic areas of
the body into specific regions (delineated from, but implied by,
their immediate surroundings), but also formalizes the kind and
degree of trespass permitted. This phenomenology of the body
makes possible the playful hide-and-seek between the erotic and
its cognition found in the world of fashion. The changing styles
of women's clothing continually vary the amount of information
about the erotic areas of her body that the female conceals from,
or reveals to, the male.)

How do intimates come to learn each other's secrets? To answer
this question we must first distinguish mundane secrets from
crucial secrets.[26]

A person's *mundane secrets* include his ordinary appearance
before he prepares his presentable self and the ordinary means by
which he becomes presentable. He usually sets aside one or more
locations—which have been called his "backstage"[27]—where he

feels he can safely lapse from his respectable demeanor into his bathrobe-and-slippers behavior and where he can safely store the indecent means (e.g., deodorant cans) he uses to make himself decent. The longer acquaintances associate, the better the chance that one will accidentally stumble into these backstage areas and see the other with his presentable self unbuttoned. Intimates indicate the extent of their trust in each other by daring to increase this chance still further. They actually invite each other into, and eventually even give each other free run of, these backstage areas, particularly the home. Here is an illustration, culled from various pages of the Japanese novel, *Kokoro*, by Natsume Soseki, of the way a progressing relationship is manifested in part through progressive access to the home and the consequent progressive probability that one intimate will come upon the other before the latter can compose his customary character:

> But I did not yet know where Sensei lived. . . . "Would it be all right if I visited you [Sensei] at your home now and then?" . . . After that day I began to visit Sensei at regular intervals. . . . I began to visit Sensei two or even three times a month. . . . My visits were becoming more and more frequent. . . . There was, however, one incident that marred my general impression of [Sensei's] married life. One day, I was standing as usual in their front hall, and was about to announce myself. I heard voices coming from the living room. An argument, rather than an ordinary conversation, seemed to be taking place.[28]

Living together represents the ultimate development of the intimates' trust in each other to tolerate their little lapses, for its maximizes the opportunity each has to monitor the other's mundane secrets, the dirty laundry of his life. (When nonintimates are forced to live together, in such institutions as jails, army barracks, and college dormitories, each has great difficulty in keeping others from catching him with his presentation down. The inability of the inmates of total institutions to control the dissemination of information about their mundane secrets is a torture for some, a temptation for others.)

Crucial secrets concern particulars that are more discrepant from the general self-presentation a person tries to project and embody more of his being than mundane secrets. "In men who are hard," wrote Nietzsche, "intimacy involves shame—and is precious."[29] In other words, in men who wish to appear hard, intimacy involves revealing the soft spots that will discredit the image of themselves they wish others to hold; for this reason, it is to be ventured with only a few. Moreover, a person fears that nearly everyone who discovered his crucial secrets, unlike his mundane secrets, would discontinue their relationship.

Whoever wants to tell his crucial secrets to another must first determine whether he can trust the other with them. He must first decide whether the other will reject him and their relationship once he learns these crucial secrets ("Well, that changes everything. You certainly didn't expect me to continue to associate with you when you tell me you're a ... "). Before confiding a crucial secret, one person usually attempts to ascertain the other's probable response by first observing the latter's reaction when the former either (1) reveals another secret that is only moderately crucial; (2) discusses his secret in the abstract; or (3) concretely imputes his crucial secret to a third party. For example, a male who wishes to tell his friend that he is a homosexual may begin by confessing that he likes very young girls; if his friend shows no disgust, he can move on to reveal that he also finds young boys not unattractive; if his friend is still unrepulsed, he may gradually increase the age range of the men he admits he fancies. Or, he may begin by discussing the nature of sexuality in general, move on to discussing Freudian theories of bisexuality, and finally discuss his own sexual inclinations in particular. Or, he may begin by casually remarking that a common acquaintance of theirs is homosexual, and, if his friend is not put off by that fact, then reveal that he himself knows because he is, too.

Whoever wants to hear another's crucial secret may take certain steps to enhance his apparent trustworthiness. First, he can try to show he "understands," he has become aware of the other's crucial secret intuitively, without himself asking about it and without the other having to articulate it ("You don't have to say it. I already know"). "The friend," Nietzsche perceived, "should be a master in conjecture and in keeping silent: you must not want to see everything."[30] A person who exhibits compassion for what the other has not yet expressed is likely to encourage him to express it. When the latter finally begins to talk about it, the former can ensure that he will receive many more crucial secrets by appearing "sympathetic," by claiming he really appreciates what having such a secret must mean to a person, bolstering his claim either by alleging that he has been close to someone with similar statuses, experiences, or inclinations, or even admitting to having had them to some extent himself ("I know what it must be like. My roommate in college was . . . " "Something like that once happened to me too." "I used to feel that way myself sometimes"). Second, just as he can get his acquaintances to volunteer harmless information about themselves by volunteering harmless information about himself, so he can increase the likelihood that his intimates will volunteer their crucial secrets by first volunteering his own (or what appear to be his own). Since crucial secrets concern crucial weaknesses, whoever knows a person's crucial secrets knows the best points at which to attack him. Accordingly, one person will often confide a crucial secret to another in order to give him a *psychological hostage*. This will serve as the former's guarantee that he can be trusted with the latter's secrets, for by informing the latter of one of his own weak points, he has put himself at the latter's mercy. When both sides exchange psychological hostages, they reach a state of mutual trust or, more precisely, mutual deterrence, for neither can now harm the other without having unacceptable damage inflicted upon himself in return.

Each intimate can enhance the probability that the other will respond in the hoped-for way to his exposure of crucial secrets if he carefully chooses the time and place for their unveiling. In another passage from *Kokoro*, one of the characters discusses his difficulty in finding an opportunity to confide his secret to his friend:

> I decided to confide my secret to K. Actually, I had been wanting to do so for some time. But I had found myself incapable, when talking to K, of seizing, or creating, the right moment to introduce the subject casually. ... I watched K closely, hoping that he would give me a chance to confide in him. But not once did he emerge from his forbidding aloofness.[31]

Conversely, each intimate can enhance the probability that the other will respond in the hoped-for way to his own questions concerning the other's crucial secrets if he asks them discreetly, that is, at those times and places when and where the other is unusually disposed to disclose. The "right time" for inquiry and revelation is when each feels especially close to the other—as, for instance, when they have both just finished listening to a favorite concerto together. The "wrong time" is when each feels especially distant from the other—as, for instance, when one is self-preoccupied with a toothache or headache, when one has been offended by the other, or when one has observed the other engaging in behavior unbecoming his image of an intimate. The "right place" for inquiry and exposure is where the two of them are alone together or effectively alone without external distractions—as, for instance, at home or at a secluded table in a restaurant. The "wrong place" is where the two of them have external distractions or are surrounded by lesser acquaintances who might eavesdrop—as, for instance, at a loud party or long cafeteria table ("Talk louder. I can't hear you over all this noise. You said you're a what?").

Eventually, intimates may achieve that utopian relationship in which they are "completely open" with each other. They have no more old crucial secrets they have held back from each other, and they do not transform any recently occurring items into new crucial secrets. Their information exchange is completely unconstricted by the fear that telling anything to each other would damage their relationship. Thus, in this ideal state, each will not be afraid to give the other his critical opinion ("Paul, I'm going to lay it on the line with you because you're my friend. She's just not your type!").

Since it is so dangerous and so difficult for a person to confess his crucial secrets, it would seem his safest and easiest course would be to convey them to no one at all. But there are at least two reasons why he may wish to reveal them—one rational, one subrational.

In order to receive from his intimate physical and psychological favors (detailed in the next chapter), he must let the other know what is bothering him. If he wants his intimate's help in the recouping of his losses, he must inform him of the cause and extent of his misfortune. For instance, if he wants his friend to lend him $5,000 immediately, he may have to say that he needs the money because he lost at the races the $5,000 he "borrowed" from his company, and the auditors are coming Monday. Most requests for "important favors," in fact, entail the revelation of crucial secrets, for an important favor concerns what an individual needs done that he can neither do himself nor get most people to do for him, and what one needs desperately but cannot obtain easily is a weakness.

It has often been noted that one person feels closer to another when the latter reveals his weaknesses to him, at least within certain limiting conditions.[32] In a discussion of rhetorical techniques, Aristotle remarks, "We feel friendly...towards those who are honest with us, including those who will tell us of their own weak points."[33] Recent animal studies seem to have found an ethological basis for this ethnological behavior. A review of Konrad Lorenz's *On Aggression* contains the following comment:

> The interrelationship of aggression and of bonds in which individuals are not easily interchangeable, is carefully and convincingly demonstrated.... Although aggression antedates personal bonds in evolution and can be found without such bonds, the fishes, birds, and mammals in which personal bonds have evolved independently are invariably species with high levels of aggression.... It is perhaps time, then, to re-examine the psychoanalytic theory of friendship and to question whether aim-inhibited aggression is not as important in friendship as aim-inhibited

sexuality.... Aim-inhibition of aggression occurs in response to the most remarkable behavior patterns. Depending on the species, the submitting animal either performs the exact opposite of threatening movement ("I am NOT fighting you!"), or defenselessly offers its most vulnerable part ("You win! Do with me what you will!"), or imitates the movements characteristic of the sexually inviting female ("I am no threat to a strong male like you!"), or imitates juvenile behavior ("I am just a baby!"). These submissive or appeasing gestures trigger off strong inhibitory reactions; it is important to note that they do not simply dissipate aggressive impulses; rather they stimulate strong inhibitory impulses.[34]

There is a suggestive parallel between the ways certain animals and humans establish personal bonds with other members of their own species by using most of the above techniques, such as performing the exact opposite of threatening movements or imitating female or juvenile behavior. But there is a striking parallel between the way certain animals and humans establish personal bonds with other members of their own species by the technique of offering each other access to their most vulnerable parts: as animals bare their throats, so humans bare their secrets.

COMPLICATIONS

The picture of each other that would-be intimates acquire may be distorted or, at least, deficient. It may be incomplete because their receiving or transmitting processes have accidentally malfunctioned, or because certain elements of their projected image have been intentionally falsified.

One person may simply misunderstand what the other is trying to tell him about himself; indeed, one may be incapable of understanding. Nietzsche asserts:

[No] friendship or love affair...can endure once one discovers that one's partner associates different feelings, in-

tentions, nuances, desires, and fears with the same words.
(Fear of the 'eternal misunderstanding'—that is the benevolent genius which so often keeps persons of different
sex from rash attachments to which their senses and
hearts prompt them ...)[35]

Though members of different social categories (e.g., men and
women) use the same language signals, they do not always attach
the same meanings to these signals, making errors in cross-cat-
egory image reception likely. Furthermore, since no two members
of a society, especially modern society, are likely to belong to all
of the same social categories, they are bound to misinterpret some
of the revealed elements in certain areas of each other's life.[36]
Misunderstanding, moreover, is multiplied by intracategory variation (e.g., among women). For instance, during periods of rapid
and uneven social change in sex mores—like today—some women
will continue to regard their vaginas as cups containing their
secret essence, to be drunk only by those whom they choose to be
their intimates, while other women, who no longer feel their
essence to be bottled up between their thighs, will spread their
sexual favors more widely. If a man cannot tell how "modern" the
girl is who has just permitted him to sleep with her, he may
misconstrue the kind of relationship she now expects to have.

   Those whose relationship is evolving to higher stages have more
opportunity to form complete and accurate images of each other,
but ironically they seem to have less ability to do so. Familiarity
may breed contempt, but intimacy breeds consecration. Emerson
remarks:

   We over-estimate the conscience of our friend. His
   goodness seems better than our goodness, his nature finer,
   his temptations less. Everything that is his—his name, his
   form, his dress, books and instruments—fancy enhances.
   Our own thought sounds new and larger in his mouth.[37]

Such perceptual distortion becomes especially acute under the
glaucoma of emotions—positive in love, negative in hatred.[38]

Stendhal has called positive perceptual distortion *crystallization,* which he defines as "that process of the mind which discovers fresh perfection in its beloved at every turn of events."[39] The Roman Epicurean Lucretius has provided us with one of the best catalogs of this philopathology:

> For men are generally by passion swayed,
> Assigning every virtue to a girl,
> Which are not truly hers.
> And so we often see an ugly girl, a girl deformed,
> The object of a man's love, blindly admired...
> And so a dark-complexioned girl may be described
> As 'Honey-dark.'
> A girl who's foul and filthy in her ways,
> As 'unadorned'...
> A wooden, skinny girl is called 'gazelle.'
> A plump and stubby girl 'Incarnate grace,'
> And 'all pure wit.'
> A large ungainly one 'a marvel and a walking majesty.'
> If ceaseless stammering impede her speech
> 'She has a lisp.'
> If silent through stupidity her 'modest bearing' is admired.
> A nagging spiteful gossip 'Virtue's very torch.'
> Another wasting right away and on the point of death
> Is called 'a slender wisp of love.'
> And if she's nearly dead with bronchial cough,
> Her lover calls her 'frail.'...
> The thick lipped girl 'a living kiss.'
> Other examples of the kind were tedious to tell.[40]

"Love," they say, "is blind." But this maxim is misleading, for it is not exactly the case that the lover does not see his beloved at all; rather, he sees her worst features obscured and minimized and her best features clarified and magnified. "Love," we should rather say, "isn't actually blind; but it is astigmatic."

(Note that these positive perceptual distortions provide one reason why people want to be loved. Since the loved one knows that his lover will always enlarge his virtues and lessen his vices, he need exert less effort to control his image-producing behavior. He can be confident that his lover will not add his unseemly items to the phenomenological construction the latter makes of him—or at least not give them the negative evaluation they deserve: "It's just so cute the way he's so oblivious to everything that he keeps walking into parking meters.")

Turning from the receiving to the sending side of a relationship, we can discover at least one way a person can unintentionally transmit to another an incorrect image of himself. The sender may feel the image to be true, but the receiver will eventually discover that it bears little resemblance to the way he really is. For instance, what he reveals as his crucial secret actually may have been his true weak point in the past, but it is now no longer an essential defect in his character—his self having evolved faster than his self-conception in the meantime.

But more interesting is the way one person can present a true picture of himself to the other while misrepresenting his intentions for their relationship. First, he can imply falsely that he wants their relationship to be an intimate one. *False intimacy* occurs when one person reveals to another what appear to be his crucial secrets without wishing to engage in the continuing intimate relation usually implied by the revelation of such secrets. The other person is often so certain their relationship will continue to be an intimate one that he reveals his own crucial secrets in return, only to discover at some future time that the bag containing what he took to be his intimate's essence—which he has been left holding—is actually empty.

In this connection, Georg Simmel points out:

> Certain external situations or moods may move us to make very personal statements and confessions, usually reserved for our closest friends only, to relatively strange people. But in such cases we nevertheless feel that this "intimate" *content* does not [give] the relation an intimate [*form*].[41]

External conditions that promote false intimacy are those in which strangers are forced to remain together in close company for a long, but finite period of time. Some instances include cross-country car and bus trips and transoceanic ship voyages. An example may be drawn from Lenny Bruce's autobiography:

> This is one indication of the character of men in [the merchant marines]. Their attitudes and relationships, personal as well as towards their work, are of a temporary nature. You may form friendships of remarkable intimacy, sharing the details of each other's lives, and then never see each other again.[42]

Internal conditions that create a momentary desire for an intimate relation are feelings of loneliness (see Chapter 2), and the ingestion of alcohol or drugs. An example may be drawn from E. M. Forster's *Howard's End*:

> ... nor was it by any means the first time that [Leonard Bast] had talked intimately to strangers. The habit was analogous to a debauch, an outlet, though the worst of outlets, for instincts that would not be denied. Terrifying him, it would beat down his suspicions and prudence until he was confiding secrets to people whom he had scarcely seen. It brought him many fears and some pleasant memories. Perhaps the keenest happiness he had ever known was during a railway journey to Cambridge, where a decent-mannered undergraduate had spoken to him. They had got into conversation, and gradually Leonard flung reticence aside, told some of his domestic troubles, and hinted at the rest. The undergraduate, supposing they could start a friendship, asked him to "coffee after hall," which he accepted, but afterwards grew shy, and took care not to stir from the commercial hotel where he lodged.[43]

Strangers often have an easier time revealing crucial secrets to each other than acquaintances do. Strangers do not have to contend with the discrepancy between their secret and their surface characteristics. Unlike acquaintances, each stranger has not yet had time to construct the public image of the other, which the latter's secrets would normally contradict. Similarly, a person need be less afraid to give his sexual secrets to a stranger, like a prostitute or a "one-night stand," who has never seen him before and will never see him again, than to give them to an acquaintance, who has and will—for someone cannot harm you who does not have your public structure on which to hang your private parts.

The second way a person can unintentionally misrepresent his intentions to the other concerning their relationship is to imply falsely that he does *not* want their relationship to be an intimate one. *False nonintimacy* occurs when what a person takes to be his important qualities do not correspond to what his culture defines as a person's essential aspects, whereas what he takes to be his casual qualities do correspond to what his culture defines as a person's essential aspects. One of R. D. Laing's case histories contains the following description of a person who behaved in this way:

> It was quite characteristic of Peter, and of this type of person, that it should be this sort of thing in his life [a Platonic friendship with a "pure" girl] that he tended to keep most concealed from others, whereas he had no inhibitions about speaking about infantile promiscuous sexual incidents, masturbation, and adult sadistic sexual phantasies.[44]

Whoever receives secrets that are not socially defined as secrets is likely to underrespond to these intimacy overtures by turning them into a joke; whoever receives casual utterances that are socially defined as secrets is likely to overrespond by pouring out his own crucial secrets in return. The first underresponse will wound the confessor to the core; the second overresponse will astonish and annoy him ("I wonder why he told me all those things? I never gave him any indication that I wanted to be his friend, did I?").

The person to whom secrets are directed too readily or repeatedly may begin to suspect that these confidences are neither critical features of a psychic landscape nor indicative of a desire for an intimate relation. An individual is unlikely to bank his essential weaknesses with another unless he first tests the potential trustee extensively in order to determine how secure his secrets will be. Nor can they be his privileged communications with intimate intent if they are retold often, for this redundancy indicates that his psychological state is so damaged or warped that, like a scratched record, he cares not who hears his tune, but is condemned to play it over and over again to whomever comes along.

The picture of each other that would-be intimates obtain may be distorted or deficient not only for these unintentional reasons, but also for intentional ones. Each person may deliberately misrepresent himself in order to induce the other to desire to become his intimate. He may make his attributes appear better than they are and his intentions for their relationship more noble than they are. In the sexual sphere, this misrepresentation is called "seduction." In the previous section we saw that carnal knowledge is only an instance of more general secret knowledge, so here we can consider *seduction* to be a general process by which one person misrepresents himself in order to *convince* another that the latter will be neither hurt nor sorry should he reveal intimate knowledge of himself. (Accordingly, we can consider *rape* to be a general process by which one person, without such persuasive misrepresentation, *forces* another to reveal intimate knowledge of himself, as in "the rape of the mind.") In the previous section we also saw that a person often engages in sex, especially for the first time with a particular partner, less for physical pleasure than for psychological satisfaction, so here we can assert that he may attempt to seduce another less to overcome the modesty by which she guards her sexual organ than to overcome the reserve by which she shields her secret essence. Ortega y Gasset has interpreted the Don Juan myth as an instance of this thesis:

> From spectator and public the man passes, by means of the [*seduction*], to an individual relationship with the

woman. Starting a [*seduction*] is an invitation to a *tête-à tête*, a furtive spiritual communication. It begins, therefore, with a gesture, a word which disregards and as it were removes the conventional mask, the woman's surface personality. Then, like the moon which emerges from among the clouds, the concealed woman begins to radiate her hidden vitality and relinquish her fictitious countenance before the man. This moment of spiritual denudification, that brief period in which the superficial, impersonal woman is transformed into the real, individual woman ... produces in the man the greatest spiritual delight. Don Juan's vice is not, as a plebeian psychologist assumes, brutish sensuality. On the contrary, historical figures who, by their traits, have contributed to the ideal character of Don Juan, were distinguished by an abnormal frigidity towards sexual pleasures. Don Juan's crime is in compelling woman after woman to "open up."[45]

All seductions, which attempt to obtain guarded knowledge of sex in particular or self in general, proceed through two stages. First, the seducer imagines what sort of person could honorably and successfully seek an intimate relation with the one to be seduced. Second, he will attempt to represent himself as possessing the attributes of this person and as using the techniques, described in the previous section, that this person would use. In *Dangerous Liaisons*, one of the characters, Vicomte de Valmont, who is modeled after Don Juan, describes how he accomplished a nonsexual seduction:

> At last I know him inside out, that fine romantic hero! He no longer has any secrets to withhold from me. I told him repeatedly that virtuous love was the supreme good, that one sentiment was worth more than ten intrigues, and that I myself was in love and timid, until finally he found my way of thinking in such close agreement with his own that, in his enchantment with my candor, he

told me everything and swore friendship to me without reserve.[46]

Returning to the other side of a relationship, we can see several defensive strategies used by someone who is afraid that his would-be intimate is trying to seduce him into revealing where his essential secret lies hidden. There are two kinds of *intimacy blocks* that he can put in the other's path toward true and important knowledge about himself.

The first kind of intimacy block is the *runaround*, leading a would-be intimate into an indiscerniable detour around what a person wants to keep secret. It allows the person to withstand the would-be intimate's endeavor to raise the intensity level of their relationship without causing him to lower it when he recognizes his failure. In other words, he conceals his secrets from the other without letting him know that something is being hidden from him. When the other seeks to pry into his secret apertures, he may divert the latter's penetration either by asserting falsely that he has no weakness in the place where the other is probing ("No, I never had many sexual hang-ups. Just the usual"), or by camouflaging his critical weakness behind a front of false faults (Nietzsche aphorizes: 'Talking much about oneself can also be a means to conceal oneself"),[47] or by telling his crucial secret casually, as though it was not crucial (Smiling: "Yes. I was addicted to heroin for a while"), or by giving a vague and evasive response and changing the subject ("Mmm. Yeh. Sorta. Sometimes. By the way, did you happen to see the movie at the . . . ").

The second kind of intimacy block is the *stone wall*. This consists of putting a conspicuous barrier around what a person wants to keep secret. It is more effective than the runaround at impeding the inquirer's endeavor to raise the intensity level of their relationship, but it is also more likely to cause him to lower this level when he recognizes that something important is being kept from him. When the other seeks to pry into his secret apertures, he may blunt the latter's penetration either by refusing to elaborate an obviously incomplete reply or by refusing to reply at all. In using the stone-wall defense, a person may concede that their relationship is one in which the would-be intimate at least has the right to attempt to inquire into his secret preserves ("There are some things I'd rather not talk about"), or he may not ("None of your business").

(Parenthetically, I should point out that intimates who feel obligated to appear to be completely open with each other sometimes also give each other the runaround in order to continue to appear honest with each other, while avoiding the transmission of certain information they feel would needlessly damage each other or their relationship. Each may tell the other a white lie in order to keep him ignorant of the truth "for his own good"—as opposed to a black lie, in which he keeps the other ignorant of the truth for malicious reasons. In telling both white lies and black lies, a person tries to keep the other ignorant of the fact that he is being kept ignorant of the facts—for the good of their relationship.)

Whoever learns the crucial weaknesses of another acquires a power over him that is enormous, especially when the latter has no reciprocal knowledge of the former's vulnerable points. Some people, who may be called *confidence men,* are so motivated by a desire to acquire this power over others that they will pose as their intimates in order to seduce their secrets from them. Madame de Merteuil, another of the pleasant characters in *Dangerous Liaisons,* is one of the more outspoken of such people:

> Having descended into my own heart, I studied the hearts of others in it. I saw that there is no one who does not have a secret that it is important for him not to reveal. This is a truth which Antiquity seems to have known better than we, and of which the story of Samson may be an ingenious symbolic representation. Like Delilah, I have always used my power to discover that important secret. How many modern Samsons there are whose hair I keep between the blades of my scissors! I have ceased to fear them; they are the only men I have sometimes allowed myself to humiliate.[48]

Although it is obvious that a person would be afraid to give his secrets to someone whose intentions toward himself were suspect, he may also be afraid to give his secrets to someone whose good intentions were beyond doubt but whose ability to avoid wounding unwittingly was still in question. A few years before the publication of *Dangerous Liaisons*, Voltaire is said to have exclaimed "May God defend me from my friends; I can defend myself from my enemies!"

It is this fear of *betrayal*—whether intentionally from enemies or unintentionally from friends—that causes a person to want to keep his secrets buried in his own backyard until he receives extensive assurances that he can safely entrust them to another. A person who entrusts his secret weaknesses to another is open to two kinds of betrayal: (1) the betrayer may disseminate the knowledge of his points of vulnerability, encouraging others to attack; (2) the betrayer may attack him at his vulnerable points himself.

1. Once a person has opened up to another the Pandora's box of his soul, he has no way to take back the information concerning his critical aspects that spilled out, short of killing whoever has come into possession of it. Having yielded to his intimate partial control over the publication of his own memoirs, he must trust his intimate to keep them to himself. However, there are several reasons why intimates may betray each other's secrets to the world.

First, intimates who have only pretended intimacy feel free to make each other's secrets public if that will advance their own economic or social ends.

> Then one of the twelve, who was called Judas Iscariot, went to the chief priests and said, "What will you give me if I deliver Him to you?" And they paid him thirty pieces of silver. And from that moment he sought an opportunity to betray Him.[49]

In those times and places in which sexual access to women is socially regulated, a man can enhance his social status by boasting

that he has entered territory that should have been off limits to
him, whereas a woman can soil her social standing should news of
her indiscretion leak out. In a somewhat different sexual context,
Plato cautions:

> No, the proper course, surely, is to show favor . . . not to
> those who, when they have had their will of you, will
> flatter their vanity by telling the world, but to those who
> will keep a strict and modest silence.[50]

Second, intimates may carelessly tell each other's secrets to one
of their other intimates who has less concern about keeping the
secrets quiet. In a letter to John Adams toward the end of his life,
Thomas Jefferson wrote:

> I had for some time observed in the public papers,
> dark hints and mysterious innuendos of a correspondence
> of yours with a friend, to whom you had opened your
> bosom without reserve, and which was to be made public
> by that friend or his representative. . . . And if there had
> been at any time a moment when we were off our guard
> and in a temper, let the whispers of these people make
> us forget what we had known of each other for so many
> years, and years of so much trial.

Third, intimates may be forced to tell each other's secrets to
another intimate with whom they are obligated to be completely
open. One index of the order in which a person ranks his various
intimate relations is to be found in whose secrets he will tell
to whom. If A tells B's secrets to C, then A indicates that his relationship with C is more intense than his relationship with B.
On this dimension, a person's most important relationship is with
the intimate whose secrets he will absolutely not reveal to any
of his other intimates and to whom he will tell the secrets of all
of his other intimates.

In practice, this kind of betrayal is not so dangerous as it seems, for a person's intimates usually have little to do with one another and little interest, other than curiosity, in one another's secrets. Rarely does anyone act on his knowledge about the weaknesses of his intimate's intimate, except to perhaps smile slightly to himself whenever he sees him, because he knows something about the other that the other does not know he knows. The following situation, however, occasionally arises.

Intimate A is being kept by B from learning a certain piece of knowledge (such as B's critical opinion of one of A's attributes) because B feels that their relationship would be irreparably damaged if A ever found out about it. But B may confide this potentially destructive piece of knowledge to one of his other intimates, C. If C then casually reveals it to D, who feels it is his duty to report it back to A, the circuit, suddenly complete, shorts. Emotion-charged information immediately flashes around it, shocking each intimate and burning out every relationship:

a between intimates A and B, because A has learned the damaging knowledge B tried to keep from him;
b between intimates B and C, because B has learned that C has betrayed his confidence; and
c between intimates C and D, because C has learned that D is a gossip and busybody.

Several hundred years ago, Pascal noted perceptively:

> I set it down as a fact that if all men knew what each said of the other, there would not be four friends in the world. This is apparent from the quarrels which arise from the indiscreet tales told from time to time.[51]

The fourth and final reason for this kind of betrayal is that intimates may feel that their obligation to keep each other's secrets lasts only as long as their relationship does. As long as their intimacy continues, each knows that the other will angrily terminate their relationship should either reveal the other's secrets. But when their intimacy has died of other causes, intimates (now ex-intimates) may feel there is now no reason for them to continue to ensure the safety of the secrets they were once quite willing to shelter.

2. Since only the intimates of an individual know his points of vulnerability, they are in the best position to attack him. Their assaults can take various forms for various reasons. One intimate can wound the other merely by changing his opinion of him for the worse because of the faults the latter was foolhardy enough to admit to. An extreme instance of this sort of assault may be seen in part of a poem by the nineteenth-century Irish-American, John B. O'Reilly, "The Lost Friend":

> My friend he was; my friend from all the rest;
> With childish faith he oped to me his breast;
> No door was locked on alter, grave, or grief;
> No weakness veiled, concealed no disbelief;
> The hope, the sorrow, and the wrong were bare,
> And, ah, the shadow only showed the fair.
> I gave him love for love; but deep within
> I magnified each frailty into sin;
> Each hill-topped foible in the sunset glowed,
> Obscuring vales where rivered virtues flowed.
> Reproof became reproach, till common grew
> The captious word at every fault I knew.
> He smiled upon the censorship, and bore
> With patient love the touch that wounded sore;
> Until at length, so had my blindness grown
> He knew I judged him by his faults alone.

A friend, in fact, has even been humorously defined as "one who knows all about you but likes you just the same."

One intimate can hurt the other merely by mocking the weaknesses he rashly revealed. For example, he can make fun of his friend's Brooklyn background until his friend—depending on how critical his weakness is, how savagely abused it is, and how momentarily sensitive he is—explodes in anger.

One intimate can stick his knife into the other's soft spot in the heat of passion. In recounting a quarrel with his wife, the husband in Leo Tolstoy's *The Kreutzer Sonata* took pains to stress, "Her every word is venomous; where she alone knows that I am most sensitive, she stabs."[52]

Finally, one intimate can try to use his knowledge of the other's vulnerable points to ruin him when they have ceased to be intimates and have become rivals or enemies. Lord Chesterfield gives his son the following piece of fatherly advice:

> There is an incontinency of friendship among young fellows, who are associated by their mutual pleasures only, which has, very frequently, bad consequences. A parcel of warm hearts and inexperienced heads, heated by convivial mirth, and possibly a little too much wine, vow, and really mean at the time, eternal friendships to each other, and indiscreetly pour out their whole souls in common, and without the least reserve. These confidences are as indiscreetly repealed as they were made; and then very ill uses are made of these rash confidences.... Trust them with your love tales, if you please; but keep your serious views secret. Trust those only to some tried friend, more experienced than yourself, and who, being in a different walk of life from you, is not likely to become your rival.

Two contradictory proverbs advise the person who must decide whether to confide his secrets to his intimate: "It is better to be deceived by a friend than to mistrust him," as opposed to "Don't tell your secret to a friend, and you'll not fear him should he become an enemy."

It should be added that the intimates of an individual may assault his trust in ways other than verbal, for they acquire not only *knowledge* of his weaknesses, but *access* to them as well. A woman who has allowed an intimate to seduce her sexually on the assumption that he would help her out of any consequent "troubles" may find herself abandoned. A man who has allowed an intimate to come near his prized possessions may find his prized possessions stolen or destroyed. Anyone, in fact, who has allowed an intimate to partake of his presence may find his presence the worse for wear. Three-quarters of the homicides in this country are committed by the friends, loves, spouses, or other intimates of the deceased[53]—proving that crime in the home is far more dangerous than crime in the streets.

In this chapter, the *information* dimension of an intimate relation has been considered and a fourth major force uncovered that transforms isolated individuals into interlinked intimates: *The potentially damaging secret knowledge of each other's weaknesses that both acquire.* As soon as their essential secrets erupt through the safeguards that normally contain them, either because the need of precautions to conceal them has diminished or because the force of pressures to reveal them has intensified, each intimate comes to feel that the other knows too many of his vulnerable points for him to terminate their relationship safely and easily.

CHAPTER 5

Do Me a Favor

As GEMEINSCHAFT evolved into gesellschaft, an individual's intimates replaced the community as the foremost agency facilitating his transactions with his environment. Interposed between an individual and his environment, intimates mediate their interaction. As an interpolated membrane, an individual's intimates are semipermeable: on the one hand, they protrude into his environment in order to aid him in obtaining from it what he wants; on the other hand, they wall him off from his environment in order to aid him in avoiding from it what he fears. On both hands, an individual's intimates constitute extensions of his organs that increase his ability to deal successfully with his circumstances.

Emerson has suggested that the intimates of an individual can perform for him what I will call *physical favors* in order to augment the effects of his successes and ameliorate the effects of his failures on his physical existence:

> The end of friendship...is for aid and comfort through all the relations and passages of life and death. It is fit for serene days and graceful gifts and country rambles, but also for rough roads and hard fare, shipwreck, poverty and persecution.[1]

Emerson's friend Thoreau has stressed their performance of what I will call *psychological favors* in order to augment the effects of his successes and ameliorate the effects of his failures on his psychological well-being:

> Most contemplate only what would be the accidental and trifling advantages of Friendship, so that the friend can assist in time of need, by his substance, or his influence, or his counsel; but he who foresees such advantages in this relation proves himself blind to its real advantage. ... We do not wish for Friends to feed and clothe our bodies—neighbors are kind enough for that—but to do the like office to our spirits.[2]

In this chapter I will consider both these sets of services—the physical and the psychological—by which the intimates of an individual strengthen his personal power and buffer his personal stability vis-à-vis his environment.

As acquaintances become intimates, they become able to ask each other for these ecological aids. The more intense their relationship, the more and greater favors they can ask for. Until their relationship reaches a certain point, they feel obligated to make a specific repayment for each favor received. Beyond this point, the closest of friends (as well as most lovers and spouses) do not feel obligated to give, or expect to receive, a specific repayment for each service rendered; rather, each feels the total amount of favors he gives and receives will average out over the course of their relationship.

Physical and psychological favors will be described in the first two sections of this chapter. Problems of testing each intimate's willingness to supply favors, problems of giving and receiving favors, and problems of repaying favors will be the topics of the Complications section.

PHYSICAL FAVORS

The intimates of an individual can enhance his ability to pluck from his environment the fruit of his desires while turning aside the thorns that forestall him. Thus, each intimate can function as an attachment to the other's effector organs that extends the range over which he can procure his provisions and overcome their obstructions. In other words, insofar as one intimate aids the other in the *manipulation* of his circumstances, he serves as his "third hand."

Francis Bacon has pointed out that each intimate can use the other to overcome both his temporal and his spatial limitations:

> Men have their time, and die many times in desire of some things which they principally take to heart; the bestowing of a child, the finishing of a work, or the like. If a man have a true friend, he may rest almost secure that the care of those things will continue after him. So that a man hath, as it were, two lives in his desires. A man hath a body, and that body is confined to a place; but where friendship is, all offices of life are as it were granted to him and his deputy. For he may exercise them by his friend.[3]

A man can fetch what he desires by intruding his intimates instead of himself into his local environment ("While you're up, would you please get me a glass of water?") or more distant reaches ("While you're in town, would you please buy me some salami?"). He can use his intimates in this way because they may be temporarily in a position to aid him, i.e., may be located nearer than he is to the objects he wants. But he may also take advantage of their relatively permanent location. He may, for instance, ask his friend who lives in New York to put him up whenever he goes there for a visit. Although he could get his own glass of water, go to town himself, or find his own place to stay in New York, in each of these cases, it would inconvenience him much more to do these things himself than it would inconvenience his intimate to do these things for him (with "inconvenience" measured in terms of expenditure of time, energy, and money).

A less common way each intimate can extend the other's ability to maneuver around his environment is to take over the position in which the other is, for one reason or another, imprisoned—thus freeing him to use his own two hands. The classical account of the famous friendship between Damon and Pythias (actually Phintias) is the most extreme example of the way one intimate can provide this stand-in service for the other. It is told how Pythias, having been condemned to death by the tyrant Dionysius, wanted first to settle his affairs. In order to do so, however, he would have to leave the town where he was held. But since his life was at stake, there seemed to be no guarantee that he would return. His friend Damon stepped forward and offered to be executed in Phythias's place if he did not return by a certain date. On this surety, Pythias was allowed to leave. To make a long story short, Pythias did return at the last moment to face his death. Dionysius was so moved at finding friends who loved each other more than they loved life itself that he pardoned Pythias.

Only pre- and post-adults and the disabled call upon their intimates actually to supply a provision or solve a problem each time they need a particular service. The adult and the able usually prefer to receive aid from their intimates in a more all-purpose form —like money. (Money is the most effective penetrating solvent an individual can squirt around his environment to loosen its hold on desired objects and to lubricate his progress toward desired ends.) Therefore, the favors an individual seeks from his intimates are often financial ones. By lending or giving him money, his intimates can indirectly strengthen his hand relative to his circumstances.

Just as each intimate can help the other to overcome his physical limitations, so each can help the other to surpass his social limitations. Again it is Bacon who points out that a person's intimate may perform the services for him he cannot perform for himself, either because he desires to present to the world a certain image of himself or because he is locked into certain roles:

> How many things are there which a man cannot, with any face or comeliness, say or do himself? A man can scarce allege his own merits with modesty, much less extol them; a man cannot sometimes brook to supplicate, or

> beg; and a number of the like. But all these things are
> graceful in a friend's mouth, which are blushing in a
> man's own. So again, a man's person hath many proper
> [i.e., role] relations which he cannot put off. A man can-
> not speak to his son but as a father; to his wife but as a
> husband; to his enemy but upon [like] terms: whereas, a
> friend may speak as the case requires, and not as it
> suiteth with the person.[4]

It is not only their position in physical space that allows the
intimates of an individual to help him achieve his ends, but also
their position in the institutions that constitute social space. An
individual who wants a job in a particular institution can contact
those of his intimates who are already employed there or who
themselves have intimates already employed there. In Natsume
Soseki's *Kokoro*, a mother encourages her son to make use of his
friend Sensei in this manner:

> "This is the sort of occasion when one tries to make use
> of one's contacts," said my mother. "Now, what about this
> man Sensei that you are constantly talking about?"
> That was the extent of her understanding of my friend-
> ship with Sensei. She could not be expected to see that . . .
> he was not the sort of person that would go out of his
> way to help me find a position.[5]

(The potential prevalence of patronage and nepotism—hiring
friends and relations—especially in political and academic institutions,[6] is indicated by the abundance of rules against them.) An
individual who wants to get the most for his money can turn
to those of his intimates who are conveniently located in the
institutions in which he wants to spend it. "A friend in the market
is better than money in the chest," goes a proverb, especially if he
can "get it for you wholesale" or if he can get a good buy. A
person may request his friend the butcher, for instance, to save
for him the best cuts of meat. Finally, an individual who wants
what it is against the house rules to have can call upon those of

his intimates who administer these house rules to obtain it for him. He may ask his friend the usher, for instance, to show him to an unsold box seat at the theater where his friend works, or he may ask his friend the city building inspector to overlook a code violation in the tenement he owns.

Each intimate can call upon the other for aid not only because of the position of the latter's helping hand but also because of its dexterity. A man can sew on his own buttons, but he will often find it more efficient to have his girl friend do it for him, for she is likely to be much handier at that sort of thing. *Manchild in the Promised Land* provides an illustration of how an individual can take advantage of his intimate's skill:

> Bucky was going to miss me a lot while I was away. I was his important friend. Since food was the most important thing in the world to Bucky, I was always showing him where some food was and how to get it.[7]

Correspondingly, each intimate may be not only more physically facile than the other but also more socially skilled. One intimate can use another to accomplish interpersonal tasks he has difficulty doing himself. A woman, for instance, may find it easier to have her husband talk to her young brother about his wayward ways than to talk to him herself.

Not all the manipulatory favors an individual wants from his intimates involve their handling third things for him. A person who wants sexual favors from his intimate usually does not want his intimate to be merely the medium through which he manipulates the genitals of a third party; instead, to paraphrase Marshall McLuhan, he wants his intimate to be the message itself, for he derives his satisfaction directly from the very act of manipulating his intimate. (To satisfy his sexual desires, especially on a regular basis, of course, is one of the most important favors an individual may ask of his intimates, for what they can do for him in this area is usually much better than what he can do for himself.)

The intimates of an individual can help him to achieve his ends not only by doing things for him, but also by helping him to do things for himself. They can increase both his information about the environment and the number of alternative organizations by which he can collate this information. Thus, an intimate can function not only as a multiplier for his effector organs but also as a magnifier for his receptor organs. In other words, insofar as one intimate gives another *advice* about how to deal with his environment as well as manipulating it for him, he constitutes his "third eye" (or "third ear") as well as his "third hand."

In this context also it was Bacon who observed that an individual can overcome his intellectual limitations by directing the eye of his intimate upon his ecological problems:

> Certain it is that the light that a man receiveth by counsel from [a friend] is drier and purer than that which cometh from his own understanding and judgment; which is ever infused and drenched in his affections and customs. . . . It is a strange thing to behold what gross errors and extreme absurdities many (especially of the greater sort) do commit for want of a friend to tell them of them; to the great damage both of their fame and fortune.[8]

His intimates may be in a position to see (or to hear of) a different selection of the opportunities and obstacles than he is. Aristotle notes that intimates can help each other thread their way through their physical environment because both can see more together than either can see separately:

> Two are better than one, or (as Homer puts it): 'When two upon a journey go, one sees before the other.' For indeed two are better able to 'see' a thing . . . than is one.[9]

Each intimate's ability to see (or hear) what the other cannot is especially important in warning an individual of impending danger ("Look out!"). And it is not only the physical position of intimates that allows them to do so, but their social position as well. In the biblical parable of the friendship between David and

Jonathan, Jonathan was in a position to alert his friend David that Jonathan's father Saul, the king, was planning to kill him.[10]

The ocular equivalent to manipulatory dexterity is a wider range of vision. One intimate who sees more of a certain area than the other often does so because he has inhabited it for a longer time—i.e., he has had more "experience" with it. An individual who has become interested in pornography, for instance, may ask a friend who has read more lewd literature than he to recommend those books worth reading.

Finally, an individual's intimate can help him to verify his experiences—as Hamlet's friend Horatio helped him do[11]—because his intimate's eye (and ear) is independent of his own ("Do you see what I see?"). The importance of this experiential validation is less apparent when intimates honestly confirm each other's perceptions than when they dishonestly deny them.

The intimates of an individual can also array themselves around him to safeguard him from peril. Thus, each intimate can function as a further growth of the other's epidermal shell that shields him from attack. In other words, insofar as one intimate gives another *protection*, he serves as his "second skin."

The biblical "Greater love hath no man than this, that a man lay down his life for his friends," [12] and the apocryphal "A faithful friend is a strong defense: and he that found such a one hath found a treasure,"[13] are enduring expressions of the fact that intimates have always called upon one another to help stave off danger. Since the human body is so constructed that it is especially vulnerable to attack from the back and sides, intimates need each other to complement each other's incomplete defensive systems. By positioning themselves spatially shoulder-to-shoulder or back-to-back, both can fight off attacks on each other more effectively than either can ward off attacks on himself. Moreover, the intimates of an individual can serve him as a secret weapon, a reserve armament, a fist behind his back, which he can bring into play whenever he has need of it. "Rip and I got real tight," writes Claude Brown. "If anybody messed with him and I heard of it, I wanted to fight them. And it was the same with him if anybody messed with me."[14]

In times of peace, at least, civilization has reduced attacks on one's existence as a physical entity relative to attacks on one's existence as a social entity. Most of the assaults on an individual now come not from persons qua persons but from persons qua role-incumbents of institutions. Therefore, he must now seek to be protected from assaults less by his strong friends than by his "influential" friends. The latter can help him because they occupy certain social positions, usually ones in the same institution from which the social aggression against him emanated and at a higher level than the official who originated the aggression. In the seventeenth century, a friend at the king's court could discount an individual's taxes in the same way that, in the twentieth century, a friend at the police court could fix his traffic tickets.[15]

When we read in the Apocrypha, "A faithful friend is the medicine of life,"[16] we can see that the intimates of any individual who has been injured in some way can help to restore him to health. Thus, each intimate functions as an adjunct to the homeostatic mechanisms of the other's body that return him to normal in the areas where he has become damaged or deficient. In other words, in addition to acting as his second skin, insofar as one intimate aids in the *rehabilitation* of another, he acts as his "first aid" as well.

Since the physical survival of an individual at times demands that he receive help immediately after he has gotten into trouble, and since only his intimates are both willing and able to extricate him before it is too late, this function of intimates has been institutionalized in many physically dangerous activities, where it is known as the "buddy system." Especially in swimming, two individuals, who may even be strangers, are required to act as though they were buddies by rescuing each other immediately should one of them plunge into difficulty. Moreover, intimates may also serve each other as life preservers when one of them needs restoration of longer duration. An individual who is too incapacitated physically to sustain his existence by himself is likely to resort to his intimates to nurse him back to health.

The aprocryphal caution "Woe to him that is alone when he falleth; for he hath not another to help him up"[17] is not meant to restrict our attention to literal tumbles and re-erections, but instead to expand it to include the more figurative ways in which an individual can collapse and be resurrected by his intimates. Intimates provide each other with several kinds of *insurance* to ease each other's passage through various kinds of crises.

When an individual finds himself in such extreme situations as disasters (floods, droughts, explosions) or total institutions (concentration camps, prisons, mental hospitals), in which his provisions are in short supply, he often enters into an (unspoken) compact with his intimates to ensure the equal distribution of the resources that are available. Claude Brown's reform school days provide an example:

> Wiltwyck was different from the other places I had been in. Some guys had been there for years, and just about everybody had at least one real good friend or partner. When two or three guys were partners, they would share everything they got hold of—packages from home, food and fruits that their parents brought them on visiting day, things they stole, and stuff like that. It took me a long time to find a real partner, one I would share my loot ... with.[18]

When an individual's living quarters have been destroyed, say, through a fire, or disrupted, say, through a family quarrel, he often turns to his intimates to take him in until the crisis passes. Edward Albee satirizes the idea of seeking refuge with intimates when disaster hits home in his play *A Delicate Balance*:

> If we come to the point ... if we are at home one evening, and the ... terror comes ... descends ... if all at once we ... NEED ... we come where we are wanted, where we know we are expected, not only where we want; we come where the table has been laid for us in such an event ... where the bed is turned down ... and warmed ... and has been ready should we need it.[19]

When illness, unemployment, bankruptcy, or robbery have drained an individual's economic reservoir, he often draws upon the well of his intimate's financial reserves. A recent insurance advertisement, however, suggests that intimates have become negligent of late in supplying this service:

BACK IN 1890, IF YOU BECAME DISABLED,
FRIENDS PASSED THE HAT.
OUR PAUL REVERE LIFE INSURANCE
COMPANY FIGURED OUT A BETTER WAY.

A GOOD THING.

PEOPLE JUST DON'T SEEM TO HAVE
FRIENDS LIKE THOSE ANY MORE.

Finally, when scandal has pulled the rug out from under an individual's social standing, he often falls back on those who stand by him. These intimates alone will try to clear his name and reconstruct his reputation.

The following exerpt from a *New York Times* article on Mart Crowley, author of the well-received play *The Boys in the Band*, lists many of the above-mentioned recuperative favors that intimates supply:

And he has not forgotten the people who stood by him through the trouble spots. People like Natalie Wood, who paid for his analysis for six months; Dominick Dunne, vice president of Four Star TV, who dragged him to dinner parties for free meals and gave him a contract to write the pilot for a TV show for Bette Davis; Jennifer Jones, who always invited him to her home when he was snubbed by the rest of Hollywood; or Billy Wilder's wife, Audrey, who used to give stern advice while she dished up knockwurst and sauerkraut. "These," he says, "are the real friends who are happy for me now.

R. J. and Marion (the Robert Wagners) kept me alive
in Rome one winter. Marion used to take me to Gucci
and buy me shoes. They know how much they've carried
me through, how many times I've passed out on their
living room floor. My friends are responsible for saving
me from death in a hotel room somewhere."[20]

PSYCHOLOGICAL FAVORS

Damage to an individual's physiological, economic, and social
supports may lead to his psychological collapse as well, which in
turn may weaken his physical foundation still further.[21] Adversity
may constitute a blow to his *psychological strength*, i.e., to the
will by which he attempts to compel his environment to accommodate itself to his own rhythms and by which he withstands his
environment's attempt to compel him to accommodate himself to
its own rhythms. (Actually, psychological strength can also wane
temporarily without any physical impairment occurring. That "depression" by which a deficiency in determination is manifested
may come on for no apparent reason at all.) The cry of one who
has given up and sees "no point in trying anymore" may be heard
in Job's lament of his misfortunes:

> Why is light given to him that is in misery,
>   and life to the bitter in soul,
> who long for death, but it comes not,
>   and dig for it more than for hid treasures;
> who rejoice exceedingly,
>   and are glad, when they find the grave?[22]

With the ebbing of his psychological strength, an individual has
more difficulty in keeping steady the rudder of his *self* (here
defined as the way he customarily deals with his enviroment).
The collapse of his inner equilibrium will cause him to waver in
his transactions with his environment as he begins to acquiesce to
external pressures instead of resisting them. Those who were ac-

quainted with his predisaster self may find strange his post-disaster self, and an alien appearing where once stood he whom they knew and loved ("Job's just not himself since the reversal of his fortunes").

When the intimates of an individual who has suffered some physical catastrophe hear of it, they often fear that his psychological strength may be impaired as well. They will rush to him, as much to cure the sickness of his soul as the illness of his body:

> Now when Job's three friends heard of all this evil that had come upon him, they came each from his own place. ... They made an appointment together to come to condole with him and comfort him.[23]

In general, the intimates of an individual who begins to fall, mentally as well as physically, can provide him with *revitalization* by serving as a trampoline, as an Antaeus-ground, from which he can bounce back reinvigorated. Cicero urges them to do so:

> The third view is much the worst of all, that as a man values himself, so should he be valued by his friends. Many times it happens that some friend may be very low in spirit, or become deeply discouraged about bettering his lot in life. Now it is not the part of a friend to be towards his friend as the friend is towards himself, but rather to put forth every effort to spur on his friend's lagging spirits, to give him hope and a more optimistic attitude.[24]

An intimate's medicine for melancholy consists of both purgatives and tourniquets. Since the very articulation of anguish seems to act as a catharsis, the intimates of an individual can provide him with just the opportunity he needs to express his distress. Close observation, however, informs us that these intimates do more than merely listen to him passively. They seem to be actively evincing the same or similar sorrow themselves:

> And when [the friends of Job] saw him from afar, they did not recognize him; and they raised their voices and wept; and they rent their robes and sprinkled dust upon their heads towards heaven. And they sat with him on the ground seven days and seven nights, and no one spoke a word to him, for they saw that his suffering was great.[25]

The intimates of a desolate individual imagine themselves placed in the same difficult situation and then display their own reaction to it. Although their discomposure is composed out of their own uniquely stylized responses, its expression is usually similar to his.[26] As soon as the individual confronts his own sorrow as it is reflected back to him from the faces of his intimates, his own distress is diminished still further.[27]

Besides purging from him the bile of his festering emotions, the intimates of an individual may apply to him a tourniquet that isolates the injured portion of his personality from the rest. Their treatment consists of reassurances designed to relieve him of responsibility for his plight ("It's not your fault." "It happens to everybody at one time or another"). In this way they keep his vitality from bleeding out in the vain attempt to heal (i.e., justify) his wounds by himself. Ben Hecht recalls how one of his intimates used to help him to justify his defeats by allowing him to reconceptualize them in a way that minimized his losses:

> This is one of the chief values of my friendship, as it is of his. We enable each other to play the strong man superior to his fate. Given a friend to listen, my own disasters change color. I win victories while relating them. Not only have I a friend 'on my side' who will believe my version of the battle—and permit me to seem a victor in my communiques—but I have actually a victory in me. I am able to show my friend my untouched side. My secret superiority to bad events becomes strongest when I can speak and have a friend believe in it.

These psychic tourniquets also keep the poison of an infected part
from spreading throughout a whole psychological system. Erving
Goffman, in "Cooling the Mark out," writes that the intimates of
a debilitated individual can help him to quarantine the diseased
part of him before it contaminates all of him:

> One must also note that there is a tendency today to
> shift certain losses of status from the category of those
> that reflect upon the loser to the category of those that
> do not. When persons lose their jobs, their courage, or
> their minds, we tend more and more to take a clinical or
> naturalistic view of the loss and a nonmoral view of their
> failure. We want to define a person as something that is
> not destroyed by the destruction of one of his selves.[28]

Even if some physical failure has not undermined an individual's psychological strength, there may be certain flaws in the way
he deals with his environment that make its cave-in always
imminent. His intimates can shore up the foundations of his
psychic house by propping up his *self-esteem* (here defined as his
evaluation of the way he relates to his environment). Unless they
provide him with *support*, once he begins to devalue his own
abilities, he may rapidly deplete his reserves of psychological
strength as well.

The mere fact that people whom he considers powerful or
beautiful, people whom he considers worldly, wealthy, or wise,
think him worthy of their intimacy—enough so to put themselves
at his disposal for whatever favors he needs—is often sufficient
to sustain an individual's self-esteem under normal conditions
("I must be doing something right"). But he needs his intimates
as a crutch to lean on, particularly during periods when the
storms of his environment blow especially fiercely or when he is
especially weak.

His environment can be particularly unfriendly insofar as many
of those in it feel they have reason to attack him. In this situation,
his intimates can help him to maintain his self-esteem by convey-

ing to him only the good things others say about him behind his back while filtering out the bad. Even if his opposition manages to get through to him, his intimates can then vindicate his worth by denying the denigration. The following exerpt from a *Life* magazine editorial illustrates the fact that even the President of the United States was not ungoverned by these sociological laws:

> As the number of critics of [President Johnson] has grown, the number of people he really listens to has shrunk.... A man can take only so much. Then he seeks the companionship of those who believe in him and tell him so.[29]

Self-esteem may have an even more difficult time weathering an inclement local environment specifically dedicated to its destruction, as are jails, concentration camps, and mental hospitals. In order to preserve their self-esteem, inmates of these total institutions find it especially necessary to seek the help of old intimates without or new ones within.[30]

For his part, an individual's self-esteem may be less able to resist even normal erosion if he possesses what are commonly known as "faults" or, in the extreme, "stigmas." The world does not take kindly to the limper or the tax evader; less so to the leper or the traitor. All faults and stigmas, at one time or another, may precipitate psychological prostration. But by tolerating—or at least trying to ignore—his shortcomings, the intimates of the faulted or the stigmatized provide a brace for his efforts to bolster his self-esteem. As Cassius says to Brutus in Shakespeare's *Julius Caesar*, "A friend should bear his friend's infirmities."[31]

Besides these relatively permanent chinks in an individual's armor, there are times when his self-esteem is temporarily weaker than usual. When he is uncertain about a decision he has made, or has to make, his intimates may reassure him that his choice is indeed the best. Nor may they merely agree with him; sometimes, in order to remain in continual agreement with him, they may even go as far as contradicting both themselves and him. In

their effort to remain agreeable, they may find themselves constantly playing the devil's advocate if he keeps switching positions
in order to articulate for himself all the arguments for and against
all the alternatives. In spite of themselves, they become transformed into the yielding opponents he wants instead of the willing supporters they took themselves to be. I recorded the following
vignette I once discovered I had played out with one of my more
agreeable intimates (A):

> I: I've been trying to decide whether to get a job in
>   California or New York City. I've sorta decided on
>   New York.
> A: That's a good choice.
> I: The people in New York are more interesting.
> A: You're right.
> I: But California's so fantastically beautiful. New York's
>   so filthy; it's like living in a sewer.
> A: Well, that's certainly true. New York might take too
>   much getting used to. California's so much cleaner
>   and prettier.
> I: But then there has to be more to a place than scenery.

The intimates of an individual can also help him to bring his
self-conception (here defined as the way he thinks he relates to
his environment) into alignment with his *self* (here defined as
the way he actually relates to his environment). One intimate can
provide another with *insight* by mirroring him to himself. "Yet
your friend's face is … your own face, in a rough and imperfect
mirror," observes Nietzsche.[32]

An intimate can help him to become self-aware indirectly by
becoming the model against which he defines himself through
comparison and contrast.[33] Below, we will see the special use to
which he puts the paradigm of his intimate when the latter is the
paragon of the virtues he himself wants to emulate.

Each intimate can also help the other to learn about himself
directly. Each can tell the other what he thinks of him and, especially, what he thinks is wrong with him. Although he usually

tolerates and supports the defects he thinks the other cannot correct, he often feels it is his duty to inform him of the flaws he thinks the other could rectify. La Rochefoucauld wrote: "The greatest test of friendship is not to make a friend aware of our faults; it is to make him see his own."[34] And Thoreau concurred:

> Friendship is not so kind as is imagined; it... consists of a certain disregard for men..., the Christian duties and humanities, while it purifies the air like electricity. ... When he... treats his Friend like a Christian... then Friendship ceases to be Friendship, and becomes charity.[35]

Each intimate, for instance, may make the other aware of blemishes on the image he is attempting to present to the world ("You have crumbs on your chin").

Beyond merely revealing aspects of the other's self to him, each intimate may evaluate them negatively. Claude Brown provides a humorous illustration of this ad hominem criticism:

> I told her that I was sorry for laughing at her and that I hadn't meant to hit her so hard. I asked her if she wanted to make friends, and she said all right. We shook hands and started talking about the things we disliked in each other. She said I just thought I was too bad and was always messing with somebody. I told her that she was all right, but should should stop licking the snot off her lip when her nose was running. Also, I thought she looked crazy always pulling her bloomers up through her skirt.[36]

It is usually hard to take the sudden discovery of some unsuspected flaw, such as "bad breath." The flaw itself may present less of a threat to self than its revelation presents to self-esteem: it is bad to be blemished, but it is worse to appear ignorant of the imperfection as well.

Because intimates may shake each other's self-esteem in this way, each is often leery of telling the other of his faults, especially

his major ones ("Even his best friends won't tell him"). Criticism
of these faults, however, will be good for his self in the long run
even if it is bad for his self-esteem in the short run. Therefore, the
best of intimates will offer it regardless of the immediate consequences. Montaigne writes:

> One needs very strong ears to hear oneself freely criti-
> cized; and since there are few who can stand it without
> being stung, those who venture to perform this service for
> us give us a remarkable proof of their friendship. For it
> is a healthy affection that dares to wound and offend us
> for our own good.[37]

One individual who must criticize a part of another will find
his task made easier if he supports the other as a whole. Thus,
intimates can be more critical than acquaintances, for their relationship is more total. In order for one intimate to find serious
fault with another, however, he often feels he must reaffirm the
totality of his affection for him at the very moment when he
affirms his particular indictment against him. Thus, he is likely
to preface his critique with that universal (social) qualifier: "I
really like you, but..."

There is a parable by Samuel Johnson, "Felicia and Floretta,"
whose moral concerns the possibility that even the best of friends
may permanently scar a relationship when they attempt to remove
a blemish. The following excerpt from it provides an illustration of
how one intimate tried—unsuccessfully, as it turned out—to soften
her censure of the other by setting it in the context of a com-
mendation.

> In a few months, Felicia, with great seriousness, told
> Floretta that, though her beauty was such as gave charm
> to whatever she did and her qualifications so extensive
> that she could not fail of excellence in any attempt, yet
> she thought herself obliged by the duties of friendship to
> inform her that, if ever she betrayed want of judgment,
> it was by too frequent compliance with solicitations to

sing, for her manner was somewhat ungraceful and her voice had no great compass.

Finally, the intimates of an individual can help him toward *self-improvement* (here defined as the upgrading of the way he usually deals with his environment). Since his success in obtaining the satisfactions he seeks from his circumstances is determined, in part, by chance and, in part, by the way he deals with them, his intimates can both improve the effects of his chance successes and effect the improvement of his chance of success.

Intimates can help an individual to increase the psychological effects of good fortune in the same way they can help him to curtail the psychological effects of bad fortune. The smile on the face of an intimate, empathizing with his good luck, intensifies his pleasure as much as the frown on the face of an intimate, empathizing with his bad luck, diminishes his pain. Cicero writes:

> How could you derive true joy from good fortune if you did not have someone who would rejoice in your happiness as much as you yourself. And it would be very hard to bear misfortune in the absence of anyone who would take your suffering even harder than you.... For when fortune smiles on us, friendship adds a luster to that smile; when she frowns, friendship absorbs her part and share of that frown, and thus makes it easier to bear.[38]

Good luck automatically increases an individual's psychological strength; sharing it with his intimates increases his feeling of mastery over his environment still further. And his intimates, in turn, can increase his exultation even more by helping to convince him that he himself was somehow responsible for his own good fortune ("You really deserved it").

Besides merely reinforcing the psychological effects of an individual's chance success in obtaining what he wants from his environment, his intimates may increase his chance of success as well by motivating him to approach his environment in a more elevated manner. They may act as a psychological pulley supplying just the amount of moral *uplift* he needs to help him raise his self up to its potential. Love has even been defined as "that relationship between one person and another which is most conducive to the optimum development of both."[39] We have already seen that the intimates of an individual may aid his endeavor to better his self by modeling the qualities he wishes to possess. Aristotle observes, "Each seeks to transfer to himself the traits he admires in another."[40] Osmotically, the virtue of the better flows into the lesser. We have also seen that the intimates of an individual may consciously make him aware of his faults; we should now add that they do so not merely to improve his self-knowledge, but to improve his self as well. If he does not respond to their criticism, they may go further and threaten to end their relationship unless he polishes out of his personality the tarnished character traits they disapprove of. (In fact, merely to have intimates in the first place, an individual must edit out some of his more repellent parts.)[41] Finally, they can help him to experiment with new modes of dealing with his environment. On the one hand, they can continue to relate to him in their accustomed manner in order to help him to return to his old self should his experimental self turn out badly; on the other hand, they can try to help him to stabilize in his new self should his experimental self turn out well. Thoreau puts it this way:

> We are sometimes made aware of a kindness long passed, and realize that there have been many times when our Friends' thoughts of us were of so pure and lofty a character that they passed over us like the winds of heaven unnoticed; when they treated us not as what we were, but as what we aspired to be.[42]

An individual whose intimates would be glad to supply him with necessary services need not become dependent on any nonintimate for these services. Should some nonintimate give him trouble (i.e., attempt to extort too high a price for a service), he can tell him to go to hell. If a garage mechanic, for instance, insists it will cost $200 to fix his transmission ("How much!"), he may instead be able to prevail on one of his automotive-skilled friends to fix it for him at half the price. Or, if he can find an intimate he likes to satisfy his sexual needs, he no longer has to associate with those who sufficed him sexually but who appalled him personally.

Intimates, moreover, may find that the potential of each to count on the other for a physical favor may itself constitute a greater benefit of intimacy than the specific favor each actually receives. When a person knows that his intimates are behind him, he can move forward more aggressively. If he knows that his intimates are available to help him should he need their assistance, he can take greater risks in his transactions with his environment in order to achieve greater gains. The little guy whose best friend is a Golden Gloves champion can act tougher than he otherwise could, and the man whose best friend is a millionaire can invest his own money in more speculative enterprises than he otherwise could.

Each intimate's potential to count on the other to supply him with a variety of psychological favors as well as physical ones encourages him to undertake more difficult tasks than he otherwise would. Wordsworth somewhere says, "There is a comfort in the strength of love: 'twill make a thing endurable, which else would overset the brain, or break the heart." Since the writing of books is one such continually frustrating self-assignment, we might expect it to be an activity in which the intimates of the author feed his fortitude with sundry sustenances. Sure enough: a cursory examination of book dedications and acknowledgments shows that it has recently become almost a literary convention for an author to acknowledge the contribution of his wife, who supplied not only miscellaneous physical services, such as typing, editing, and advice, but more important, an assortment of psychological services, ranging from buffering his failures to enhancing his successes. The following acknowledgment implies that it has become customary for a wife to act as the uninvoked tenth muse who helps her author-husband blot up the uncongenial outpourings of the other nine while underlining the inspired:

Finally, it is considered good form to say that one's wife has borne, with infinite patience and understanding, the trials and dolors of the literary work; I cannot in all conscience say this, since my own wife has been fully as impatient as I to see the book finished. But she has done something far more important than show patience and understanding; she has consistently and immoderately admired my efforts chapter by chapter, and with this indispensable support to my ego, I was able to finish at all.[43]

COMPLICATIONS

Three problems may complicate the favors intimates give each other to aid their environmental transactions: (1) *assurance* of forthcoming favors; (2) *dependence* on current favors; and (3) *obligation* for past favors.

1. In order to feel secure vis-à-vis his environment, an individual must learn how much he can count on his intimates for assistance. Accordingly, he will often devise certain *tests* in order to see how far each of his intimates will go to help him. On the one hand, he must discover the lower limits of his relationship with an intimate in order to determine the minimum amount of aid he can count on from him. The more readily his intimate will supply the little favors he requests, the higher this minimum. (Conversely, the more readily his intimate will repay the little favors he himself supplies, the more disposed he will be to grant his intimate larger ones. "If you lend a friend five dollars and never see him again, it's worth it," goes a modern maxim.) On the other hand, he must also discover the upper limits of his relationship with an intimate in order to determine the maximum amount of aid he can count on from him. Cicero points out the great variation on this end of the scale:

> If a man is wise, then, he will keep a close check both on the direction which his feelings of friendship are taking and on the speed with which they are developing, so

that he may, so to speak, drive them like a tried and tested team, watching the development of his friendship by putting his friends' characters to the test now here, now there. Often when men are asked for small loans they make it abundantly evident how little we may rely on them; others, who find it unthinkable to get excited about small loans, show their true colors when a larger request is made of them. But if we do find some individuals who would think it shameful to put money ahead of friendship, where shall we find those who would not put honors, public office, military command, civil authority, or wealth ahead of friendship.[44]

Intimates have always demonstrated their dependability by doing physical favors for each other on request. In the late Middle Ages, to perform a difficult service for a lady (e.g., slaying her dragon) was an institutionalized way of proving one's love for her. Sometimes, one intimate will set the other a hypothetical situation in which he would need an extreme service from him in order to discover whether the other would perform it for him. Sartre suggests that these hypothetical favors usually involve a conflict between loyalty to an intimate (the smallest unit of moral reference) and loyalty to society (the largest unit of moral reference):

> Thus to want to be loved is to want to be placed beyond the whole system of values posited by the other and to be the condition of all valorization and the objective foundation of all values. . . . The woman in love demands that the beloved in his acts should sacrifice traditional morality for her and is anxious to know whether the beloved would betray his friends for her, 'would steal for her,' 'would kill for her,' etc.[45]

There is no necessary correlation, however, between willingness to perform extreme hypothetical favors and willingness to perform extreme actual ones. In regard to an actual moral conflict between loyalty to the intimate and obedience to social norms, Cicero has written:

> He used to say, too, that friendships were violently and in many cases quite properly broken up when men demanded of their friends something that was morally reprehensible, for example, that they assist in immorality, or aid in an illegal act. In these instances, men who refused their help, however honorable such refusal might be, nonetheless could be charged with violating the laws of friendship by those they refused to go along with; and these latter, who made bold to demand complete compliance from their friends, would say that they were showing, by the very fact of such a demand, that they themselves would do anything whatever for a friend's sake. This sort of complaint, he said, not only frequently destroyed friendships of long standing, but even became the source of enduring enmity.[46]

The most extreme favor one can give and ask for, of course, is the sacrifice of one's life. Some intimates would sacrifice their lives for each other in theory but not in practice; other intimates would never seriously consider sacrificing their lives for each other until they were suddenly confronted with just such a decision (e.g., whether to run into a burning building to save their friend).

Willingness to supply psychological favors constitutes as much a test of the intimacy level of the relationship as willingness to supply physical ones. Such a psychological favor as "criticism," which indicates that one intimate puts the well-being of the other even ahead of the continuance of their relationship, usually suffices to convince the latter of the depth of the former's feeling for him.

But note that those who have ulterior motives for wanting to appear intimates may also employ this technique to assure their victims of their affection. The two villains of Choderlos de Laclos's *Dangerous Liaisons* employ this tactic to persuade the innocent and unsuspecting Cecile Volanges that they have her best interests at heart:

Madame de Merteuil also told me she would lend me some books that talk about [love] and will teach me how to behave, and also how to write better than I do. You see, she tells me all my faults, which proves she likes me....

And then when [Monsieur de Valmont] came he seemed no more angry than if I had never done anything to him. He only scolded me afterward, and then very gently, and in such a way.... Just like you; which proved to me that he had great friendship for me too.[47]

Although the examinee himself sometimes initiates tests he knows he is prepared to pass, it is much more common for the examiner to do so, even though he too is certain the other will pass them. He needs to give his intimate these tests especially when his own world momentarily appears extremely bleak and he feels incapable of dealing with it, for he must then reassure himself that at least someone remains willing to help him. Objectively unnecessary requests for "support" usually serve this subjective purpose ("I'll never finish my dissertation and it won't be any good." "Sure you'll finish it and it'll be just fine. Don't worry so much about it").

2. Whenever an individual attempts to facilitate his relationship with his environment by inserting his intimates between himself and his circumstances for the automatic transmission of his desires into actuality, he may find that the disadvantages offset the advantages. True, he no longer has to shift for himself and can rely on the extra power of his intimates' overdrive. But when he ceases to gear himself into the world directly (manually transmitting his will into reality), he may find that he has given up total control over his life and has increased the chance of breakdown. In short, when an individual loses his autonomy, when he begins to count on his intimates to do for him what he used to do for himself, he may discover that he is worse off now than he was before.

All the potential dividends of an intimate relation may develop into fatal *dependencies*:

a If he uses his intimates to extend his range of manipulation, he may find that their clumsiness has destroyed what was almost in his grasp. Should he ask them to perform an important favor, he may have no way of knowing, until it is too late, whether or not they actually did it. Asking an intimate to mail an important letter entails the risk that the intimate may forget or the risk that he would insult his intimate were he to remind him of his commission again.

b If he assumes his intimates will supply him with sound advice, he may find that, in following their incompetent counsel, he is brought to ruin. And if he assumes they will verify his vision when it is correct, he may begin to doubt his own sanity should they be incredulous about what he has seen.[48]

c If he drops his own guard in the presumption that they are protecting him, he may find that he is knocked down. And if he over-reaches himself in the expectation that they will rehabilitate him should he get into trouble, he may find himself friendless when he is flat on his back.

d If he seeks out his intimates when he is despondent over his failures in the anticipation that they will revitalize him, he may find that they actually deepen his despair, either through a frivolous response that indicates they are less able to sympathize with his problems than he thought, or through a fervent response that indicates they hold him more responsible for his plight than he does himself. And if he presupposes their psychological support, he may find that it is not forthcoming ("You're right. You are pretty worthless and your future does indeed look bleak"). Not only may he no longer be able to do anything without their constant reassurance,[49] he may also discover that they are actually aggravating his weaknesses. The exchange between Cassius and Brutus, referred to earlier in this chapter, in fact continues thus:

> Cassius: A friend should bear his friend's infirmities,
> But Brutus makes mine greater than they are.
> Brutus: I do not, till you practice them on me.
> Cassius: You love me not.

Brutus: I do not like your faults.
Cassius: A friendly eye could never see such faults.
Brutus: A flatterer's would not, though they do appear
         As huge as high Olympus.

e If he takes it for granted that his intimates are mirroring him
accurately when in fact they are not, he may find himself so
puffed up by their flattery that he will experience the inevitable
deflation that occurs when someone reveals the truth to him at
last, as did the child who told the emperor about his new
clothes. And if he becomes accustomed to having them heighten
his elation over his successes, he may find that he is unable to
sustain his good spirits by himself or that their bad mood brings
down his good mood.

f Finally, if he believes his intimates to be aiding his attempts at
self-improvement, he may become disappointed in several ways.
First, had he thought they were helping him to correct his
faults, he may discover that they are taking too much delight
in this sort of social work. Their constant criticizing, which at
first he found edifying, may turn into nagging. As Confucius
said, "In friendship, repeated scoldings can lead only to estrangement."[50] Second, had he thought they were helping him
to experiment with novel ways of dealing with his environment,
he may discover that they have actually imprisoned him in his
old personality. (He may be afraid to try on his new selves
before those who, having known him in the past, will think
him affected for attempting to be someone they know he is not,
and who will continue to respond to him in the same way they
have always responded to him.) Third, had he thought he was
picking up their virtues, he may discover that he has actually
been picking up their vices. Fourth, had he thought he would
like the new self in which they were stabilizing him, he may
discover that their influence on his self-development has been
negative, for he does not welcome the new character they are
bringing out in him ("I hate myself when I'm around them").
Fifth, had he thought his intimates were all pulling together to
make him a better person, he may discover that they all have

different goals in mind, and that they are actually pulling him apart.

When one intimate becomes aware that the other has become dependent upon him for a particular favor, the former may be tempted to abuse his power over the latter. He can force him to do his bidding by threatening to terminate the service. Those who engage in personal relations professionally may even attempt to create the dependency they wish to abuse. Thus, the female spy will seduce the government official in order to get him to betray his country if he wishes to remain in her favor.

Because he is dependent on his intimate for a certain service in one area of his life, he must put up with all the latter's disservices in other areas. One way he can try to moderate his intimate's disfavors is to create in him a counterdependency, which he himself can threaten to terminate. The only other way is to screw up his courage to break off the relationship entirely and attempt to face the world again alone, without the service. Although it is only a possibility that interpersonal bonds will become interpersonal bondage, that famous philosopher of paranoia, Schopenhauer, feels such subjugation is certain unless one heeds the following counsel:

> There is one thing that, more than any other, throws people absolutely off their balance—the thought that you are dependent upon them. This is sure to produce an insolent and domineering manner towards you.... The only way to attain superiority in dealing with men is to let it be seen that you are independent of them.... To become reconciled to a friend with whom you have broken is a form of weakness; and you pay the penalty of it when he takes the first opportunity of doing precisely the very thing which brought about the breach; nay, he does it the more boldly because he is secretly conscious that you cannot get on without him.

His intimate may simply stop supplying him with the physical and, especially, psychological services to which he has become addicted. Since he can now neither do without them nor provide them for himself—as he once could—he is likely to become angry with his intimate for falsely enticing him (he believes) into a relationship with the implicit promise to continue to provide him with these favors forever. If his intimate ceases to supply him with his former favors, he can always blame his intimate ("She's incapable of loving anyone"). But if his intimate begins to supply these same services to a third party, he will have to blame himself. His withdrawal symptoms are compounded when he realizes it was his own deficiency, relative to the third party's, that caused his intimate to cease to serve him. His jealousy of the third party is an expression of his growing awareness that his own relative lack led to his absolute loss.[51]

We have seen that intimates may suffice each other too well in some areas. But they may not suffice each other well enough in others ("Somehow, she just doesn't satisfy me completely"). His intimates may be unable or unwilling to perform for him all the favors he needs. Intimates may *specialize* in providing each other with certain services and not others. The friend of a good-time Charlie may find him a good drinking companion at happy times, for Charlie is skilled at enhancing elation, but at sad times, Charlie's attempts to cheer him up are clumsy. Moreover, intimates may be capable of doing each other certain favors, but may not want to. A bibliophile may refuse to lend his friend any books from his large library, even though he would readily give him anything else he requested. Usually, as individuals become more intimate, they are willing to perform services for each other that involve greater cost to themselves. Sometimes, however, one intimate may be more willing to be counted on as a potential donor of an extreme service, which he will probably not have to perform, than to be called upon as an actual donor of a mundane one. Someone was once quoted as saying, "I might give up my life for my friend, but he had better not ask me to do up a parcel."

3. Another set of problems each intimate may face when he asks the other for a favor concerns his *obligation* to repay it. Until their relationship reaches a certain stage, one good turn requires

a re-turn. Even that apostle of self-sufficient individualism, Nietzsche, occasionally felt obligated to refund a favor to a friend:

> Gast was always prepared to drop whatever he might
> be doing to come to Nietzsche's assistance whenever he
> was needed. In the face of this, Nietzsche would indeed
> have been the monster of ingratitude he is sometimes
> painted as being if he had accepted Gast's devotion with-
> out feeling some sense of obligation towards him. But
> this in fact he did feel. Gast was by profession a com-
> poser, and Nietzsche is well known to have done all he
> could to further his friend's career, securing or attempt-
> ing to secure performances of his music whenever he
> could and praising Gast's mediocre talent as that of "an-
> other Mozart."[52]

Several social theorists have conceived of personal relations in
terms of the economic model of exchange of goods and services.[53]
Here I will mention only a few of the many ways in which intimates who feel obligated to return favors discharge their debts, as
well as noting some of the difficulties each method entails. The
economics of intimacy is complicated because most transactions
are more intricate than the elementary case in which tit is immediately returned for tat.

First, the favor one intimate repays to another need not be the
same as the favor he was given. A wife may give her husband
access to her genitals in return for access to his wallet. (Ian Watt
has even suggested that the apparent lack of sexual desire shown
by Western women from the eighteenth century until recently
resulted from their need to counterbalance the relative increase
in economic rights men achieved during this period. Seeming not
to desire sex themselves, women could exchange it, *noblesse
oblige*, for economic security.[54]) Nor need he even requite one
physical favor with another physical favor. Behaviorists who think
they are observing one-sided affairs overlook the psychological
services by which one intimate settles his accounts for the physical

favors another has given him. The friends of the man who has everything may pay their meal tickets to his banquets with their support for his self-esteem.

Second, one intimate need not repay the favor at the same time he was given it. But if he does not, he is under a diffuse obligation to the other to return whatever favor the other needs, whenever the other needs it. In this case, the former must be prepared to drop everything in order to answer the latter's call for aid.

Third, the favor one intimate repays to another need not have precisely the same value as the favor he was given. In fact, if he does attempt to equate exactly his restitution with the service he received, he will encounter two very serious problems. He is likely to find it extremely difficult to equate favors that are not to be repaid in the same coin with which they were given. And, he is likely to find that he has insulted his benefactor, for, by not keeping up the pretense that their friendship is more than mere, he has made their relationship appear crassly economic.[55]

An individual who asks for a favor will feel an obligation to return more for it if his intimate gives it grudgingly. Having to plead with an intimate for a service so increases its cost that only a person who is in dire need will stoop to mortgaging himself by begging for what is begrudged. Conversely, an individual who asks for a favor need return less for it if his intimate gives it willingly. Since intimates who are glad to be of help seem not too inconvenienced by the performance of their services, their favors are purchased at a lower price. Accordingly, the person who receives what is freely given will be extremely grateful for the discount.

An individual who receives the favor he wants without openly asking for it, or with merely hinting he desires it, has made an extremely good buy; as no implicit contract was established by his request, he need make only a token repayment. Even so, he will sometimes adopt the strategy of refusing to accept the favor that he desires, which his intimate is quite willing to supply unasked, in the hope that his intimate will continue to urge it on him anyway. In this way, he acquires the favor marked down 100 percent from its usual price tag. In fact, he now even makes it seem that he is doing his intimate a favor by allowing his intimate to do him a favor. By letting it be known that his intimate is doing him the favor against his will ("Well, if you insist"), he rejects any responsibility for its return. Of course, in following this tactic, he risks the possibility that his intimate will not insist, which leaves him in a decidedly unfavorable position.

The Swedish sociologist Vihelm Aubert suggests that many of the arguments between intimates over whether their obligations to each other have been discharged results from the above-mentioned problems: that many favors are incomparable; that they are given with varying degrees of willingness; and that they are requested with varying degrees of articulation:

> The dual aspect of love, sexual or otherwise, as simultaneous expressions of supply and demand, makes it difficult to gauge the terms of exchange between lovers. The dualism makes concepts of justice largely inapplicable in love relationships. Although strong feelings of outraged justice are frequent in unhappy marriages, attempts to clarify the rights and wrongs meet with notorious difficulties. They are usually ascribed to the intensity of the emotions involved, of love and of hatred, but they may also be related to the cognitive problems of assessing the respective contributions to the relationship. Normal social rules about equitable exchange of contributions and sanctions approach their limit of applicability when the borderline between a gift and a demand is obliterated, as it frequently is in love.[56]

We have thus far looked at the favors intimates exchange from the point of view of the intimate receiving them. We will now switch our perspective to that of the intimate giving them.

Why do intimates bother to do favors for each other? First, one intimate may do another a favor because he is compelled by his dependency on the other for certain services, which the latter may cease to supply should he refuse. A religious virgin may submit to the sexual advances of the man she loves because she is afraid he may leave her if she does not. Second, one intimate may do another a favor because he has an obligation dating back to services in the past. A visitor who has asked a friend to put him up for a while must take out the garbage if he is asked. Third, one intimate may do another a favor in order to make the latter obligated to perform for him the services he needs.[57] An aspiring politician may work to get his friend elected senator in order to obligate the latter to support his own Presidential ambitions. Fourth, one intimate may do another a favor in order to induce the latter to return support for his self-esteem in the form of gratitude. A woman may continually give presents to her friends in order to bask in their appreciation. Finally, one intimate may do another a favor in order to empathize with his joy—thus delighting himself indirectly by delighting another. A hippie may himself luminesce in the light of the ecstatic expression that beams forth from the face of the friend he has just turned on.

On the other hand, since each of the intimates who are involved in this upper middle level of personal relations still has his own interests at heart, there are times when one will feel that it is not worth his while to do the favor the other asks. He may expect that the requested favor will be intrinsically unpleasant, and he may foresee no equivalent service he will need from the other in return. A person whose friend asks him for help in moving—a tiring, dirty job—may hesitate or refuse if he anticipates that he will not require similar help from his friend for a long time to come. Second, he may expect that his value to the other will decrease if he does the favor requested. A woman may not want to sleep with her lover because she may feel that he will begin to take her too much for granted afterward.[58] Third, he may anticipate difficulty in getting the favor refunded. A man may not want to lend money to his friend because he may feel that he will lose both his money and his friend.[59] Finally, he may decide that the resources he would have to give up in granting the favor are limited, inconvenient to do without, or irreplaceable. A person may not want to lend his friend a cigarette if he is running out, a bicycle if he expects to have occasion to use it, or a book if he has spent hours underlining it to his taste.[60] The most limited, inconveniently drawn upon, and irreplaceable of all his resources is, of course, his time—which his friends are often thieves of.

Although there are occasions when these self-interested reasons cause one intimate not to want to do a particular favor for another, it is usually also in his interest not to refuse the other's request for aid directly. If he does so, he is likely to damage the relationship permanently by spoiling the other as a source of services for himself ("What do you mean, you won't do it for me?" the other will retort, and then attempt to extort the service from him anyhow by transforming the request into a demand supported with past claims or future cautions: *obligation* continuation: "Look at all I've done for you"; *dependency* continuation: "Just don't ask me for any more ...!"). In order to preserve the relationship without performing the service, he can use the strategies of *avoidance, procrastination,* or *excuse.* When one intimate thinks another is going to ask him for a favor, he can avoid the request by avoiding the intimate. Thus, if he suspects his friend wants to borrow some money, he can fail to answer his door or telephone. When one intimate receives a direct request from another for a favor, he can withhold it by delaying its execution in hopes that the other will forget about it, get someone else to do it, or do it himself. Thus, if his friend asks to borrow some money, he can keep forgetting to go to the bank to get it. Finally, when one intimate is asked by another for a favor, he can claim that, although he would like to supply it, he cannot, either because he lacks the resources requested or because he has an obligation (which he hopes his intimate will recognize as higher) to distribute them elsewhere. Thus, if his friend asks to borrow some money, he can claim that he does not have any to lend at the moment or that he has already promised all he could spare to someone else. Since all these strategies are based on making the nonperformance of the favor look like a chance occurrence, there is a built-in limitation to the number of times they can be used successfully. A person can be away from home, can forget to go to the bank, or can be out of spare cash just so often before his friend begins to suspect that he really does not want to lend him any money at all.

Cynics, like La Rochefoucauld, have asserted that intimacy is *nothing but* the exchange of the benefits described in this chapter for individual profit: "What men call friendship is just an arrangement for mutual gain and an exchange of favors; in short, a business where self-interest always sets out to obtain something."[61] In the next chapter, however, I will show that the closest of intimates are connected not merely by *mutual benefits*, but by *mutual being*. Consequently, their relationship cannot be adequately described in terms of the cost and value of the favors they give and receive. They would find the whole economic rhetoric used to describe lesser intimacies to be completely inappropriate for describing their own transactions. If the economics of intimacy constitutes the substructure of personal relations, for close friends, at least, it is a phenomenologically invisible one. Should it surface in their consciousness at all, they consider their relationship to be breaking down.

Close intimates (including the best of friends, most lovers, and many spouses) do not see their intimacy in economic terms, because the economics involved is not the mundane one of scarce resources (in which each receives according to his contribution), but the utopian one of infinite resources (in which each receives according to his need), which is hardly an economics at all. Cicero seens to be making the same point in the following passage:

> The second view was that which limits friendship to an exact exchange of duties and kindnesses. This, of course, demands a far too nice and narrow calculation of friendship to make sure that there is a precise balance between income and outgo. In my opinion true friendship is too rich, yes, too affluent, for this sort of thing, and does not keep a sharp eye out for fear it may give more than it has received. It does not need to worry for fear something may be lost or drop on the ground, or that a friend may receive more than is coming to him.[62]

Mutual benefits can be fruitfully analyzed as an exchange of benefits only when two separate parties are involved. Close intimates, however, see themselves as being only one party with a single interest. The absence of separate self-interest is particularly clear when one performs a favor for the other. He does so not because he is obligated to but because he wants to; not to benefit himself but to benefit the other. He derives no individual profit from his favor—unless one wants to take into account the indirect advantage he obtains, for, having expanded his self and his interests to include the other (as I shall show in the next chapter), his egoism *à un* has become an egoism *à deux.*

Although Montaigne the moralist was born a century before La Rochefoucauld the cynic, he seems to have had the latter's views in mind when he attempted to refute the proposition that all friendships consist solely of a self-seeking exchange of services:

> In this noble relationship services and kindnesses, which keep other friendships alive, do not deserve even to be taken into account, by reason of the complete fusion of the wills. For just as my own love for myself is not increased by the help I give myself at need, whatever the Stoics may say, and as I feel no gratitude to myself for any service that I do myself; so the union of such friends, being truly perfect, causes them to lose consciousness of these duties, and to hate and banish from their thoughts these words that imply separation and difference: benefit, obligation, gratitude, request, thanks, and the like. Everything being in effect common between them—will, thoughts, opinions, goods, wives, children, honour, and life—and their agreement being that of one soul in two bodies, according to Aristotle's very proper definition, they can neither lend nor give one another anything. This is why the lawmakers, to honour marriage by some imaginary comparison with this union, forbid gifts between husband and wife, intending thereby to infer that everything should belong to each, and that they have nothing to divide or share out between them. If, in the sort of friendship of which I am speaking, one could give to the other, it would be the one who received the

benefit that would be laying his friend under an obligation. For since the principal study of each is to confer benefits on the other, it is the one who provides the matter and occasion that plays the truly liberal part, by giving his friend the pleasure of acting towards him as he most desires. When the philosopher Diogenes had need of money, he used to say that he asked it *back* from his friends, not that he asked them for it.[63]

In this chapter, the *ecological* dimension of an intimate relation has been considered and a fifth major force uncovered that transforms isolated individuals into interlinked intimates: *the favors each intimate derives from the other that facilitate his transactions with his environment.* These favors further either his actual physical exchange with his circumstances or his potential psychological ability to deal successfully with his surroundings.

CHAPTER 6

Couples

EVERYONE in the community was connected inter-subjectively to everyone else insofar as they all participated in the common "geist" of the gemeinschaft.[1] In society, however, anyone who wishes to become the intimate of anyone else must create his own intersubjective couples. In the last chapter, I considered how the individual's intimates have replaced the community as the outer membrane that separates him from his environment. In this chapter, I will consider how the individual's intimates have dissolved the inner membrane, which was deposited during the decline of the community, that separates him from themselves. Montaigne, in his continuing struggle to convince mankind that these interpersonal connectives of common being deserve a higher value than those interpersonal connectives of common benefits, posits the former to be the core of intimacy while excluding the latter even from its definition:

> For the rest, what we commonly call friends and friendship are no more than acquaintanceships and familiarities, contracted either by chance or for advantage, which have brought our minds together. In the friendship I speak of they mix and blend one into the other in so perfect a union that the seam which has joined them is effaced and disappears.

... It was some mysterious quintessence of all this mix-
ture which possessed itself of my will, and led it to
plunge and lose itself in his; which possessed itself of his
whole will, and led it, with a similar hunger and a like
impulse, to plunge and lose itself in mine. I may truly
say "lose," for it left us with nothing that was our own,
nothing that was either his or mine.[2]

Accordingly, the first section of this chapter will investigate the
ways intimates achieve their *Communion*.

Although it is necessary for both intimates to establish a common being in order to create a personal relation of the highest
order, it is not necessary for each of them to lose all individuality
and become exactly like the other in the process. In fact, in acquiring a more focused ground against which to contrast himself,
each intimate actually sharpens his self. Accordingly, the second
section of this chapter will investigate the ways intimates intensify
each other's individuality through their *Contrariety*.

Both communion and contrariety, however, are extremely unstable. Since both of these processes involve each intimate's very
being, each attempts to make their relationship, and hence his
transformed self, more durable. Accordingly, the third section of
this chapter will investigate the ways intimates lock themselves
together through their *Commitment*.

Finally, the Complications section of this chapter will investigate some of the intimates' difficulties in accomplishing their
communion, contrariety, and commitment, and some of the draw-
backs of successful accomplishment.

How do intimates achieve their intersubjective integration and
differentiation? Georg Simmel provides the clue in one of the
most important insights he—or for that matter any Western social
theorist—ever had. "Man," he said, "has the capacity to decom-
pose himself into parts and to feel any one of these as his proper
self."[3] This capacity of man to commit what I will call a *psychic
synechdoche* has significant consequences for his social relations:
if a person can particularize himself, then he can give himself
totally to another or withhold himself totally from another, merely

by relinquishing or retaining what he particularized himself in. I have already discussed one such psychic synechdoche in Chapter 4: the secret. Here I will describe the rest.

COMMUNION

Observers of social life have often noticed that intimacy involves some merger between the selves of individuals, but they have not been able to describe the nature of this merger concretely or consistently. Thus, in one place Aristotle describes this psychological union in terms of what the intimates have in common by quoting the Greek proverb: "Two bodies and one soul."[4] In another place, he describes it in terms of the similarities between the intimates by referring to an intimate as "a second self"[5]—a phrase better known to us in Cicero's Latin version, "alter ego."[6] In still a third place, he describes it in terms of one person's selfless desire for the continued existence of his intimate by referring to a friend as "one who desires the existence and preservation of his friend for his friend's sake."[7]

The moderns have not done much better, for the descriptions of the highest level of intimacy they have offered are also vague and abstract. Freud describes it in terms of the loss of ego boundaries between the intimates:

> Normally, there is nothing of which we are more certain than the feeling of our self, our own ego. This ego appears to us as something autonomous and unitary, marked off distinctly from everything else.... There is only one state—admittedly an unusual state, but not one that can be stigmatized as pathological—in which it does not do this. At the height of being in love the boundary between ego and object threatens to melt away. Against all the evidence of his senses, a man who is in love declares that 'I' and 'you' are one, and is prepared to behave as if it were a fact.[8]

Sullivan describes the highest level of intimacy in terms of each intimate's view of the other as an extension of himself: "When the satisfaction or the security of another person becomes as significant to one as one's own satisfaction or security, then the state of love exists."[9] And Erikson describes it in terms of the fusion of identities: "The young adult, emerging from the search for and the insistence on identity, is eager and willing to fuse his identity with that of others. He is ready for intimacy."[10]

These writers and others have attempted to elucidate more concretely the nature of the intersubjective integration they had abstractly defined the essence of intimacy to be. But in the end they were reduced to similes ("Souls, which wrap around each other like two vines . . ."), reduced to trying to convey intuitively through poetry what they could not clarify conceptually through prose. In order not to becloud further an already misty subject, I will endeavor to make my own concrete explication of the inter-subjective unification of intimates as prosaic as possible. I will proceed first by discriminating the self of an individual into its material and immaterial components, and then by delineating the ways intimates combine these components in order to connect their separate selves into a single whole.

The most obvious of a person's material components in which his self can be embodied is his body. Accordingly, intimates may foster the fusion of their souls through conjugating the members of their body. They can temporarily incorporate certain unde-tached anatomical aspects into each other. During the sex act, for instance, each intimate may secrete his fingers, toes, tongues, genitals, etc., within the other's body. But they can also arrange for a more permanent swap by irrevocably severing certain of their anatomical aspects—those that are easily disconnected, such as locks of their hair, or even those that are not, such as drops of their blood. Although intimates usually transfuse their blood only metaphorically, in some cases they become "blood brothers" by ritualistically trickling some blood into each other from, say, a pricked finger. Intimates may even discuss interchanging other body parts, as when lovers say to each other, "I give you my heart." Again this usage is usually metaphoric, though the medical advances in the field of organ transplants may cause intimates in the near future to ponder the more literal possibilities. But all these examples of the ways intimates have become of one spirit by becoming of one flesh reveal the poverty of their imagination when compared to Plato's great myth on the origin of lovers— which, regrettably, because of its length, I can present only in abridgment:

> First of all I must explain the real nature of man, and the change which it has undergone—for in the beginning we were nothing like we are now.... each of these beings was globular in shape, with rounded back and sides, four arms and four legs, and two faces, both the same, on a cylindrical neck, and one head, with one face one side and one the other, and four ears, and two lots of privates, and all the other parts to match. They walked erect, as we do ourselves, backward or forward, whichever they pleased, but when they broke into a run they simply stuck their legs straight out and went whirling round and round like a clown turning cartwheels.... Now when the work of bisection was complete it left each half with a desperate yearning for the other, and they ran together and flung their arms around each other's necks, and asked for nothing better than to be rolled into one.... And so, when this boy lover—or any lover, for that matter—is fortunate enough to meet his other half, they are both so intoxicated with affection, with friendship, and with love, that they cannot bear to let each other out of sight for a single instant. It is such reunions as these that impel men to spend their lives together, although they may be hard put to it to say what they really want with one another, and indeed, the purely sexual pleasures of their friendship could hardly account for the huge delight they take in one another's company. The fact is that both their souls are longing for a something else—a something to which they can neither of them put a name, and which they can only give an inkling of in cryptic

sayings and prophetic riddles. Now, supposing Hephaes-
tus were to come and stand over them with his tool bag
as they lay there side by side, and suppose he were to
ask, Tell me, my dear creatures, what do you really want
with one another? And suppose they didn't know what to
say, and he went on, How would you like to be rolled
into one, so that you could always be together, day and
night, and never be parted again? Because if that's what
you want, I can easily weld you together, and then you
can live your two lives in one, and, when the time comes,
you can die a common death and still be two-in-one in
the lower world. Now, what do you say? Is that what
you'd like me to do? And would you be happy if I did?
We may be sure, gentlemen, that no lover on earth
would dream of refusing such an offer, for not one of
them could imagine a happier fate. Indeed, they would
be convinced that this was just what they'd been waiting
for—to be merged, that is, into an utter oneness with the
beloved. And so all this to-do is a relic of that original
state of ours, when we were whole, and now, when we
are longing for and following after that primeval whole-
ness, we say we are in love.[11]

The self of an individual can be corporealized not only in
anatomical aspects, but also in physiological movements and
rhythms as well. Accordingly, intimates may harmonize psychologically to the extent they can synchronize physiologically. Thus,
intimates may feel that they have brought all their physiological
rhythms together when their "two hearts beat as one."[12] Since
individuals may become soul partners by coordinating their pos-
tures and gestures, intimates often become dancing partners simply to have the opportunity to do so. Copulation provides them
with still another occasion for physiological reciprocity, for not
only must they synchronize their time of arousal, but they often
find that the physical pleasure each derives from orgasm is ex-
celled by the psychological pleasure both derive from simultaneous
orgasm. Participant observers of the sex act between intimates

have always stressed the fact that, as its climax approaches, the individuality of each dissolves and pools into a common liquidity. Violette Leduc's fictionalized autobiography, *Thérèse and Isabelle,* contains the following narration of sexual intercourse between lesbian lovers: "I was receiving what she was receiving: I was Isabelle. My efforts, my sweat, my rhythm were exciting me too. The pearl [Isabelle's clitoris] wanted what I wanted."[13]

An individual's self can reside in his conduct or demeanor.[14] Consequently, intimates may create a common consciousness by picking up each other's mannerisms. They may dress in a similar fashion, walk and gesture in the same way, and constantly reiterate identical favorite words. Claude Brown seems to feel that this was what his old friend Tony was up to:

> People started saying that [Tony] was my partner. He turned out to be a real nice guy, so I didn't mind. He stayed close to me and used to try to dress the way I did. He'd buy clothes from the same people I got mine from. ... I guess he wanted to start acting just like me, and he had to start someplace.[15]

Even if intimates do not conduct themselves in the same way, each may still feel implicated in the quality of the other's behavior and the success it brings him. Each may be as pleased with the wealth of learning the other expresses as with the wealth of fortune he accumulates. Emerson, for one, claims to evaluate his friend's deportment as though it were his own:

> I must feel pride in my friend's accomplishments as if they were mine, and a property in his virtues. I feel as warmly when he is praised as the lover when he hears applause of his engaged maiden.[16]

Social scientists have pointed out that a person's self inhabits the objects he possesses or owns almost as much as it inheres in his body or behavior.[17] Intimates, then, may join their internal spirits to the extent that they join their external objectifications.

They may fuse insofar as they feel the same way about each other's objectifications. The Latin proverb "Love me, love my dog" implies that those who want to love an individual must also love his dog (or any of his self-objectifications), for his dog (or any of his self-objectifications) constitutes, he feels, one of his essential parts.

Intimates may also wall each other in by dispossessing themselves of their own objectifications in order to give them to each other as gifts. In this way, each surrounds the other with concrete manifestations of his own self:

> Then Jonathan made a covenant with David, because he loved him as his own soul. And Jonathan stripped himself of the robe that was upon him, and gave it to David, and his armor, and even his sword and his bow and his girdle.[18]

Washington Irving once wrote:

> There is after all something in those trifles that friends bestow upon each other which is an unfailing indication of the place the giver holds in the affections. I would believe that one who preserved a lock of hair, a simple flower, or any trifle of my bestowing, loved me, though no show was made of it; while all the protestations in the world would not win my confidence in one who set no value on such little things.

The keepsakes or "intimacy trophies"[19] that intimates exchange include pictures, personal creations, and group membership insignia (like fraternity pins or high school rings). One lover or spouse may literally put on the part of the other's identity derived from his institutional affiliation, as does the Vassar girl who wears her boy friend's Yale sweatshirt.

In the extreme, intimates can go all the way in conjoining this component of their selves: each may surrender exclusive control over all of his possessions by transforming them all into common property. Aristotle has observed:

> As the proverb truly says, "friends have all things in common," for friendship is an expression of community. Brothers and comrades go shares in everything, other friends share this or that part of their possessions and to a greater or lesser extent according to the warmth of their friendship.[20]

Today, perhaps the ultimate example of common property is the joint checking account. Intimates also acquire property in common when they act in conjunction with each other to create or to obtain a material object that objectifies their common self. Examples: Intimates who are academic colleagues can pool their ideas to author a book jointly. Intimates who are living together can pool their resources to buy house furnishings and appliances. Intimates who are married can pool their biological and social characteristics to have a baby. Aristotle also observed:

> Children are a bond between the parents—which explains why childless unions are more likely to be dissolved. The children do not belong to one parent more than the other, and it is the joint ownership of something valuable that keeps people from separating.[21]

An individual can inspire his relatively intangible parts with his self in the same way that he can embody or objectify it in his relatively tangible parts. One set of a person's incorporeal constituents in which his self can be lodged include his tastes, opinions, attitudes, and ideas—especially those he regards as uniquely his own, those he contrasts with other people's. As with their more material aspects, intimates may become of one mind to the extent to which they develop and share (and become aware that they share) similar tastes, opinions, attitudes, and ideals—especially those that set them both off from other people around them.

"A friend," remarked an anonymous maker of maxims, "is someone who hates the same things you do."

Another set of unsubstantial self segments consists of an individual's personal culture: the books he has read, the movies he has seen, the concerts he has attended, the places he has visited, the education he has received—in short, his selection from the cultural artifacts available in his society, especially those he feels have influenced him the most ("It's the most important book I've ever read. You've got to read it!"). It is in this sense that intimates develop a common culture. Each gets the other to read the books he has liked, both attend the same movies, they travel together, etc. Since an individual articulates his experience in terms of his personal culture, the more the cultures of intimates become common, the more readily each can recognize any reference the other makes ("Doesn't she remind you of the girl in *Portnoy's Complaint?*" "You mean the one who...?").

Still another set of a person's immaterial elements are those remembered incidents of his life that, taken all together, constitute his autobiography. In "Marriage and the Construction of Reality," Peter Berger and Hansfried Kellner suggest that intimates may have stitched in the past one of the seams that hold them together in the present:

> It is not only the ongoing experience of the two partners that is constantly shared and passed through the conversational apparatus. The same sharing extends into the past. The two distinct biographies, as subjectively apprehended by the two individuals who have lived through them, are overruled and re-interpreted in the course of their conversation.... The couple thus construct not only present reality but reconstruct past reality as well, fabricating a common memory that integrates the recollections of the two individual pasts.[22]

There are three ways intimates can experience their past in common. Each can tell the other more and more incidents that happened before they became intimate, until one can remember the other's past almost as well as his own. The theme of the Japanese novel *Kokoro*, by Natsume Soseki, centers around the difficulties one friend had in confiding his autobiography to another.

> Since my past was experienced only by me, I might be excused if I regarded it as my property, and mine alone. And is it not natural that I should want to give this thing, which is mine, to someone before I die? At least, that is how I feel. On the other hand, I would rather see it destroyed, with my life, than offer it to someone who does not want it.[23]

Each can also tell the other developments that have occurred since they had become intimate but during the times they have been separated spatially, in order for each to keep his knowledge of the other's biography up-to-date. (Intimates express their desire to acquire the latest information about each other by asking, "What's new with you?" or "What have you been doing?") But the most important way intimates create a common past is to experience together a constantly receding common present.

A shared past is supposed to be one of the strongest factors leading to a shared present. Moreover, an individual is supposed to evaluate his intimates by the standard of a loose *seniority system*, in which the importance of a relationship ought to be correlated with its longevity. But moralists of all periods would not have continually felt the need to remind us that our old friends should be more important to us than our new ones[24] unless the interpersonal link forged by a common past is weaker than has been thought to be the case.

A person can identify his self with still other of his components: the expressions of his thoughts, feelings, desires, and self-definitions. Although he may attempt to communicate his "I think..." "I feel..." "I want..." or "I am..." to anyone, these communications, and hence the self that rides on them, become qualitatively transformed whenever he tells them to an intimate who understands him immediately and totally. All communication involves some degree of what George Herbert Mead referred to as "calling out in the other that response an individual calls out in himself";[25] but it is Communication with a capital C when he actually succeeds in accomplishing this completely. As long as this state of total Communication lasts, the self component that consists of the speaking "I" will seem to inhabit both the speaker and the listener, the one as much as the other. A taker of LSD describes in the following words what he means when he defines the essence of intimacy to be the selfless state an individual experiences during perfect Communication:

> That is intimacy, an ultimate intimacy not obtained by shared confessions of guilts, Oedipus complexes, or secrets, but by a mental unification analogous to sexual intercourse, a joining of thought processes so total that the listener could just as easily be the speaker. In short, one gets inside the other's head.[26]

Intimates, it seems, speak to one another with but a single tongue.

The outcome of this total rapport between intimates is that, as soon as one learns of any particular stimulus the other has experienced, he can anticipate the other's response. In her "Testament of Friendship," Vera Brittain has written:

> After a year or two of constant companionship, our response to each other's needs and emotions had become so instinctive that in our correspondence one of us often replied to some statement or request made by the other before the letter which contained it had arrived.

Conversely, as soon as one learns that the other has behaved in a particular way, he can divine his motive. In his "Essay on Friendship," Michel de Montaigne has written:

> It is beyond the power of all arguments in the world to upset my certainty of my friend's intentions and judgments. No action of his could put before me in any aspect that I should not immediately discern its motive.

> Our souls traveled so unitedly together, they felt so strong
> an affection for one another, and with this same affection
> saw into the very depths of each other's hearts, that not
> only did I know his as well as my own, but I should
> certainly have trusted myself more freely to him than to
> myself.[27]

Each intimate's ability to predict and understand the other's responses to various situations allows them to be together in spirit even when they are apart in space. As they go their separate ways, each carries with him a mental image of the other, allowing him to compare the other's imagined response to a situation with his own.

There are certain times when intimates in each other's presence experience most intensely the coalescence that results from perfect understanding. One occurs when they have ceased to Communicate verbally and are content merely to observe and appreciate each other's existence in silence. Another occurs when they begin to discuss some topic from opposed points of view and then, over the course of their conversation, gradually merge their two perspectives into a single outlook. A third peak experience of unification occurs when they suddenly discover they have something important in common. A look of sublime rapture comes over both their faces as the one begins to define himself to the other while the latter begins to nod his head rhythmically, punctuating the former's speech with responses like, "Yes" "I know" "I understand" "I'm the same way" "I'm like that, too."

The intimates' feeling of oneness is enhanced especially when they are encapsulated together in an encounter, engaged either in intense intercourse—verbal or sexual—or in intense—reciprocally contemplative—silence. Their mutual engrossment in each other transforms their phenomenological experience of the time and space coordinates along which each, in his individuality, usually orients himself to the world. Time, as measured objectively outside their encounter, seems to cease inside it. Whatever time the intimates do perceive consists only of that measured by the progressive evolution of their Communication. Within their encounter, both intimates experience the duration of time equally. As Alfred Schutz would say, both of them "grow older together."[28] But when they step out of the time capsule of their Communication back into the world, they find that objective time has flowed much faster outside the sphere of their encounter than the subjective time has passed within it. Instead of the brief moment they had felt to elapse since they entered the time ship of their Communication, they discover they have time-traveled to a point much beyond that which they had expected ("Look how late it's gotten. How fast time flies when we're together!"). Space, too, is qualitatively transformed. The spatial environment surrounding the intimates in their encounter, which outsiders see, also disappears for the insiders. In *Thérèse and Isabelle,* Violette Leduc provides an illustration of how the external environment seems to fade away during sexual intercourse:

> We hugged one another for one last time, we were joining two tree trunks together into one.... I hugged her, but I couldn't annihilate the shrieks [of the children outside], or the yard, or the boulevard and its plane trees. ... [At last] I hugged her, suffocating the tree; I hugged her, stifling the voices; I hugged her, annihilating the light.[29]

Briefly, then, to the extent that each intimate becomes the total environment to which the other is responding while external temporal and spatial distractions disappear, both intimates feel that they are being transported from the mundane world to a spiritual retreat. And, in the encloister of their encounter, the soul of each intimate becomes enraptured with the soul of the other.[30]

When two individuals are in love, they are totally oriented to each other even when they are spatially separated from each other. Each finds his usual phenomenal world fading away as he focuses in on the other. Denis de Rougemont has written what is possibly the best statement of love's phenomenological destruction of the world:

'The lover is alone with all that he loves.' [wrote Novalis] ... it can be held that his maxim states ... that passion is by no means the fuller life which it seems to be in the dreams of adolescence, but is on the contrary a kind of naked and demanding intensity; verily, a bitter destitution, the *impoverishment* of a mind being emptied of all diversity, an obsession of the imagination by a single image. In the face of the assertion of its power, the world dissolves; 'the others' cease to be present; and there are no longer either neighbours or duties, or binding ties, or earth or sky; one is alone with all that one loves.[31]

In this sense, then, love is a form of consciousness contraction. But in another sense, love is a form of consciousness expansion. For though the whole world shrinks to the size of the beloved, the size of the beloved expands to fill the whole world. The illumination and magnification of his loved one's light and lens intensifies certain aspects of the lover's life (even while diminishing others). The beloved generates an orientational field for the lover that gives new vitality and meaning to certain aspects of his existence (even while taking away old vitality and meaning from others). "Love," goes one proverb, "makes any place agreeable." "Love," goes another proverb, "makes one fit for any work." Ralph Waldo Emerson has written what is possibly the best statement of love's phenomenological reconstruction of the world:

But be our experience in particulars what it may, no man ever forgot the visitation of that power [love] to his heart and brain, which created all things anew; which was the dawn in him of music, poetry and art; which made the face of nature radiant with purple light, the morning and the night varied enchantments; when a single tone of one voice could make the heart bound, and the most trivial circumstances associated with one form is put in the amber of memory; when he became all eye when one was present, and all memory when one was gone; when the youth becomes a watcher of windows and studious of a glove, a veil, a ribbon, or the wheels of a carriage; when no place is too solitary and none too silent for him who has richer company and sweeter conversation in his new thoughts than any old friends, though best and purest, can give him; for the figures, the motions, the words of the beloved object are not, like other images, written in water, but, as Plutarch said, 'enamelled in fire.' ... The passion rebuilds the world for the youth. It makes all things alive and significant.[32]

(Whether the emphasis is put on love's destructive potential or love's reconstructive potential accounts for whether love is considered a disease, as the ancients thought,[33] or a medicine, as the moderns think.)

Although *self-conception* is not, properly speaking, a part of the *self*—for it is more metacomponent than component—it constitutes another means by which intimates bind themselves together. To the extent that two individuals define or conceive of their relationship as being intimate, it becomes intimate. But, being a matter of definition, this connection is subject to great cultural and individual variation. Different societies, and different individuals within a society, begin to apply the social category of intimate to a relationship at different points in its development. When a relationship suddenly falls over the brink into the category of intimate, it is consequently intensified by being so defined. (In this connection, it is interesting to note that love, too, is, in part, a matter of social definition. "There are many people who would never be in love if they had never heard love spoken of," goes one of La Rochefoucauld's finest maxims.)[34]

Terms of *self-reference* may also be transformed into terms of *pair-reference*. Since an individual usually considers one of his most central components of self to be his name, those who would be intimates may want to make their names the same. Married people, of course, attempt to show that the distinct identities represented by their separate first names are ultimately tied together into a two-pronged social unit by their common last name.

But even friends sometimes adopt—or do not mind if others give them—a common nickname (e.g., "the Minnesota Twins").

Still other components of a person's self consist of the ways he deals with various aspects of his environment. In the previous chapter, I suggested that the person whose self was completely determined by his environment was in a very bad way indeed; here I will reverse the emphasis to point out that a person's environment—both natural and social—must circumscribe to some degree, at least, the range of possible ways available to him for dealing with it and, hence, limit the number of selves possible for him. Consequently, intimates may superimpose these components of their selves to the extent that they succeed in constructing a common environment to which they both must respond.

Intimates can create a common natural environment in several ways. They can constantly associate with one another in order to maximize the amount of time their total environment impinges on both of them simultaneously. And they can develop common interests, such as smoking marijuana, in order to be concerned with the same partial segments of their environment (e.g., drug lore). Even when they are physically separated, their common interests will still facilitate integrating the separate environments experienced by each into a common environment experienced by both. After they come together again and one of them asks the other, "What's happening?" the other need not tell everything that is happening, but only those matters of common concern ("We'd better cool it, man. I heard the narcs are planning a bust soon"). In this way, each intimate becomes a kind of detachable sense organ for the other, while both have the opportunity to equalize their responses, and hence this component of their selves, to the stereo inputs of two slightly different environments.

An individual's social environment, especially as it is made up of those he considers significant, has a far more crucial effect on his identity than his natural environment. Intimates may create a common identity to the extent that each manages to overlap his social circle with the other's in order to become fellow foci of the same *social ellipse*.

There are several ways intimates can merge their social circles to circumscribe a common social oval around themselves. Each can formally introduce his newly acquired intimate, *as such*, to his own significant others—his family and his friends. ("Mom and Dad, I'd like you to meet *my girl friend* Judy.") Or each can informally indicate to his own significant others that his newly acquired intimate is such by interacting with him in front of them the way intimates, rather than mere acquaintances, would. Thus, the families and friends of each of the two individuals will eventually surmise that both of them are intimates if they see the two of them always together; if they observe them holding hands, kissing, or embracing amorously; if they notice them airing their dirty laundry in public together at the laundromat; if they hear them talking about each other with detailed knowledge; or if they discover an important favor one did for the other. Members of an individual's social group who themselves do not obtain direct evidence concerning the identity of his newly acquired intimate will usually credit hearsay evidence, i.e., gossip. Gossip often consists of crude kinematic indicators of relationship level, such as "who is seen with whom where." ("Guess who Sam is sleeping with. Guess who I saw leaving his apartment with him at eight o'clock this morning"). Each individual not only informs his own associates that the other is now his intimate, he also "blackballs" those of the other's associates he does not like. The resulting double social circle is not necessarily contracted, however, for while some old associates are dropped, some new ones, which the intimates have met together, are added.

The members of the intimates' common social environment can enhance their common identity passively merely by providing them with topics of conversation. William Hazlitt, an early nineteenth-century essayist, once remarked, "Discussing the characters and foibles of common friends is a great sweetener and cement of friendship." Intimates construct a common response to each of the significant members of their common social surroundings by exchanging information about his biography, opinions about his person, and gossip about his predicaments. They also discuss their own relationships with him, exchanging complaints and advice. In *The Eye*, Vladimir Nabokov provides an illustration of how much a common social reality encloses intimates within its walls, while excluding strangers:

> Mukhin and the majestic Roman Bogdanovitch have long known the family, while Smurov is comparatively a newcomer, although he hardly looks it. None could discern in him the shyness that makes a person so conspicuous among people who know each other well and are bound together by the established echoes of private jokes and by an allusive residue of people's names that to them are alive with special significance, making the newcomer feel as if the magazine story he has started to read had really begun long ago, in old unobtainable issues; and as he listens to the general conversation, rife with references to incidents unknown to him, the outsider keeps silent and shifts his gaze to whoever is speaking, and, the quicker the exchanges, the more mobile become his eyes, but soon the invisible words of the people around him begin to oppress him and he wonders if they have not deliberately contrived a conversation to which he is a stranger.[35]

Each member of the social group intimates wrap around their relationship can also enhance their common identity actively by treating them together as a package. For example, their common friends may ask one intimate about the other, or they may give them both a common present or may invite them out as a couple.[36]

The self-components that a pair of individuals share with each other but not with those around them unite them far more than those they have in common with everyone.[37]

The self-components that bound a pair of individuals together at the beginning of their relationship (such as their Communication in their sexual encounters) often give way during their relationship's later phases to other intertwined self-components (such as their common objectifications in children and house furnishings).[38]

The extent to which each intimate tries to give the other his
own self-symbols or to collect the other's self-symbols measures the
degree to which he wants to increase their communion. One intimate may convince the other that his intentions concerning their
relationship are serious by constantly attempting to obtain me-
mentos from the other. (All the self-embodiments and objectifications listed above may serve as such souvenirs.) Conversely, one
intimate may test the strength of the other's attachment to him by
assessing the amount of his own self-symbols—particularly his
tastes, opinions, attitudes, and ideals—the other has adopted. The
personal lives of two psychologists may be used to illustrate this
sociological process:

> One day . . . Romundt announced his intention of be-
> coming a Roman Catholic. . . . To have been born a Cath-
> olic was one thing; but to decide to become one after
> having listened to Nietzsche for ten years—no, that he
> could neither understand nor forgive. The need to im-
> press his opinions upon his contemporaries and to call
> them his friends only if they agreed with him was present
> in his nature beyond question. . . .[39]

> [Freud] was tortured, therefore, by periods of doubt
> about Martha's love for him and craved for repeated re-
> assurances of it. As commonly happens then, special tests
> were devised to put the matter to the proof, and some of
> them were inappropriate or even unreasonable. The chief
> one was complete identification with himself, his opin-
> ions, his feelings, and his intentions. She was not really
> his unless he could perceive his 'stamp' on her.[40]

CONTRARIETY

So far, we have seen that, when two individuals become intimate, each gives up his individuality insofar as the components

that make up his identity combine with the components that make up the other's. But each intimate has not only lost the old sources of his singularity, he has also acquired new ones.[41] If anything, he has become more of an individual than he was, though in a different way than he had been.[42]

Although intimates may mystically merge many of their self-components, they may not be able to make all of them mingle. First, pace Plato, each intimate may neither press all his anatomical aspects into the other, nor harmonize all his physiological rhythms with the other's, nor mimic all the other's conduct, nor share all his possessions. Second, each intimate may never match the whole range of the other's tastes, opinions, attitudes, and ideals, may never assimilate all the other's personal culture, and may never succeed in making the other's past as real to himself as it is to the other. Third, each intimate may not share all his partner's interests; consequently, he may interact with a somewhat different segment of their common environment. Each may also feel he has been differentiated from the other by certain experiences that occurred when they were spatially separated, which he simply cannot convey to the other in words. Finally, each may be unable to overlap totally his own social circle, and the self-component determined by it, with that of his partner; each may interact to a somewhat different degree with a somewhat different selection of their set of common friends. (For instance, when one married couple visits another, the same-sex pairs may have more intercourse than the cross-sex pairs. Or, to take another instance, an individual may retain a confidant from his old social group, whose private responses to him assure his keeping part of his self independent from his new intimate.)

A person will feel more individuated when he performs a psychic synechdoche with one of his unfused self-components *after* he has amalgamated most of his other self-components with his intimate's than he would have felt *before* he had done so. Each of the unalloyed aspects of his identity now stands out more sharply against the background of those that had melted together than it had before there was any basis of comparison. As soon as a person becomes able to contrast what was once merely one of his personal peculiarities with the corresponding feature of someone with whom he has many traits in common, he finds it transformed into a distinguishing, and hence individuating, characteristic.

Communication between intimates, both imagined and actual, also affords them opportunities to intensify their individuality. An individual's mental image of his intimate, which he internalizes to play the accompaniment for his own responses to the situations he encounters, may strike dissonant as well as sympathetic chords. Consequently, he is constantly presented with occasions when he can contrast his personal responses with those he takes to be his intimate's. He often has the opportunity, in other words, to hone his singularity against the grinding wheel of his internalized companion. It is important to notice further that when he sharpens his self against a single intimate or *specified other*, the edge produced is much finer[43] than that effected by his coarser (less defined) reference group or *generalized other*,[44] whose place his intimate has taken.

When intimates are in each other's presence, the topics of conversation provide them not only with areas in which to synthesize their points of view, but also with arenas in which to polarize them. Each intimate, moreover, may feel his individuality crystallize when he is trying to define himself to the other and the latter begins to shake his head in counterpoint ("No" "I don't know what you're talking about" "I'm certainly not like you at all there").

Intimates can stretch out their differences without tearing apart their relationship only because there are so many threads to their mutual identity. For instance, a husband and wife may be bound to each other by so many of their self-components that he can be dovish on the Cold War while she is hawkish without jeopardizing their marriage. Those whose union is more tenuous, such as the newly acquainted, must discover and express what the other considers to be a tolerable position on this subject, for a strong disagreement may abort their embryonic relationship. (The agreeableness that observers have found to characterize most conversations between acquaintances[45] results from their awareness that the slightest heat, which any friction generates, would be enough to unstick their flimsy fastenings.)

How much polarization, how much individuation of this sort, can a relationship withstand? The answer depends on the strength of each intimate's attachment to the topic relative to the strength of each intimate's attachment to the other. One of the best examples of the stress polarizations put on personal relations occurred at the end of the 1960s. In the academic world, the Vietnam War had become a topic of such salience that a difference of opinion on it caused even old friends to cease to speak to one another; in the outside world, where this concern was less important, even casual acquaintances could disagree about it without damaging their relationship.

A person can make his whole self coincident either with those of his self-components that are united to his intimate's or with those that are opposed—both in varying proportions at the same time or oscillating back and forth over time. This fact accounts for his perplexing experience that in his personal relations his individuality seems sometimes to be diminished and sometimes to be enhanced. Furthermore, he shares and opposes a different selection of his self-components in each of his intimacies, which accounts for his feeling that each of them is unique—a feeling Montaigne articulates inarticulately thus: "If I were pressed to say why I love him, I feel that my only reply could be: 'Because it was he, because it was I.' "[46] (I think it was the feeling that intimacies are essentially incomparable that motivated the large number of people who told me that personal relations cannot be generalized about, and that any sociology of intimacy such as I was attempting is impossible.) A person feels that his personal relations bear little resemblance to one another insofar as he himself in any one of them bears little resemblance to himself in any other. Each intimate relation involves a different selection from his set of self-components. Each intimate relation intensifies and diminishes the individuation of different aspects of his self. Each intimate relation, in short, literally transforms him into a different individual.

COMMITMENT

The compound self both intimates derive from their communion and the new individuality each intimate derives from their contrariety are extremely unstable (for reasons to be considered in the next section). Each intimate, therefore, may wish to ensure the durability of their relationship as though his very existence depended upon it—which, in the sense we have seen, it actually does. Intimates, like college professors, want tenure. And in order to guarantee that their relationship will continue, they must make a *commitment* to each other.

A commitment, however, so hardens a relationship that it becomes extremely difficult for each intimate to break out. Therefore, each must be very careful with whom he establishes so strong a bond. For this reason, a relationship will first go through a *probationary period*, in which each intimate has time to evaluate his interaction with the other, before he decides whether to put it on a more permanent basis or to end it. After this probationary period, intimates, again like academics, go "up or out." Should they decide to up intimacy, they can solidify their relationship with each other through three degrees of commitment.

The first level of commitment is "going steady," or the *exclusion* of other intimate, or potentially intimate, relations. At this stage, each intimate decides he will attempt to intensify only this relationship, and he will take on no new relationships that may develop into intimate ones. This level is most clearly visible in love relations, where lovers reach a point at which they decide not to go out with, nor have sex with, anyone else. Friends, too, may develop a proprietary regard for each other insofar as they do not want each other to Communicate with third parties. Goffman notes, "We feel a slight disappointment when we hear a close friend, whose spontaneous gestures of warmth we felt were our own preserve, talk intimately with another of his friends (especially one whom we do not know)."[47]

The second level of commitment is "living together," or the creation of a *common space*. Living together maximizes the num-

ber of occasions intimates can conjoin themselves and thickens the
glue that cements their psychological joints together. Intimates
who live together have more opportunities to experience common
circumstances than do those who live apart: they can be in each
other's presence more often; they can decorate their living quarters to suit their common taste; they have a common place in
which to entertain and confront their friends as a pair. Intimates
who live together can more easily harmonize their physiological
rhythms, such as eating, sleeping, and sex. A common household
expedites the transformation of individual self-objectifications into
mutual ones in that it provides a single storage place where all
objectifications may be kept together and in that it necessitates the
pooling of money for the purchase of such common objects as
furniture and appliances. Living together increases the chance
that the intimates can reestablish whatever Communicating encounters they had to break off.[48] And, in general, intimates who
live together become more conscious of all aspects of each other's
existence.[49]

It has recently become more acceptable for heterosexual pairs to
partake of the advantages of living together without the disadvantages of marriage. Several experts on the subject of this arrangement were interviewed by *Life* magazine:

> One advantage of the arrangement, of course, is that it
> is so easily entered into—no blood tests, no papers, no
> waiting. In fact, there is often so little to be said about so
> unset and undetermined an undertaking that, most often,
> nothing is said at all. "People fall into it," says Linda Le
> Clair. "It's a nonverbal thing."
>
> Take Deedee and Mike at Columbia. "We began
> studying together," she says. "Then, I made his dinner
> before we studied. Then we came back and I made him
> coffee. At first, I let him out. Then he let himself out,
> then he stayed and I made him coffee in the morning.
> Then he went shopping for groceries and in a week he
> was here all the time."[50]

This interview indicates the way intimates who live together come to minimize the politeness that characterizes the domicilic interactions between guests and hosts and come to localize their once separate eating and sleeping patterns.

The third level of commitment is "marriage," or the creation of a *common future*. Because individuals organize their lives temporally as well as spatially, they can merge their identities, in part, by merging their temporal organizations[51] as well as their spatial ones. Reflected in a seemingly endless procession, as in the facing mirrors of a barbershop, a person's memory and imagination reveal to him the various positions he has assumed and might yet assume in the dance of his life. Insofar as individuals exist in this temporal series, they may try to become one with each other by interweaving their past, as we have seen; but they may also try to make their present oneness endure by intertwining their future.[52]

Intimates can integrate their individual futures by setting for themselves a common project during which they remain together, and then by making plans to coordinate their activities in order to bring about their goal. For instance, they may want to take a trip together:

> Nietzsche's letters to [Rohde] are full of protestations of friendship and of plans for a future the two were to share. The friends supposed during these years that their future careers would in any case follow parallel paths, but they discussed particular enterprises they might undertake together, the most dearly-loved of which was the visit to Paris.... Nietzsche's letter to Rhode of the 16th January 1869 in which he tells of his probable appointment to Basel is touching in its anxiety to convince him that he cannot very well refuse the appointment, even though this cherished plan would no doubt fall through because of it.[53]

Any project to be undertaken in common, however, is usually too limited to guarantee that the intimates will remain together in the future should the fortune of one or the affection of the other diminish. Accordingly, intimates may make promises or take oaths to "cast their lot together," to "stand by each other come what may," and they may assert that their affection for each other will remain, under all conditions, "constant" and is, in any event, "eternal."

Nota bene: one's future, in Western society at least, is one's most prized possession (or particularization). To commit it to another is the most important gift one can give.

COMPLICATIONS

Intersubjective interconnections, so sought for as the ultimate in intimate relations, before their construction are (1) difficult to attain and (2) difficult to avoid and after their construction are (3) difficult to maintain and (4) difficult to abide.

1. An individual will often find it difficult to construct psychological bridges to others because so much rides on the attempt; for it is with the components of his very being that he attempts to erect these psychic spans. When, in order to secure a relationship, he presents to another aspects of himself with which he is totally identified, he will experience any rejection of his particular gifts as a rejection of his total being—and so great a blow is likely to cause his own insecure internal scaffolding to sway dangerously.

Conversely, a person may be reluctant to yield his self-components to potential intimates for fear that they may not merely accept them, but may actually devour them. He may be afraid that his potential intimates will swallow up and annihilate his individuality. Here is how R. D. Laing describes the anxiety a person may feel when he believes his basic being to be threatened in this way:

> A firm sense of one's own autonomy is required in order that one may be related as one human being to another. Otherwise, any and every relationship threatens the individual with loss of identity. One form this takes can be called engulfment. In this the individual dreads relatedness as such ... because his uncertainty about the

stability of his autonomy lays him open to the dread lest in any relationship he will lose his autonomy and identity.... Engulfment is felt as a risk in being understood (thus grasped, comprehended), in being loved, or even simply in being seen.[54]

Since the intimates of an individual determine the direction in which he is going to be recreated, he must be careful to become intimate only with persons whose potential transformations of him he thinks will be beneficial. On one hand, if he is happy with his present self-conception, he may wish to become intimate only with those whose future transformations of him will naturally evolve from it and be easily integrated with it. Thus, an introverted, sensitive boy may be leery of forming a liaison with an extroverted, partygoing girl, and vice versa. On the other hand, if he is unhappy with his present self-conception, he may wish to become intimate only with those whose future transformations of him will revolutionize it and eventually replace it. Thus, an introverted boy may look forward to forming a liaison with an extroverted girl, and vice versa.

A person may dread, moreover, the loss of a single self-component as much as the loss of all the rest of his psychological parts if it is the one with which he identifies his whole self most intensely. Emerson illustrates a fear felt by many intellectuals: that if an intimate relation causes them to lose the originality of their ideas, they will lose their *raison d'être*.

I do then with my friends as I do with my books. I would have them where I can find them, but I seldom use them.... Though I prize my friends, I cannot afford to talk with them and study their visions, lest I lose my own.[55]

In short, even though a person may be conscious that he is missing an opportunity to obtain a high yield for the investment of the old resources of his individuality, he may still prefer to hoard

his self-components rather than risk them on any potentially intimate relationship that comes along. Even though he may be aware
that no individuality ventured is no individuality gained, he
may still prefer not to put in all his self-components in one
basket.

The commitment by which intimates try to preserve their fragile
fusions and fissions may also involve a problem of communication.
Usually each intimate does not simply tell the other that he is
pledged to him; instead, he confirms his commitment by performing a symbolic act. Unfortunately, intimates are not always aware
of all the personal meaning inherent in each other's actions.
On the one hand, each may misunderstand the intent of the
other's gesture and not appreciate the extent of the interpersonal
warranty it implies; on the other hand, each may wonder why he
has so hard a time getting the other to do him a particular favor,
such as lending him his money, his books, or his body, little realizing that this is the favor by which the other signs his interpersonal sureties. Misunderstandings about commitment are especially prevalent in the relations between men and women; until
recently, at least, a woman in our society usually ratified her commitment to a man when she first gave herself to him sexually,
whereas a man usually ratified his commitment to a woman only
when he proposed to marry her. (Consequently, women wanted
marriage for the commitment it entailed and the concomitant
stabilization of the relation. Since the attractive power of a
woman's main manifest qualifier—her physical attractiveness—
reaches its peak relatively early in her life, she was often anxious
to captivate a man into committing himself to more durable bonds
before her bargaining power— her power to attract and hold his
orientation—declined. For most women, even in our present "lib-
erated" age, this search for a stable relationship, this longing to
marry before it is "too late," is still the rule.)

Marriage presents a special problem of commitment. In the
course of the past few centuries, it has been normative in the
West for heterosexual lovers to get married in order to bring their
relationship up to *commitment level two*. During this period,
heterosexual lovers had to get married to procure the right that

other kinds of intimates presume: the right to secure the psychological integrations of their relationship through living together. (All intimates become aware of the importance of this privilege when it is abrogated, as it is, for instance, in prisons and concentration camps, where the authorities usually do not allow friends to move in with one another at will.) But if marriage generates a minimum of relationship durability by allowing the couple to live together, it also engenders a maximum of relationship unbreakability by committing them to a lifetime together. In other words, in order to achieve any of the benefits of *commitment level two*, heterosexual lovers must go beyond it to *commitment level three*, with all its disadvantages. Marriage, therefore, represents a qualitative escalation of commitment that may be greater than either intimate would care to contract for without an extensive probationary period in which to give the matter much thought. The marriage ceremony itself, at least in its most popular version, that given in Book of Common Prayer, includes a last-chance warning for each partner to reconsider whether he actually wants to lose the uncommitted freedom to form his own future: "... and therefore is not by any to be entered into unadvisedly or lightly; but reverently, discreetly, advisedly, soberly, and in the fear of God." Although heterosexual lovers may not mind having their futures bound together to some extent, they may not want to be roped into a relationship whose exiting (divorce) procedures are so exacting as to compel them to remain together during extreme vicissitudes of fortune—"... for better for worse, for richer for poorer, in sickness in health ... "—and fluctuations of affection that would cause intimates who are less committed to each other to split up.

2. Just as a person's physiological defense mechanisms will attempt to repel an unwanted corporeal invader in order to preserve the integrity of his body, so a person's psychological defense mechanisms will attempt to repulse an unwanted personal invader in order to preserve the integrity of his self. This may occur when one individual considers the other to be polluted and wants to maintain his own purity. Since intimacy would involve his openness to the other's self-system, he may fear the other's impure self-components may begin to contaminate his own self-system. For

example, in spite of their other qualifiers, he may be wary of becoming too intimate with cigarette smokers because he may fear their psychological weakness in resisting biological and social pressures, revealed by this habit, might soon become his own.

One occasion in which an individual must take action to keep from integrating his self-components with another's occurs when neither particularly wants the resulting intimacy, but external forces compel them to intersect their selves. Although a limited supply of funds and housing in a college town may force two nonintimates to live together, each of them is likely to take steps to ensure his independence from the other. Each may keep his own food in separate parts of their refrigerator, may create private alcoves in their common abode, may keep different hours, and, in general, may attempt to segregate as many of his self-components as he can within their overall state of forced integration.

Another occasion in which an individual must take action to keep from integrating his self-components with those of another occurs when the other wants to increase the number of points of connection while he does not. The former may turn aside the latter's encompassing tentacles by being reticent about his private life, by keeping his own friends, by turning off the other's sexual advances, by declining the other's gifts, by divulging his own past only with reluctance, by refusing to live with the other, and by being noncommital about sharing a common future ("We'll see how it goes").

Those who continue to associate with each other after one has had to place certain self-integrations off limits for the other are said to have an "understanding" with each other. That is, certain privileges and restrictions have been written into the *microsocial contract* of their association. Friendship, for instance, with its limited license, is often offered as a consolation prize to those who have lost at love. A conversation Claude Brown reports between himself and a homosexual named Baxter illustrates the way partial intimates may establish the *ground rules* of their relationship:

> [Baxter] "It's like, I just like you, and I know we couldn't have anything goin' in that love vein, but, well, I just like you."

[Brown] "Yeah, well, I like you too, man. And as long as we both understand how things are, there's no reason why we can't go on bein' friends. But, like, it's gotta be friends like this, man, everybody understandin' where he is."[56]

3. Once intimates manage to attain their communion, they discover they have to struggle to sustain it. Two of its most important constituents, volitions and cognitions, are continually falling out of alignment.

First, intimates may find it difficult to keep each of their organic rhythms in tempo. When these physiological pulsations get out of phase, each intimate will find that, in order to accommodate the other's rhythms, he must readjust his own. In other words, when intimates are out of step, either each will have to compromise his own desires to a large extent or both will have to compromise their own desires to a small extent in order to reestablish their common cadence. Thus, if one intimate is sexually aroused while the other "just doesn't feel like it," there are three alternatives: (1) the former will remain unsatisfied, (2) the latter will grudgingly submit, or (3) both will abridge their usual program of sexual intercourse. In any event, what's sauce for the goose is often cinders for the gander.

Second, intimates may find it difficult to preserve their communication as Communication, for Communication processes are easily disrupted.[57] On the one hand, the bubble of their Communication may burst under internal stresses. Intimates may eventually reach a point where one simply can no longer understand or tolerate what the other is trying to convey. On the other hand, it may burst under external pressure. The intimates may be forced to separate. A third person may intrude.[58] The static of outside distractions may drown out their own signals. In either case, once the spell is broken, it is difficult to conjure up again.

The preservation of contrariety also presents a problem. The continuum between the complete synthesis of all self-components and the complete antithesis of all self-components forms a precarious passage, and fancy footwork is sometimes all that keeps intimates from falling together, on the one side, or falling apart, on the other. They discover they must continually make minor readjustments in their psychological distance from each other in order to avoid merging their identities totally (becoming in all respects a single person) or separating them totally (becoming in all respects two solitary individuals).

And even though their commitments to each other are supposed to give their relationship a lifetime guarantee, intimates often find it difficult to keep their relationship from wearing out. The collapse of *commitment level one*, the breakdown of the exclusiveness of going steady, results in jealousy.[59] The collapse of *commitment level two*, the breakdown of the common space of living together, results in separation. The collapse of *commitment level three*, the breakdown of the common future of marriage, results in divorce.

Today, the institution of marriage has lost many of the social functions it once had. We have seen that cross-sexed couples need no longer go through its front entrance in order to live together. But the hinges on its rear exit have likewise loosened. The present easing of divorce procedures, together with the more fundamental ideological reevaluation that now emphasizes the importance of the caprice of individual inclination relative to the rigidity of formalized social structures, has weakened the ability of the marriage institution to enforce the commitment of its member-pairs to a common future ("Why should we stay together if we don't love each other anymore?"). Because the difficulty in leaving marriage is decreasing while the opportunity of entering into its benefits without its obligations is increasing, marriage has become less necessary in sustaining an intimate relation at the same time it has become less successful in doing so. Those who would be intimates, however, find it unfortunate that no new social institution has replaced marriage to aid them in protracting their personal relations. They must now do it themselves, without social support.

4. Having finally effected a durable relationship with each other, intimates must now endure its effects. Many arguments between intimates stem from the fusion of their selves, for although

each intimate no longer has total control over the disposition of his self-components, he can use the lever of what partial control remains to him to look out for his own interests. No longer sole master of his house, he still has some say in its upkeep.

When two individuals have become one with each other's body, each has, as it were, doubled the amount of his surface area that is exposed to sickness and accident. Each must now bear up not only under his own ill health, but also under that of his intimate. Furthermore, squeezed together as they are inside a common body, each becomes a victim of what he takes to be the other's self-abuse. For instance, if one believes eating properly is good and drinking excessively is bad, he will feel himself dying a little whenever he discovers his intimate skipping a meal or taking a nip. The unhappily married husband in *The Kreutzer Sonata* makes the following complaint about his wife:

> What was terrible, you know, was that I considered myself to have a complete right to her body as if it were my own, and yet at the same time I felt I could not control that body, that it was not mine and she could dispose of it as she pleased, and that she wanted to dispose of it not as I wished her to.[60]

When two individuals have become intimates to the extent that they share in each other's virtues and successes, they discover they have become implicated in each other's vices and defeats as well. Responsible as they are for each other's behavior, they themselves can be contaminated by each other's faults and failings, embarrassed by each other's blunders and bankruptcies. In other words, intimates can debase each other as much as they can ennoble each other. And by acquiring an intimate, an individual doubles both his opportunities to be ashamed and his degree of shame. He may now be ashamed not only of his own ignoble deeds and unsuccessful actions, but also of those of his intimate. He may now feel shame not only for his own behavior, but also for causing his intimate to suffer.

When an individual has objectified his self in an object, the fate of this object becomes his fate. He gives up complete dominion over this section of his self as soon as he begins to share this object with his intimate. If his intimate, then, consciously or accidentally mistreats his self-objectification, he will experience it as though it were he himself who was being mishandled. Should the friend to whom he lends his beloved sports car smash it up, he will feel as damaged as his car. Moreover, when two intimates objectify their selves in the same thing, they must agree on its care. If their ideas differ, their arguments may become vehement in proportion as each is defending an offshoot of his own self. The husband in Tolstoy's novella bewails another of his problems thus: "Besides, the children were a new cause of dissension. As soon as we had children they became the means and the object of our discord."[61]

When intimates invest their selves in the total resources of their relationship, each may dispute the way the other is distributing them. Fights over finances are especially common in marriage. A husband may feel his vitality being drained away by the way his wife spends his money; a wife may feel her vitality being choked off by the way her husband constricts her purchasing power.

When an individual acquires a new intimate, he is acquiring an *identity appendage* that is large enough to alter his social group's reaction to him in general and their evaluation of him in particular. Intimates, that is, affect each other's reputations. "'Tis thus that on the choice of friends our good or evil name depends," wrote the eighteenth-century poet and dramatist John Gay. And the twentieth-century black autobiographer, Claude Brown, came to a similar conclusion about the way his potential intimacy with a girl named Sugar would affect his social standing:

> I thought about Sugar, how nice she was, and how she was a real friend. I knew she wanted to be my girl friend, and I liked her a lot. But what would everybody say if I had a buck-toothed girl friend.[62]

When an individual acquires an intimate who, in a fit of depression, attempts to commit psychological suicide by destroying his own self-components—carving up his body, ceasing to care for his health, burning and breaking his possessions, losing his job, or alienating his social group—the individual must try to cheer up his intimate in order to keep him from being so self-destructive. If he begins to annihilate these self-embodiments and objectifications, he will be attacking what are now his intimate's essential elements as well, and, consequently, his intimate will have a vested interest in keeping such self-mutilations to a minimum.

An individual may not like the new individuality that his contrariety with his intimate brings out in him, especially when some of his newly articulated self-components stand out with a lower evaluation than they previously had. When he compared himself with others before he met his intimate, he may have felt himself to be intelligent. But when he compares himself with his intimate now, he may feel himself to be dumb.

Finally, once both intimates handcuff themselves to each other by means of their commitments, each must resign himself to losing the various kinds of freedom that these commitments constrict. *Commitment level one* requires each intimate to give up his potential to find a better intimate *with whom* to spend his life. *Commitment level two* requires each intimate to give up his potential to chose without restriction *where* he is going to spend his life. (So a wife may have to suffer the slum or suburb in which her husband, to be near his work, wants to live.) And *commitment level three* requires each intimate to give up his potential to decide independently *what kind* of life he is going to spend.

In sum, once two individuals have melted themselves into a common body, tempered themselves with common standards of behavior, plated common objects and a common social group around themselves, scraped off the impurities of other potential relationships, immersed themselves in a common environment, and pointed their two-edged intimacy toward a single future, each may find himself the subject of more stress than he had forseen. In consequence, a person must choose his intimates carefully: not merely is he known by the company he keeps, but, in the above respects at least, he *is* the company he keeps—and he may suffer for it accordingly.

In this chapter, the *intersubjectivity* dimension of an intimate relation has been considered and a sixth major force uncovered that transforms isolated individuals into interlinked intimates: *the blurring of their boundaries through the merging of their self-components.* As individuals become intimates, they fuse their self-components in communion, fission them in contrariety, and forge them in commitment. They bind their basic beings together, in other words, by losing their old selves in each other, by creating each other anew, and by attempting to immortalize their relationship.

PART TWO

Ruins

CHAPTER 7

Making Up

IN PART ONE, we saw how two individuals can join together and generate an intimate relationship; in Part Two, we shall see how their intimacy can degenerate and their relationship fall apart.

Like any human construction, intimate relations are subject to deterioration. Even the best of them suffer countless minor malfunctions that, unless continually corrected, will eventually destroy the intimacy, if not the relation. As these minor breakdowns accumulate, they will both weaken the centripetal forces that hold intimates together and strengthen the centrifugal forces that drive them apart. When the centrifugal forces become stronger than the centripetal, the intimates will break up. If the intimates are so chained together that they cannot break up, however, these contained disintergrating forces will be manifested in each intimate's attempt to differentiate himself from the other as much as possible within the confines of their overall relationship. Each intimate who experiences the painful tension of the contradictory pressures both to sever and to sustain the relationship will often express it in the little cruelties by which he tries to make the other's life as miserable as his own. The relationship between George and Martha in Edward Albee's *Who Afraid of Virginia Woolf?* is the paradigm.

"A man," said Samuel Johnson, "should keep his friendships in repair." In this chapter I will consider the *reintegration mechanisms* by which intimates attempt to keep their relationship in repair. In other words, I will consider how intimates "make up" when their intimacy is threatened with breakup. Integrations that have a tendency to become loose can be tightened by *preventive maintenance* before they become loose, or by *corrective maintenance* afterward. The various ways in which a relationship can need preventive or corrective readjustment call for various types of interpersonal tune-ups.

One factor that affects the degree to which intimates are integrated is the external environment surrounding their relationship. This environment may increase the strength of some of the forces holding intimates together without regard to their wishes. The intimates themselves, however, may adopt a "do-it-yourself" attitude toward their degree of integration and may deliberately seek out environments that (they expect) will tighten up their relationship. Accordingly, the first section of this chapter will consider how the integrity of their relationship is intensified whenever intimates pass through certain consolidating circumstances: those that are fertile and benign on the one hand, those that are barren and hostile on the other. Intimates become closer, in other words, whenever they go "through thick and thin."

A second factor that affects the degree to which the intimates are integrated is the alignment of the forces holding them together. If intimates are most certain of their relationship level when the intensities of all the forces that integrate it are equal, they are most confused about where they stand with each other when the intensities of all the forces that integrate it are unequal. Regardless of whether these integrating ties were improperly laced during the early phases of their relationship or whether they have become increasingly undone over its course, if their ties are uneven, intimates must rethread their relationship in order to continue to interact smoothly. In this situation of malintegration, there are two techniques of reintegration: the *meta-intimate communication*, in which each intimate dispassionately considers the problem in the context of the relationship and attempts to "work it out" in a way acceptable to both; and the *argument*, in which each intimate passionately considers the problem in the context of his own life and attempts to "have it out" in a way acceptable only to himself.

A final factor that affects the degree to which intimates are integrated is the decline of the forces holding them together. Although I noted in Chapter 2 that it takes less energy to sustain a self in an intimate relation than in an acquaintance one, I must add here that it takes more energy to sustain an intimate relation than an acquaintance one. (For instance, although intimates can relax when they are with one another, they must get up the energy to meet.) Consequently, each force that holds intimates together keeps falling back to the more stable acquaintance level. In order to revitalize their ever-sagging esprit de corps intimates must perform periodic *ceremonies*. Unlike arguments, in which any reinvigoration is an unintentional by-product of their activity, ceremonies are intentionally designed to renew relationships. Accordingly, the last section of this chapter will consider the ways in which intimates try to warm up their ever-cooling relationship by regularly holding "revivals."

The Complications section will deal with the ways in which these reintegration mechanisms themselves can malfunction and aggravate the sickness they are supposed to cure. Also considered will be an extreme reintegration mechanism designed to keep the relationship alive even when its most intimate aspects have died.

THROUGH THICK AND THIN

The integration of intimates can be increased by two totally opposite types of circumstances: (1) barren and hostile; (2) fertile and benign. Each extreme environment, however, tightens up different dimensions of the relationship.

1. Georg Simmel has pointed out that the members of a group become bound together more tightly when the group is in conflict with its external environment.[1] Since he and his students[2] have already extensively elaborated this insight, I need not belabor

it here except to mention its application to the scheme of personal relations set forth in these pages. Hostile and barren environments increase the amount of favors intimates need from each other and hence their dependence on their relationship. Intimates who are comrades-in-arms or "two against the world" must share the scarce supplies their lean circumstances provide, must specialize in either the procurement or the preparation of these resources in order to utilize them most efficiently, and must coordinate their actions in order to fend off external attacks most effectively.

In this connection, it is interesting to note Denis de Rougemont's assertion that an environment opposed to a love relationship—especially one placing obstacles between the meetings of the lovers—is necessary not merely to intensify love, but, in fact, to sustain it all:

> Tristan and Iseult do not love one another.... *What they love is love and being in love.* They behave as if aware that whatever obstructs love must ensure and consolidate it in the heart of each and intensify it infinitely in the moment they reach the absolute obstacle, which is death.... What they need is not one another's presence, but one another's absence. *Thus the partings of the lovers are dictated by their passion itself,* and by the love they bestow on their passion rather than on its satisfaction or on its living object. That is why the Romance abounds in obstructions, why when mutually encouraging their joint dream in which each remains solitary they show such astounding indifference, and why events work up in a romantic climax to a fatal apotheosis.[3]

Marriage, then, insofar as it entails a slackening of external obstacles and conflicts, must necessarily decrease love.[4] Lovers who must part, and to a lesser extent all intimates who must separate, define the outside world that forces them to leave each other as hostile. In so doing, they are brought closer together psychologically at the very moment they are being pulled apart physically. It is for this reason that parting is said to be "such sweet sorrow."

There are several levels of adverse environments that tighten up loose relationships. On the most cosmic level, the Existentialists, in general, believe the basic structure of "being" itself is unfavorable to human existence; accordingly, every person should acknowledge the fact that he is the intimate of every other, for all mankind is bound together because all must endure a common cosmic environment that is less than man's liking and that, in fact, will eventually overcome him. All men are intimates, say the Existentialists, insofar as each of them has the common fate of struggle and death.

On a less exalted plain, the world of nature can constitute an environment inimical to individuals and hence enhancing of relationships. Protracted common dangers, such as famine or plague, and sudden common crises, such as floods or accidents, cause their victims to seek help from each other and to huddle together, psychologically as well as physically. Sometimes intimates or would-be intimates purposely go on expeditions or safaris into natural environments that are relatively more dangerous than the ones they left in order to take advantage of the fact that the relationships of those who struggle together against nature are intensified. One small confirming instance of the generalization that those who deliberately place themselves in dangerous situations increase the intensity of their intimacy may be found in the report that the second-person-singular pronoun exchanged among recently acquainted European mountain climbers switches from the V form to the T form after they reach a certain critical altitude.[5]

Society, too, can be seen as an environment that is antagonistic toward its members. Intimates who rebel against their society overtly through insurgency or covertly through crime find that they have attained the "solidarity" of revolutionaries or have become "as thick as thieves." It has been suggested that one motive behind the student disorders of the 1960s was the desire to experience the intoxicating intensification of relationships that results from these social confrontations.[6] Similarly, members of the recent liberation movements—black, women's, gay, etc.—have become aware that the common fight for freedom from the larger social unit leads to the not unpleasant subjugation to the smaller

social unit. Those who want the integrating effect of social conflict without directly participating in it themselves may merely
complain about the provocations and persecutions of groups that
are thought to oppose them. Common to all those who hold
conspiracy theories of politics, it seems, is the feeling that the
only way they can achieve meaningful relationships with others is
to personify a common opponent—be their enemy the Commu-
nists or the Establishment or the omnimalevolent "They" ("Look
what they're doing to us now!").

Social institutions represent another level of environment that
can unwittingly enhance personal relations. The more these institutions are explicitly dedicated to deteriorating the lives of their
members, the more they seem to subvert their overt intention
by unintentionally transforming their inmates into intimates. Concentration camps and prisons are the two most notorious examples,
and it has been said, "There is no warmer friendship than
that formed in jail."[7] The integrating power of these repressive
social institutions is often strong enough to overcome the segrega-
ting power of those obtrusive social distinctions, such as race and
class, that usually impede the formation of intimate relations. The
movie *The Defiant Ones* (Kramer, 1958) portrays the evolving
friendship between a white and a black who, chained together
literally as well as symbolically, attempt to escape from a Southern
prison road gang. And the movie *Grand Illusion* (Renoir, 1937)
portrays the evolving friendship among a French aristocrat, a
wealthy Jew, and a petit bourgeois who attempt to escape from
various German POW camps during World War I. In the ambiguous case of mental hospitals, where it is a matter of controversy whether or not they actually serve their patient's best interests, Goffman reports:

> The hospital provided a kind of game situation in which
> one could pit oneself against the authorities, and some
> of the relationships that flourished seemed to do so partly
> because the participants enjoyed the intrigue of sustain-
> ing them.[8]

Even when institutions are not overtly antagonistic to their members, it is often useful for those of their members who wish to become and remain intimates to make them appear so. A student, for instance, may define his university solely in terms of its worst features in order to win friends and influence people. What Goffman calls "role distance"[9] is also an effective technique to enhance intimacy. When someone intentionally gets out of his institutional role, he and his role (distance) partners become intensely, if only momentarily, united in their conspiracy to undercut the rules of the institution. A professor, for instance, may try to win the love, if not respect, of his classes by telling them not to take seriously the required assignments and examinations that he is forced to give.

Finally, a microsocial environment consisting only of a third person can intensify an intimacy. Freud has pointed out that individuals become closer when they revolt against a high-status leader,[10] and Goffman has pointed out that individuals become closer when they perform a "collusive byplay" against a third party who has momentarily lost status by acting the fool.[11] Occasionally, an individual may inadvertently unite his intimates, whose own relationship has heretofore not been very close. If something dreadful has happened to him, a conference of all his intimates is often called in order to commiserate and to decide what to do about him. Countless television dramas contain scenes of family friends with their arms around crying women whose husbands or brothers are fleeing the law or are involved in accidents or are threatening suicide or are merely missing.

2. Although some social theorists have asserted that intimates can intensify or even sustain their relationships only in opposition to their environment, we should also be aware of the ways intimates can intensify or even sustain their relationships in harmony with their environment. Rich and unthreatening circumstances seem to be able to draw people as close together as poor and threatening ones, though in a different way and for different reasons. If an antagonistic environment causes intimates to need favors from each other more, an amiable environment causes intimates to fear fusions with each other less. We have seen the

dangers an individual faces if he yields to someone else partial control over the disposition of his self-components, particularly the knowledge of his secret weaknesses. If, however, he becomes convinced that his environment does not harbor hidden enemies (waiting only for him to bare his essential being for them to leap out and bite it), he will feel freer to strip off his defensive covering and expose himself to others.

The view that the cosmos is a basically benign environment for human existence finds its ultimate expression in Buddhism. What human suffering there appears to be results merely from a misconception about the nature of things; the cosmic core of man does not really suffer. The Buddhists—to greatly simplify their manifold and complex doctrines—believe every person should acknowledge the fact that he is the intimate of every other, for his feeling that his self is separate from the selves of others is an illusion. All men are intimates, say the Buddhists, insofar as each of them essentially consists of a common cosmic substance or spirit.

On a lower level, relationships become more intense when intimates stand before the world of nature, which is seen to be not merely uninjurious but positively beneficial. Awe and wonder at the grandeur and beauty of the world will cause any fear an individual has of nature and of human nature to fall away, and he will become more at one with any of his fellow creatures who happen to be in his vicinity. Those who wish to become lovers and those lovers who wish to become still closer, therefore, will seek out or try to create intimate settings in order to intensify their intimacy. Outside, they may walk by the sea or sit under the stars or watch the moon. Inside, they may arrange soft lights, mood music, and comfortable chairs. Inhaling the right atmosphere through visual, audile, and tactile senses can be most invigorating for personal relations.

Thus, two intimates can consolidate their affair not only through opposition to society, its institutions, or a third party, but also through identification with it, with them, or with him.[12] Intimates who are unified through a *common identification*, however, often find themselves at war with intimates who are unified through a *common opposition* to their common identification.

WORK-IT-OUTS

The integrity of a relationship is affected by what goes on inside it as well as by what goes on outside it. A relationship is called "strained" whenever the bonds that hold intimates together go out of alignment. However these integrating bonds get misaligned, intimates must bring them back into balance if they want their relationship to continue with a minimum of tension. In this section, I will consider how they take the problem that is the source of their stress and work it out through *meta-initimate conversation*, i.e., through conscious conversation about their relationship itself (to be contrasted with the less conscious conversation about their relationship that all interaction between intimates entails, which I have considered in the previous chapters). Intimates use the phrases "having a serious talk" or "getting serious" whenever they wish to refer to the meta-intimate conversation in which they assume conscious control over the course of their relationship in order to work out their interpersonal tensions rationally and peacefully.

The most important form of meta-intimate conversation focuses on the relationship itself. This kind of serious talk begins with what may be called a "State of the Union Address," or "State of the Relationship Address." It occurs whenever one intimate can no longer stand the status quo of a relationship that is strained by unbalanced bonds ("Look, we can't go on like this!").

Innumerable combinations of uneven intimate bonds cause instability in personal relations. For one thing, the forces holding a pair of intimates together may have been out of balance since the beginning of their relationship and may have become increasingly so over its course because one force was prevented from developing as fast as the others. Intimates may, for instance, discover to their dismay that they have been Communicating without communicating—having a Platonic relationship consisting of an exchange of concepts without an exchange of contacts.[13] For another, the forces holding a pair of intimates together may have become unbalanced during their relationship because one intimate has let go of one of the bonds. He may, for instance, have slackened off in supplying the physical favors he had been exchanging for his partner's psychological ones. A husband who has lost his job and is no longer "bringing home the bacon" should not expect his wife to continue to fill their household with the aroma of goodwill.

The State of the Relationship Address, which results from tensions like these, consists first of a summary of the relationship's past performance, including both its perfections and imperfections ("So far we've been . . ."), and second of proposals for potential improvements ("And now we must . . ."). These proposals involve rewriting the *constitution* on which the relationship is based, either by adding amendments or by articulating articles that were ambiguous. These proposals establish or clarify the rules of the relationship. Usually, they are intended to set limits to how high or low each intimate may tune the intensity of their various integrating forces.

Consider the case in which a woman wants to set limits on her relationship with a suitor: (1) she can propose to freeze their potential ("Friends are all we can be"); (2) she can propose to cut down on their congregations ("I don't think you should stop by more than twice a week"); (3) she can propose to confine their communications. ("Unh-unh, no petting below the belt"); (4) she can propose to restrict their free flow of information exchange ("Don't ask me about that. I don't want to talk about it"); (5) She can propose to prohibit certain favors ("I'll do anything for you but that"); (6) she can propose to circumscribe their couples ("You don't own me. I'll go out with whomever I please").

It is important to recognize that a meta-intimate conversation differs essentially from other types of interaction in personal relations, even though it is intended to control them. Just because intimates who talk about their relationship agree to change some of their current interactions does not mean that they will. After they have agreed on the new regulations to govern their interactions, however, each may issue an *interim progress report*, should he find that the other has not been living up to them. The Complications sections of the previous chapters have considered some of the *transgression techniques* by which each intimate can avoid following the spoken and unspoken rules of their relationship while keeping the other from becoming aware of his duplicity. When these transgression techniques fail to deceive properly, the latter calls on the former to account for the discovered discrepancy ("Look, we said we were going to be honest with each other, didn't we?")

A second form of meta-intimate conversation focuses on the faults of one of the intimates and the damage these faults are doing to the relationship. It is these faults, in fact, that have brought the relationship to its present state of crisis. This kind of serious talk begins with what may be called a *talking-to*. It occurs whenever one intimate finds the other's behavior so increasingly intolerable that he feels he must "tell him off." In a talking-to, one intimate tells the other what he dislikes about him and what the other had better change if their relationship is to continue ("The trouble with you, Harry, is that you . . . "). Occasionally, one intimate will sense that something has gone wrong with the relationship and volunteer to be the object of a talking-to ("But what have I done wrong?"). A wife begs her husband to tell her off in the following passage from the Japanese novel *Kokoro*:

> Finally, I could not stand it any longer, and so I asked him to tell me frankly whether he found fault with anything I did. If he would only tell me what my faults were, I said, I would try if possible to correct them. His reply was that I had no faults and that it was himself that was to blame. His answer made me very sad. It made me cry and made me want to be told more than ever what my faults were.[14]

All intimates satisfy each other in many ways, but not in all ways. In fact, the more ways in which they satisfy each other, the more their dissatisfactions with each other seem to stand out phenomenologically. In this situation, each intimate is continually confronted with the choice of either ending their relationship in the hope of finding elsewhere the pleasures he is presently lacking (e.g., intellectual)—but with the fear of losing altogether the pleasures he is presently enjoying (e.g., sexual)—or of attempting to iron out the other's irritating habits or to fill in the other's exasperating deficiencies (e.g., by getting the other to read more). On the microlevel, intimates must choose between destroying or reforming their relationships just as, on the macrolevel, citizens must choose between destroying or reforming their institutions. But, as we saw in Chapter 5, it is no easy matter to straighten out an intimate. In the words of one of Claude Brown's Harlem associates:

> Johnny D. was always talking stuff about men in Harlem, saying that the only way men could be friends was that each one had to stay off his friend's toe, but that if a friend got on a friend's toe, you had to be able to tell each other about it and go on being friends. If you couldn't do that you'd have to go to war, and war certainly ends friendship.[15]

A technique one intimate sometimes uses to induce the other to mend his ways without tearing apart their relationship is to persuade a third party to have a talk with him.

A third form of meta-intimate conversation focuses on the relationship of one intimate to an outsider. This kind of serious talk begins with what may be called a *jealous j'accuse*. It occurs whenever one individual becomes so suspicious of his intimate's relationship with a third party that he accuses his intimate of betraying their (usually unspoken) commitment to exclusiveness. His intimate must then defend himself by reassuring him that his relationship with the third party is nothing to worry about. Jealously consists, in part, of A's fear that his intimate B's being and behavior will become so integrated with the being and behavior of a third party, C, that B will be less able to continue to adjust to A's being and behavior as easily as B could before B lost a degree of freedom in having to take C into account. B will then have to convince *A* that *B*'s relation with *A* will always have priority over *B*'s relation with *C* or, for that matter, with anyone else. In love relations, where such jealousy usually occurs, the beloved must convince her lover that her relations with the third party are limited, that he is "merely a friend." We can find an illustration of the *jealous j'accuse* form of meta-intimate conversations in Jones's biography of Freud, whose well-documented life is capable of providing at least as much insight into personal relations as his work:

> Fritz was engaged to a cousin of Martha's, Elise, but he had long been a brotherly friend to Martha, bringing her out and encouraging her in various ways. It was an intimate friendship, although apparently with no serious *arrière-pensée*. . . . Freud at last understood the situation, although Martha would not accept his view of it and protested that Fritz was nothing but an old friend. But it was clear to him now that Fritz was really in love with her without knowing it consciously. . . . Martha, however, would have none of his explanations. It was nothing but a simple friendship, as indeed Fritz himself assured Freud when they met a few days later.[16]

All these forms of meta-intimate conversation function to re-integrate the relationship. Thus, their presence indicates negatively that the relationship needs reintegrating but positively that the relationship is worth reintegrating. Intimates, therefore, must engage in *meta-meta-intimate conversation* about their meta-intimate conversation whenever they feel the need of this negative function ("We're going to have to have a talk about that") or the lack of this positive function ("How come we never talk anymore?").

HAVE-IT-OUTS

When the misalignment of integrating bonds has strained their association, intimates may adopt another method to reintegrate their relationship: the *argument*.[17] Normally, intimates accommodate each other's actions (including both preferences and habits) unconsciously or spontaneously. But when their respective actions become so disparate that each can no longer easily adjust to the other automatically, they must both begin to coordinate their interaction consciously. This they can try to do either through meta-intimate conversation or through contra-intimate confrontation. Though each of these two methods of reintegrating relationships may be used independently, work-it-outs often modulate into have-it-outs, and vice-versa. Fights differ from serious talks in that each intimate who is talking seriously is oriented to discovering how much he can compromise his customary way of acting in order to resolve their conflict in a way acceptable to both; each intimate who is fighting is oriented to discovering how much he can accentuate his customary way of acting in order to resolve their conflict his way.

Fights function to affirm the individuation of each intimate. Fights begin when one intimate comes to feel that an action of the other has degraded the other as a person. And since he himself is implicated in the other's being by means of the various connections described in the preceding chapters, he may further come to feel that he himself will also be degraded unless he separates himself, at least momentarily, from the other. In this situation, he will often resort to provoking an argument whose consequent self-amplification and -particularization will intensify his differentiation from the other. It is important to recognize that the argument need not be over the specific action that is felt to be contaminating, for arguments over any topic set off intimates from each other.

Arguments result in the separation of the intimates' selves because each intimate can particularize himself, by means of the "psychic synechdoche" (discussed in Chapter 6), in the side of the controversy he takes. As the distance between the sides increases, so does the demarcation between the intimates. Georg Simmel was the first to notice this process:

> The more we have in common with another *as whole persons*, however, the more easily will our totality be

involved in every single relation with him. Hence the wholly disproportionate violence to which normally well-controlled people can be moved with their relations closest to them.... Therefore, if a quarrel arises between persons in such an intimate relationship, it is often passionately expansive.[18]

Because arguments increase interpersonal distance, those who argue with each other must be relatively close, or relatively distant, to begin with; those in the middle are likely to terminate their association as soon as they begin to disagree. Thus intimates, who are tightly tied together on many dimensions, dare chance an argument to settle their differences, but acquaintances must find some other way to resolve their disagreements, for any serious argument would rip apart whatever weak connections they have. William Allingham, a minor nineteenth-century poet, penned this point in verse:

> While friends we were, the hot debates
> That rose 'twixt you and me!
> Now we are mere associates,
> And never disagree.

Strangers, who will never see each other again and hence have nothing to lose, can argue more easily than acquaintances who will and have.

Although an argument is intended to segregate intimates, it actually results in integrating them more closely if—and only if, as we shall see—it does not get out of hand and is successfully resolved. "Lovers' quarrels," goes the ancient proverb, "are the renewals of love." Georg Simmel and his students have made us aware of the ways in which internal social conflict functions to bind the members of any group together.[19] In the context of personal relations, intimates who make the continuance of their relationship problematic through argument suddenly become aware of the strength of the bonds that hold them together. Their awareness of how much they need each other—in fact, cannot do without each other—itself becomes another force fastening them to each other still more securely.

This implicit threat to end the relationship, which all arguments involve, is sometimes made explicit in the form of an *ultimatum*—the ultimate expression of the strategy underlying most of the specific tactics intimates use to win their disputes. It says in effect: "I am less dependent on our relationship than you are. I can stand ending it more easily than you can. Therefore, you must do things my way if you want our relationship to continue." Ultimatums usually concern preferences ("Unless you do X, we're through!") or tolerances ("Unless you stop doing X, we're through!"). Sometimes they are used to force or maintain commitments; for instance, the commitment to exclusiveness ("You must choose: him or me!"). Freud is reported to have presented this last form of ultimatum to his future wife at least twice:

> He told Martha he considered it urgent that she leave her mother's home (and influence). . . . ". . . If we don't get over this obstacle we shall flounder. You have only an Either–Or. If you can't be fond enough of me to renounce for my sake your family, then you must lose me. . . ."
>
> He addressed an ultimatum to her with four points, the first of which was that she was to write an angry letter to her brother calling him a scoundrel. . . . He explained to her that it was not the money as such that mattered, but that their hope of married happiness had been at stake. She was not to write to him again until she promised to break off all relations with [her brother].[20]

All ultimatums seem to boil down to the simple cliché, "Love me or leave me," i.e., "Either our relationship is going to be run my way or not at all."

Intimates who want their relationship to continue are usually careful to give each other ultimatums only when each thinks the other will choose the alternative to termination; but in the heat of a have-it-out, one intimate may give the other an ultimatum when the latter is momentarily not disposed to defer ("OK. If that's the way you want it, we're through!"). Should this occur, the ultimatum giver must either go through with the termination or back down ("No, no. Don't go. I didn't mean it. I'm sorry. We'll do it your way"). But should he back down, he not only loses the argument, but he reveals his own dependence on the relationship and therefore discredits this ploy for future use. The wife who continually cries "Divorce," like the boy who continually cried "Wolf," can no longer convince even when she is serious ("This time I mean it." "Sure you do. OK. Pack your bags again and go home to mother for a few days like you did the last time").

It takes two to argue. Intimates can have a fight only when both are in the mood for one. When one intimate is in a good mood, he will try to avoid trouble by giving way to the other's preferences and tolerating his habits. When one intimate is in a bad mood, he will try to create trouble by refusing to give way to the other's preferences and refusing to tolerate his habits. If one intimate is in a bad mood while the other is in a good mood, it is not easy for an argument to start; the more the former claims and criticizes, the more the latter appeases and apologizes. In order for a fight to begin, both intimates must be in a bad mood, i.e., each must stand his ground by refusing to yield his own wishes or to take the other's criticism of his behavior. One intimate who wants to differentiate himself from the other, then, must first cause the other's self to coalesce so that he can have something solid from which to separate his own self.

Since intimates know where each other is vulnerable, the one who wants to start a fight can attempt to change the mood and consolidate the self of the one who wants to avoid a fight by needling the latter's weak points. He may begin his assault on the other's self at its loosely integrated extremities and slowly work in toward its core by mocking the objectifications and embodiments the latter considers more and more central and, hence, increasingly sacred. For instance, the former can first make fun of the latter's alma mater, or his family, or his friends, or his job, or the book he is writing, before finally focusing the attack in on his most central synechdoches, such as his body or his personality. Another tactic is for the former to deny whatever points the latter is trying to make, no matter how trivial ("What a beautiful day!" "It's too cold").

It is not clear what causes bad moods (what psychiatrists call "depression"). They seem to come on partly through internal physiological changes and partly through external behavioral frustrations, especially in association with others ("Don't bother me. I'm not feeling well," or "I've had a hard day at the office"). In any case, a person who would pass over minor conflicts when his mood is good will blow them up into major confrontations when his mood is bad. Leo Tolstoy, whose novella *The Kreutzer Sonata* contains several well-observed arguments, portrays how in a bad mood an intimate is set off by what in a good mood she would have shrugged off:

> "I think it was on the third or fourth day that I found my wife depressed. I began asking her the reason and embracing her, which in my view was all she could want, but she removed my arm and began to cry.... I began to question her, and she said something about feeling sad without her mother. It seemed to me that this was untrue, and I began comforting her without alluding to her mother.... But she immediately took offence because I had not mentioned her mother, as though I did not believe her. She told me she saw that I did not love her. I reproached her with being capricious, and suddenly her face changed entirely and instead of sadness it expressed irritation, and with the most venomous words she began accusing me of selfishness and cruelty.... I tried to soften her, but encountered such an insuperable wall of cold virulent hostility that before I had time to turn round I too was seized with irritation and we said a great many unpleasant things to one another."[21]

When one intimate is looking for a fight in order to differentiate himself from the other (whom he momentarily finds contaminating for a reason he does not clearly understand), he needs a *pretext* to serve as its opening bell. Pretexts that set off arguments are neither hard to find nor hard to create. One intimate may simply make his preferences so contradictory to the other's that the latter cannot possibly give in to them, or the former may force the latter to behave in an extreme manner that he can then refuse to tolerate. Illustration:

> "Let's go out tonight."
> "I don't want to."
> "Well, then let's spend a quiet evening at home."
> "I don't feel like staying home."
> "Well, if you don't want to go out or stay home, what
>   *do* you want to do?"
> "Don't raise your voice to me!"

The Complications sections of the previous chapters are replete with potential conflicts inherent in the structure of interpersonal relations, any of which can serve as the pretext for a quarrel. Here is Tolstoy's description of the incipience of another argument:

> "I was all the more staggered by that second quarrel because it arose from such an impossible pretext. It had something to do with money, which I never grudged and could certainly not have grudged to my wife. I only remember that she gave the matter such a twist that some remark of mine appeared to be an expression of a desire on my part to dominate over her by means of money, to which I was supposed to assert an exclusive right—it was something impossibly stupid, mean, and not natural either to me or to her. I became exasperated, and upbraided her with lack of consideration for me. She accused me of the same thing, and it all began again.... Now I am astonished that I failed to see my real position. It might

have been seen from the fact that the quarrels began on pretexts it was impossible to remember when they were over. Our reason was not quick enough to devise sufficient excuses for the animosity that always existed between us."[22]

Once begun over the pretext, each intimate can use the history of their relationship as a resource to prove that the pretext is merely a symptom of how unfair and irritating the other has become over the course of their relationship ("I've gotten fed up with you..," "I've had enough from you..," "I've spoiled you long enough..," "Now let me tell you a thing or two..."). In other words, he can escalate the specific conflict over the pretext into a general conflict he claims they have always or increasingly had, but which he has previously concealed from the other at great pain to himself ("Remember when you.... I never forgave you for that").

> "Well, that is how things were going not long before it happened. We seemed to be living in a state of truce and had no reason to infringe it. Then we chanced to speak about a dog which I said had been awarded a medal at an exhibition. She remarked 'Not a medal, but an honourable mention.' A dispute ensues. We jump from one subject to another, reproach one another, 'Oh, that's nothing new, it's always been like that.' 'You said....' 'No, I didn't say so.' 'Then I am telling lies!'..."[23]

The exchange of opposing assertions that make up the content of the confrontation revolve around questions of fact and questions of value. Intimates debate precisely what the historical events of their relationship were ("You said...." "I never said that") as well as how to evaluate the events initiated by the one relative to the events initiated by the other ("When you did X to me, you hurt me." "Well, you hurt me more when you did Y to me"). It is interesting to note that both parties can claim, "I've done more for you than you've done for me" or "You've irritated me more than I've irritated you," because the assistance and irritation of each party are usually impossible to compare with those of the other. If one claims that the other irritated him by laughing at his mistakes, and the second claims that the first irritated him by returning less favors than he owed, no comparison is possible— each is reduced to asserting his claim as the point at issue while denying the right of the other's claim to hold the floor ("But that's beside the point." "It is not. I wouldn't have... if you hadn't . . .").

Although intimates intentionally fan the fire of their conflict in these ways as soon as it has begun, they usually ignite the precise spark that sets it off by accident. An argument usually blazes up out of the following sequence:

1 The chance combination of A's bad mood and B's specific action annoys A.
2 A deliberately provokes B, to get even.
3 B, surprised ("Why did he do that to me? I didn't do anything to him"), now deliberately provokes A.
4 The undeclared war of attacks and reprisals escalates until it reaches a point at which the intimates openly have it out.

Arguments may be single-rounded or multi-rounded in duration. In the course of the latter, *running battle* form of argument, the time-outs between skirmishes are particularly worthy of attention. During these *intermissions* in open face-to-face conflicts, each intimate engages in certain activity designed both to punish the other and to "take the temperature" of their ailing association. Since their relationship is sick, the diagnostic aids needed now differ from the ones enumerated in the previous chapters; for whereas those were supposed to indicate how high intimacy had reached, these are supposed to indicate how low it has dipped.

One of the equilibrium mechanisms of a personal relation involves each intimate's willingness to compensate for the other's behavior in order to keep the relationship going. The tests of intimacy that occur during the have-it-out crises of the relationship involve subjecting this equilibrium mechanism to extreme conditions. By making it more and more difficult for him to do so, one intimate attempts to determine how much the other is willing to compromise himself in order to make allowances for the former's misbehavior. (Note that one intimate can stretch the other's capacity to compensate for him by applying the following techniques with regular frequency and gradually increasing intensity. Should he intensify them too rapidly or too strongly, however, he is likely to strain or rupture the relationship.)

There are four common ways in which one intimate can cruelly differentiate himself from the other in order to test the degree of the other's desire to continue their relationship. All these ways involve inflicting various kinds of punishment on the other and observing his reaction. First, one intimate may become obstinate, in order to see how far the other will yield to him on minor issues (unrelated to their major disagreement) where he takes an extreme and irrational position that he stubbornly refuses to modify. Second, he may become insolent, in order to see how far the other will tolerate his worst behavior. Third, he may become hypercritical, in order to see how far the other is willing to curb his own conduct to avoid even unreasonable criticism. Fourth, he may become sullen, in order to see how far the other will go to draw him back into their usual sociability.

All these interpersonal torture tests involve *withdrawal*, the simulation of termination. When one intimate withdraws from the other, he pretends he is ending their relationship in order to observe the latter's reaction; specifically, to observe how far the latter will go to save the relationship. These mock terminations can take a more sociological form when one intimate temporarily decreases the *volume* on any or all of the forces that hold his relationship with the other together:

1. One intimate may imply that their relationship has no future, that their potential to remain intimate or to become more so is now nonexistent ("I've had all I can take from you. It's obvious we don't get along. We're just too different. We don't have enough in common. We just aren't Communicating. I don't see how we could possibly get married if we're going to keep fighting like this").

2. One intimate may suddenly break off his face-to-face inter-action with the other and storm out without arranging their next encounter. He may not tell the other where he can be found. He may be "not in" when the other calls or visits. And he may avoid seeing the other for a while, especially during their customary meeting times (e.g., by not coming home to dinner), in order to break the regular rhythm of their meetings and partings. One of Tolstoy's unhappy spouses uses this technique to torment the other:

> "I hear her go out into the hall preparing to go away. I ask, 'Where are you going to?' She does not reply. 'Well, devil take her,' I say to myself, and go back to my study and lie down and smoke.... The evening passes, she has not returned, and two different feelings alternate within me. Anger because she torments me and all the children by her absence which will end by her returning; and fear that she will not return but will do something to herself. I would go to fetch her, but where am I to look for her? At her sister's? But it would be so stupid to go and ask. And it's all the better: if she is bent on torment-ing someone, let her torment herself. Besides that is what she is waiting for; and next time it would be worse still. But suppose she is not with her sister but is doing some-thing to herself, or has already done it!... Towards morning I fall asleep. I wake up, she has still not come! ...And in me the same struggle still continues: anger that she is torturing me, and anxiety for her."[24]

3. One intimate may be cold to the other. He may not respond to the other's intimate communications while giving him various nonintimate communications in return. Thus, he may treat the other as an *enemy* by hitting or slapping him. He may treat the other as an *acquaintance* by pulling his arm or hand away when the other tries to take it or by only nodding to the other when he passes him by chance on the street. He may treat the other as a *stranger* by refusing to recognize or acknowledge him at all should they accidentally come together in the same public place. Or,

most extreme, he may even treat the other as a mere *subsocial object* by neither requesting permission nor excusing himself when he must walk or reach through the latter's personal space, or by icily turning his head away when the other is speaking. In this last case, he is denying the other's human status itself—with all the privileges a person, as opposed to a thing, is supposed to possess. Thus, by intruding his body into the other's territory or by averting his eyes away from the other's presence, he pretends that the other is not there at all, or at least not there enough to merit a social response.

4. One intimate may be unwilling to provide the other with his customary output of information about himself. He may simply cease to volunteer to relate the recent events of his life required to keep the other's picture of him up-to-date. Or, should the other ask him about them, he may simply give curt, literal answers, without elaboration. In the extreme, he may refuse to respond to the other's inquiries at all ("None of your business!").

5. One intimate may refuse to supply the other with his usual favors. When a married couple is retiring after a day of intermittent arguments, the wife may keep her husband from her bed. Conversely, one intimate may refuse to allow the other to do him the favors he plainly needs. During a lull in an unresolved quarrel, a girl may keep her boy friend from helping her hang a picture with which she is having difficulty ("Let go! I'll do it myself!").

6. Finally, one intimate may take what appear to be the preliminary steps necessary to snap his intersubjective couples and commitments to the other. He may threaten their *exclusiveness* by beginning to call up someone else to ask for a date. He may threaten their *common space* by beginning to pack up his personal belongings as a prelude to moving out.

> At about three she comes. When she meets me she does not speak. I imagine that she has submitted, and begin to say that I had been provoked by her reproaches. She, with the same stern expression on her terribly harassed

> face, says that she has not come for explanations but to
> fetch the children, because we cannot live together.[25]

And he may threaten their *common future* by beginning to make
arrangements for a long trip.

> And so the same kind of quarrel, and even worse ones,
> occurred continually: once a week, once a month, or at
> times every day. It was always the same. Once I had al-
> ready procured a passport to go abroad—the quarrel had
> continued for two days. But there was again a partial ex-
> planation, a partial reconciliation, and I did not go.[26]

If withdrawal is to test accurately the reaction to the threat to
terminate the relationship, it must look real rather than merely
revelational. Here, as elsewhere, social man faces the same problem as social scientist: he must observe without being observed
observing. And, like the social scientist, he often tries to overcome
this restriction by observing his subject indirectly through his
tracks and traces. Thus, the boy who has stormed out of his girl
friend's house during an argument may drive by her home later to
see if she is still there, waiting for him, pining ("My God! Her
light's out and her car's gone! She must have gone out with someone!").

Time-outs also serve a more positive function by providing each
intimate with the breathing space necessary to come up with new
reasons to support the position he is arguing or with new justifications for yielding it. They also provide time for him to recall how
his previous arguments with his intimate ended. Remembrance of
reconciliations past provides trust that this argument, too, will ultimately be resolved, perhaps with strategies that had previously
proved successful. If an intermission begins with a husband storm-
ing out of the house, his wife can be confident that the disruption
to their relationship will be temporary. He will eventually come
back—at least, he always has. Again, the life of Freud may serve
as illustration:

The crisis was over, though it left both [Freud and Martha] shattered. Martha even admitted that for the first and only time she had felt herself destitute of any love. What sustained her was the memory of how her lover had turned back to her in the Alserstrasse years ago after having angrily left her. She knew his tenderness would in the last resort overcome everything else.[27]

Although arguments are dangerous instruments by which to re-stitch a relationship that is coming apart at the seams—for, as we will see in the next chapter, they can easily get out of hand—nevertheless, optimism about their outcome is the main factor that allows intimates to continue to initiate them. First fights, then, seem far more critical than later ones, for intimates who lack a tradition of successful conflict resolution are not at all con-fident that they can carry their initial confrontations to satisfactory conclusions.

Arguments end either in victory for one intimate and defeat for the other or in a draw for both. Should there be a winner, should one force or convince the other to do or see things his way, he may demand *unconditional surrender* from the loser, making him admit that he was completely wrong (i.e., inferior), forcing him to apologize. ("Say you're sorry"). Or he may allow the loser to save face by phrasing his victory in terms of a *face-saving formula* ("I guess I wasn't making myself clear. But you understand now why we should do it my way") or by means of the practice of *alternative winning* ("We'll do it your way next time" or "We did it your way last time. Now it's my turn to make the deci-sion"). Finally, the intimates may agree to compromise on the problem or to forget it ("Let's not talk about it anymore").

In threatening to end the relation, arguments strain everything holding it together. Each member of the social group that pro-vides part of the intimates' paired identity is implicated on both sides of the association. Should he be present when the two inti-mates are polarizing away from each other during a quarrel, their conflict will threaten to tear him apart. (Note that he is under more internal tension than either intimate, for their external opposition leads to their internal unification.) Although he is but an innocent bystander, each intimate will try to drag him into their dispute by appealing to him to support his side—which, of course, he cannot do without incurring the enmity of the other. The best he can do is to try to dampen down their heated have-it-out with the cooling waters of his work-it-out words ("Now, calm down, let's see if we can get this settled. Why don't you...."). The worst he can do is to achieve the unintentional unification of both intimates against himself, as they both turn on him openly or collusively.

Conversely, intimates usually try to avoid quarreling in front of any member of their social group in order to protect their social standing as interpersonally competent—a social standing they would lose if they were to subject to stress the social group members whom they have entangled in their affair. Furthermore, since a relationship is a joint construction, each intimate is judged by its apparent success.[28] Once word gets around that they "aren't getting along too well," the reputation of each intimate will fall into disrepute. Hence, intimates usually resolve that they will continue to appear to be intimates in front of others no matter what their inner feelings at the moment. A husband and wife involved in a domestic quarrel are likely, when one of their friends drops in for a visit, to bring it to an abrupt halt—and to appear all smiley and lovey with each other as long as he is there—only to begin throwing things at each other again as soon as he departs.

REVIVALS

If we are indebted to the German Georg Simmel for our understanding of the reintegrating function of social conflict, we are indebted to the Frenchman Emile Durkheim for our understanding of the reintegrating function of social ceremonies.[29] Durkheim's conception of ceremonies, induced from data about primitive communities, like Simmel's conception of conflict, induced from data about social groups, has important application to personal relations in advanced societies.

First, however, two sorts of ceremonies should be distinguished: *integration ceremonies*, such as oaths and marriages, occur when an intimacy grows through an upper intensity threshold, and function to vitalize the developing relationship; *reintegration ceremonies*, such as the ones to be considered here, occur when an intimacy decays through a lower intensity threshold, and function to revitalize the dying relationship. Relationships require energy to operate, and will waste away unless their energy supply is constantly renewed. Reintegration ceremonies are the refreshments of run-down relationships.

The most important kind of reintegration ceremony, which Durkheim calls *commemorative*, concerns the temporal dimension of the association. Its purpose is to render the past, with all its archetypal energy, into the present—in other words, to give the relatively secular present continuity with the relatively sacred past.[30]

The most common references of these commemorative ceremonies are the various points at which the relationship is thought to have originated. Intimates may mark every date at which they elevated their communion or commitment with an *origin-celebration*, or anniversary. Although heterosexual intimates usually commemorate only wedding anniversaries, they may commemorate other interpersonal anniversaries they feel were important as well. Freud unwittingly provides an instance in which such celebration was perhaps excessive:

> The date of that fateful Saturday, after which they considered themselves engaged, was June 17, [1882] one which they never forgot. They even commemorated the seventeenth of every month for some years; it was February 1885 when they first forgot to mention it in their letters.[31]

Along with the various points of relationship origin, reintegrative ceremonies also commemorate personal origins and social origins. When one intimate celebrates the birthday of the other, he shows that he treasures the other's existence as much as his own; in fact, since the other has become so much a part of him, by celebrating the other's coming into being, he is actually celebrating his own as well. Although national holidays (which usually memorialize social origins) are much corrupted in modern society—insofar as what precisely they are commemorating has been lost ("Help keep the X in Xmas!")—they continue to function to renew close relationships. Intimates try to be together on holidays; if they cannot, they at least try to contact each other to keep their communication channels from closing—calling or writing to indicate that the potential of their relationship still exists. (Holidays, accordingly, have become a time for rating one's personal relations and letting go of those that are no longer live. At Christmastime, especially, some attenuating relationships are moved down from the visit stage to the send-a-present stage, while others are moved down from the greeting-card stage to the dropped-off-the-list stage.)

Intimates feel it is important for them to remember to perform these relational, personal, and social ceremonies, because their performance shows that they continue to be willing to do all they can to rekindle their constantly cooling affair. Intimates may become so dependent upon these commemorative ceremonies, however, that although their actual celebration of anniversaries scarcely warms up their association, their sudden disregard of anniversaries definitely ices it over. The wife whose husband never remembers his wedding aniversary will eventually adjust to the fact that he has no concern with such formalities, but the wife whose husband brings an anniversary present every year and then one year suddenly forgets will fear for the future of their marriage.

Intimates also engage in less formal reintegration ceremonies to recall times, other than the origin of their association, during which they were especially close ("Remember when we...?"). We have seen in the first section of this chapter that periods of intense intimacy occur when the common environment of the intimates is either especially difficult for them to deal with or especially gratifying for them to be in ("We've been through a lot together." "We've been friends through thick and thin.") *Remember when's*, then, include both bad times and good times.

In bad times, their common circumstances were extremely rough ("Remember when we were stopped by the cops and we had all that grass in the car?"), and concomitant internal crises threatened to disrupt their relationship.

> The first two weeks of Freud and Martha's separation in June 1883 were among the worst they lived through. ... Resignation, however, never suited Freud. He often expressed his satisfaction that they had been through such a terrible time. "Such memories bring people closer than hours lived together. Blood and sufferings in common make the firmest bonds."[32]

In good times, their common circumstances and relationship were particularly delicious, as, for example, when they were newlyweds walking along the Bermuda beaches together under the stars. A honeymoon, in fact, is usually so intensely intimate an experience that spouses whose relationship is languishing often go on a second honeymoon in order to attempt to reinvigorate it. Claude Brown provides another instance in which one intimate considers recalling good times in order to reintegrate a relationship. In this passage, Brown is afraid that he and his younger brother Pimp are drifting apart:

> I wanted to say, "Pimp, what happened to the day that you and I used to walk through the streets with our arms around each other's shoulders? We used to sleep with our arms around each other, and you used to cry to follow me when I went out of the house." I wanted to say it, but it didn't make sense, because I knew that day had gone.[33]

Intimates objectify many of the periods at which they were extremely close in certain objects that aid their recollection ("Listen, they're playing our song. Remember when we first heard it?"). Rereading old love letters or reviewing old snapshots are common ways in which intimates attempt to recapture their bygone past rapture.

An individual whose relationship with another has faded away almost to nothing may remind the other of the intense relationship they once had, thus drawing the other closer to him at the very moment when he must distance himself from the other still further by begging him for an important favor ("Please do it for me. Do it for old times's sake").

Intimates may find the resources to reintegrate their relationship not only in the past, but in the future as well. They may perform ceremonies not only around the origin of their relationship, but also around its potential termination. These ritual exchanges usually begin with a question that hypothesizes the end of their affair ("What would you do if I suddenly died?"). By making manifest their latent fear that their affair is fragile and must eventually end, intimates can draw closer together, at least momentarily, as they anxiously huddle before the previews of their approaching doom. In *Thérèse and Isabelle*, Violette Leduc illustrates this ominous catechism:

> 'If I died tomorrow, would you go on living?' '... When you say you would die with me, do you really mean it? Would you really like us to die together?'[34]

Besides death, breakup is the other type of termination whose possibility intimates often discuss ("What would you do if I left you?" "I don't know. Marry your sister, I guess"). Intimates who ask and answer these questions jokingly imply that they find the thought of ending their relationship to be simultaneously appalling and appealing.

A second kind of reintegration ceremony was called by Durkheim *piacular*; it is designed to expiate guilt, especially that induced by loss or death.[35] Piacular ceremonies in personal relations usually occur when intimates make up after an argument—the near-death of their relationship for which they were almost responsible. Intimates who have had a falling out must "kiss and make up" or "shake hands and make up" in order to pull themselves back together again. Having reaffirmed their individuation during their argument, they must now reaffirm their integration at its conclusion. (An argument, in fact, may be seen as a sort of *negative ceremony* or *circuitous ceremony*; for whereas most cere-

monies reaffirm the union of intimates directly, arguments reaffirm
their union indirectly. Each intimate must first devalue the other
and differentiate himself from the other during the fight phase of
the argument in order to become conscious of the other's worth
and to celebrate their relationship when the argument is over—re-
affirming the overall association that circumscribes their degree
of dissociation.)

A third kind of reintegration ceremony Durkheim discusses is
the *communion*, or common meal, usually accompanied by sacrifice.[36] During the Middle Ages, friends sealed their friendship
religiously, legally, and socially through the common meal of
"Compotacio."[37] Today, intimates who are celebrating various aspects of their relationship (their wedding anniversary, an unexpected increase in their economic resources, etc.) often engage in
the modern equivalent of a common meal at sacrificial cost—eating out in an expensive restaurant.

The last kind of reintegration ceremony I will consider is one
with which Durkheim does not deal: the *reassurance ritual*. Each
intimate may use this ritual to reassure the other that he is still
expending the energy necessary to keep up his side of their relationship. In love relations, the most common incantation intended
to ward off relationship decay is the phrase "I love you." Choderlos
de Laclos comments:

> That 'I love you' which I was so fond of repeating
> when I could hear it repeated to me in return, that sweet
> assurance which sufficed for my happiness, now offers
> me, if you have changed, only the image of an eternal
> despair. But I cannot believe that this talisman of love
> has lost all its power, and I still try to make use of it.
> [Footnote:] This sentence will be meaningless to those
> who have never had the occasion to feel the value of a
> word or an expression consecrated by love.[38]

Ortega y Gasset counters:

> [Love] lives in the realm of ceaseless confirmation. (Love
> is monotonous, incessant, boring; no one would stand for

anyone's repeating the most ingenious statement so many times and, yet, the lover demands unending reiteration that his beloved loves him. And vice versa: when someone is not in love, love bestowed upon him oppresses him and drives him mad by its utter plodding quality.)[39]

By his compliments ("Gee! You're beautiful today!") and by his gifts (e.g., flowers), a lover intends to show his beloved that she is still "always on his mind," i.e., still the center of his orientation. Each of these reassurance rituals functions as a gauge, an *amourometer*, that indicates the amount of passionate energy propelling each intimate's pursuit of the relationship. (The intimates themselves face the same problem as the social scientist who studies them in determining how many RPM—reassurances per measure of time—are sufficient to give and to receive.) Reassurances that the relationship is functioning properly, at least insofar as its energy supply is concerned, are usually given unasked. In an emergency, however, when one intimate fears that the other's fuel supply is running low, he may put in a special request for an amourometer reading ("You don't love me anymore." "Oh but I do! I do! More than anything!").[40]

COMPLICATIONS

Certain kinds of environments nurture intimate relations, but other kinds poison them. Sometimes it is difficult to tell which is which. A hostile and barren environment may cause intimates to become more dependent on each other to use scarce resources, but it may also cause intimates to compete with each other for them. Conversely, a benign and fertile environment may cause intimates to fear to fuse with each other less, but it may also cause them to enjoy their environment more than each other. Environments that are definitely disintegrating, however, are those that are beneficial for one intimate and detrimental to the other. These uneven environments cause all the benefits of the relationship to flow from one partner to the other—an imbalance that few associations can stand for long periods of time. Providing intimates with un-

equal rewards forms the basis of the divide-and-conquer strategy
their enemies can use to crack apart their relationship.

Since an intimate who is attempting to work it out seems to
be compromising himself as best he can in order to accommodate
the other, an intimate who does not want to accommodate the
other will often try to appear as though he did. In other words,
by appearing reasonable, an intimate can get his way while seeming to give it up. The other may feel intuitively that he is losing
out somehow, but such specious reasonableness is a difficult tactic
to counter.

Although I will consider the main problem of have-it-outs in
the next chapter, I think it worthwhile to include here an excerpt
from Dan Greenburg's sociologically insightful book, *How to
Make Yourself Miserable*, illustrating a rare form of interaction
in which one intimate disintegrates a relationship through the
successfully resolved argument that seemed to have reintegrated
it:

> You: "Well, our first big fight."
> Mate: "Yes."
> You: (Pause) "Do you think we have anything left?"
> Mate: "What do you mean?"
> You: "I mean do you think we still have a relationship?"
> Mate: "Of course. (Pause) Why—don't you think so?"
> You: "Well, I thought so before, at any rate."
> Mate: "What's that supposed to mean?"
> You: "That I thought so before."
> Mate: "And you don't think so now?"
> You: (Pause) "I don't know. What do you think?"
> Mate: (Pause) "I don't know. I thought so before."
> You: "But now you're maybe not so sure, is that it?"
> Mate: (Pause) "I don't know. Maybe not."
> You: "Well, since you're obviously planning to break
>   up with me sooner or later, you might as well do
>   it sooner and not prolong the agony."[41]

There are two times in a relationship when intimates need not
perform reintegration ceremonies: at its high points, when no

renewal is necessary, and at its low points, when no renewal is possible. Reintegration ceremonies, then, are performed in the continuum between these two limits.

> Ceremony was but devised at first
> to set a gloss on faint deeds, hollow welcomes,
> Recanting goodness, sorry ere 'tis shown;
> But where there is true friendship, there needs none.[42]

The slope of the effectiveness of these reintegration ceremonies changes from positive to negative at the midpoint of this continuum. Above this point, intimates who perform these ceremonies from desire actually accomplish the reintegration they intend; below this point, intimates who perform these ceremonies from duty actually poison their relationship more than they cure it.

> Brutus: A word, Lucilius,
>   How he received you. Let me be resolved.
> Lucilius: With courtesy and with respect enough,
>   But not with such familiar instances,
>   Nor with such free and friendly conference,
>   As he hath used of old.
> Brutus: Thou hast described
>   A hot friend cooling. Ever note, Lucilius,
>   When love begins to sicken and decay,
>   It useth an enforced ceremony.
>   There are no tricks in plain and simple faith.[43]

A lover often forces his beloved to perform reintegration ceremonies as proofs of her affection for him when he fears her love for him is fading ("If you really loved me, you'd ...").[44]

Occasionally, these reintegration mechanisms can come into conflict with one another. For instance, when a problem ruffles the smooth flow of interaction between the intimates, one may want to work it out while the other may want to have it out. In a cartoon from *The New Yorker*, an angry wife shouts at her unperturbed husband: "Stop being reasonable! Can't you see we're having an argument!"

Finally, when intimates are unable to adjust to each other through any of the usual reintegration mechanisms, they may adopt an extreme method to keep their relationship together. Al though its costs may be high, they will not terminate their relationship if its benefits are even higher. Should intimates be unable to reform their relationship and unwilling to destroy it, they must "make it work." The make-it-works of mismatched mates involve deliberately harmonizing behavior while resolutely supressing inclination. This drastic method, however, merely sweeps the external antagonisms of the association under the rug of each partner's psyche, transforming conflicts between both intimates into conflicts within each of them. Such *forced affairs*, of course, are no fun—being stressful by definition.

CHAPTER 8

Breaking Up

THERE SEEMS to be no necessary reason an intimate relation should not continue until one of the participants dies. (In fact, we shall see how some of the intimate bonds may even survive the death of one of the intimates, often to the dismay of the other.) However, there are several contingent reasons most intimate relations do not live out their theoretically maximum life spans. The specific stress that ultimately destroys an intimate relation may originate either within the relationship or outside it. But it is most likely that intimates who break up will do so under a combination of internal weaknesses and external pressures.

Intimacies are internally weakened when intimates discover that the life-styles to which they are individually inclined are too dissimilar to keep connected. If each intimate's internal gyroscope is constantly pulling him away from the other, the connecting bonds they have forged will be subject to great strain. Intimates manifest the resulting tensions of their relationship in continual conflicts over the problems enumerated in the Complications sections of Chapters 1 through 6, which are inherent in the processes of personal relations. One intimate may want to resolve these problems one way; the other intimate another way. For instance, on the variable of the proportion of time the intimates are together relative to the proportion of time they are apart, one may want to be in the presence of the other as much as possible, whereas the other may like to be alone a lot. When each intimate's preferred life pattern differs too fundamentally from the other's and adjusts too inelastically to the other's, all the reintegrating mechanisms they use—extreme environments, work-it-outs, have-it-outs, and revival ceremonies—will not be able to pull their disintegrating relationship back together again.

It is obvious that if these internal conflicts are major ones, the net profit each intimate derives from the association—the gross benefits he receives from the other minus the costs of their conflicts—will become a net loss relative to the break-even point of solitude. In this case, realizing their conflicts are both important and irreconcilable, the intimates will actively seek to terminate their relationship. A more interesting case occurs when the conflicts, while continual, are minor—leaving the participants in the relationship with enough of a net profit to restrain them from seeking actively to terminate it, though not enough to entice them to seek actively to maintain it should the benefits decrease or the costs increase.

In other words, these continual minor internal conflicts may so strain the relationship that it would not survive any further increase in stress level. In this connection, Samuel Johnson once wrote, "The most fatal disease of friendship is gradual decay, or dislike, hourly increased by causes too slender for complaint, and too numerous for removal." In previous chapters, I considered the persisting sources of stress that weaken a relationship. In this chapter, I will consider the immediate causes of a further increase in stress level that will finish off an already weakened relationship. These immediate causes of termination may act slowly or rapidly.

The first section of this chapter will consider the breakup of an intimate relation under the gradual impact of certain strain-producing factors that, little by little, decrease its benefits and increase its costs. Since intimates, under these conditions, can gently disengage themselves from their affair by degrees without having a traumatic deathbed scene, I will call this type of intimate termination *passing away*. This section will conclude with a discussion of how both intimates intentionally sever their remaining connections in order to cut themselves completely free of their dying relationship.

The second section will consider the rapid breakup of an intimate relation. Since close associations that are rapidly ended usually involve traumatic terminal scenes, I will call this type of termination *sudden death*. The dramatic ending may result from the official cutting of the last living tie that holds the association together, after the factors mentioned in the first section have slowly sapped the life out of all its other bonds. Or it may result from the unexpected snapping of all the seemingly solid intimate bonds at once. In either case, the last convulsions of the relationship usually demand that the intimates say a final benediction over it before laying it completely to rest.

The Complications section of this chapter will consider the ways in which a dead intimate relation may return to haunt those who killed it.

PASSING AWAY

One way an intimate relation may end is to pass peacefully away, unmourned. Intimacy may decline to acquaintance and beyond in nearly imperceptible degrees. The fact that during New Year's celebrations "auld acquaintance" are supposed to be brought to mind indicates that throughout the rest of year they are oft forgot. Unless a relationship cannot die easily (for reasons to be considered in the next section), the expiration of a relation that succumbs slowly will be both mutual and mute. When the following factors cause an intimacy to begin to end, each partner will decide independently that their relationship can no longer survive and will begin to speed up its burial on his own, without ever speaking to the other about his intentions.

There are three factors external to an intimate relation that can slowly suck the vitality out of it: (1) the intrusion of a new intimate; (2) the expansion of interaction distance over space; and (3) the aging of each intimate over time. Although these factors will necessarily debilitate an intimacy, they will cause it to terminate only when it has already been enfeebled by the internal weakness of dissonant life-styles noted in the introduction to this chapter. Intimates who were completely satisfied with their association would do all they could to avoid new entanglements that might damage their old, to keep from moving away from each other, and to resist growing away from each other as they aged. But, for analytic purposes, I will consider how these external factors erode the rivets of the relationship without taking into account any internal flaws its fastenings may already have.

1. *New Intimate*

The gradual intrusion of a third party may slowly but surely nudge one member of an intimate relation out of position. "A new friend," goes an English proverb, "makes the old forgotten." "A friend married," goes a Scandinavian proverb, "is a friend lost."

An individual who acquires a new intimate may destroy his old potential as a worthwhile personal relation for some of his old intimates. They may find that his new intimate has disqualified him, for instance, by filling the special opening of his they themselves had hoped to fill someday. The female friends of a man who gets married may consider him a less desirable associate, for he is no longer the eligible bachelor he once was.

An individual who acquires a new intimate will have more difficulty managing to have meetings with his old ones. His new intimate will cut down the amount of free time he has available to spend with his old intimates and make the scheduling of their get-togethers harder to arrange. When his new intimate has acquired a *copresence priority* higher than that of his old, he can arrange an encounter with his old intimates only when his new intimate is free to come along or is engaged in a pursuit that does not require or allow them to be together. Furthermore, his new intimate restructures his perception of the warm spots of his environment along its spatial and temporal coordinates. As he finds himself drawn more and more to his new intimate and less and less to his old intimate, the warm spots associated with the former come to outshine those associated with the latter.

An individual whose relationship with a new intimate has reached the level of exclusiveness can no longer communicate with his old intimates through his customary philemes—especially in public, where word of his behavior may return (along the information network of their common social group) to the one to whom he is now supposedly committed. A man who gets engaged, for instance, can no longer indulge in the higher kinesics with his old girl friends, without fearing that the knowledge that he is still making these now condemned communications may get back to his fiancée before he does. Phileme families that are not continually stretched to their intimate position tend to contract back to their acquaintance level.

When an individual acquires a new intimate, he decreases his output of public information about his ongoing life activities to his old intimates. Since his new intimate now receives it all first, he is left with less interest in providing his older intimates with what is now to him stale news. The quality of his information output to his old intimates declines even more drastically than its quantity. He need no longer confide any private information about himself to his old intimates, for his new one now provides him with a single storehouse for all his secrets. Conversely, his input of confidential information from his old intimates lessens once they come to realize that, as he now has no secrets from his new intimate, whatever secrets they confide to him will now pass through four ears. The arrival of a new intimate affects the exchange between the old intimates not only of present and future information, but of past information as well. When an individual acquires a new intimate, he will reperceive his old ones and reinterpret the information he has previously acquired about them. A man who marries, for example, may frequently discuss his old friends with his new wife and thus come to define them differently from the way in which he defined them before.[1]

Since an individual's resources are finite, a new intimate will reduce the amount of aid he is now able to render to his old intimates. Conversely, since his new intimate now supplies him with many of the services that were once the franchise of his old, he now needs fewer services from his old intimates. An individual who acquires a new intimate, then, becomes less valuable to his old ones at the same time that they become less necessary to him.

Finally, the intrusion of a new intimate will loosen many of the intersubjective couples that had connected an individual to his old intimates. He will have increasing difficulty in communing with them as soon as his new intimate begins to insert fresh self-components into him.[2] (For instance, the new social group members his new intimate brings may not be easily integrated with his old ones.) His new intimate will also replace his old intimates as the ground against which his identity is contrasted and focused. And, should he begin to make commitments to his new intimate, his old ones will be gradually eased out of their association. Claude Brown provides illustration of this last disintegration process:

> [Bucky had] been acting kind of funny lately, as if I didn't want him coming around any more. I guess he was feeling that me and Turk were getting tight, that Turk was taking his place with me as being my best friend.[3]

2. *Spatial Expansion*

When one intimate is forced to move away from the other, both may allow their relationship to lapse. Economic and social necessities are the major forces that pull intimates apart spatially. The company one of them works for may transfer him to a job in another city, or he may discover that his career opportunities may be much better elsewhere. Or someone to whom one of the intimates is socially handcuffed, such as a husband or a parent, may move, dragging him along.

> Mamma's Hamburg plan began to ripen.... Martha's entreaties and protests were not so vigorous as Freud wished—another source of disagreement—but to her Mamma's wish was law. In the end the departure took place, and Freud was separated from Martha for a second

time, on June 17, 1883, and now for a quite unforseeable
future. Mamma had tried to pacify him by saying they
were going to Hamburg only to see how they liked it and
would decide later about settling there. Later on Freud
often referred to this 'deception.'[4]

For whatever reason one intimate moves away from the other,
each will find that the stretching of their interaction over space
will lead to the attenuating of their intimacy over time.

Intimates who do not expect their relationship to endure the
increase of their interaction distance will see no point in expending the increased energy now necessary to keep it up. As soon as
they feel they have lost their potential for remaining intimates in
the future, they will cease trying to decelerate their relationship's
decline.

The bond that is most distended as their interaction distance is
extended is the rhythm of their coming-togethers and going-aparts.
Since it is now difficult for them to effect copresence, they can
no longer easily obtain psychological stimulation, passion polarization, or expressive exercise from each other, nor participate in
common activities with each other. Furthermore, as intimates can
receive these enjoyments most readily in face-to-face interaction,
each of the separated intimates is likely to look for a new source
of supply closer to home. Should either intimate subsequently
find someone else to supply them, he will speed up the disintegration of their relation by supplementing the disruptive effects of
spatial separation with the added disruptive effects of the new
intimate.

Intimates who are at an unnatural remove from each other cannot communicate the level of their relationship to each other as
frequently as they could when they were propinquitous. As noted,
communication philemes that go unused shrink back from the
intimate level to acquaintance level. Kinesic communications are
especially subject to retrenchment; there is as yet no technologi-
cally feasible way to transmit them over long reaches. Although
intimates who are parting always promise to keep in touch with
each other, the relatively extreme hugging, kissing, and other

intimate kinesics that accompany these departures seem to indicate that they are fully aware that their intimacy is about to decline precipitously. In intensifying their intimate communications at the moment of separation, they seem to be taking the precaution of raising their relationship to a higher level in order to draw out its anticipated downfall.

When one intimate moves away from the other, their information exchange is drastically curtailed. Hence, the image each continues to hold of the other is the one frozen at the moment of departure, despite their best efforts to keep each other up-to-date on its current modifications through letters and calls. And, as they are no longer aware of most of the changes that have taken place in each other since they separated, whatever each now has to say to the other is directed to his past self and becomes increasingly irrelevant to his present self.[5] Intimates whose isolation from each other lasts longer and longer, then, tend to talk past each other more and more.

Intimates who have become remote from each other physically, if not yet psychologically, can no longer draw easily on each other for the favors, enumerated in Chapter 5, that facilitate their dealings with their environment. Friendships, however, are more affected by this abatement of aid than love relations: friends are more attached by the actual services they receive, lovers are more attached by the anticipated services they hope to receive.

Distance also debilitates many of the intersubjective couples that had held the intimates together. Their once congruent behaviors, attitudes, opinions, etc., drift out of alignment as they can no longer coordinate them through interaction and conversation. Their once similar physical and social circumstances become different, especially for the one who moves away. Most important, intimates who are separated for any great length of time no longer add to their stock of common biographical experiences, but, in fact, increase the proportion of differentiating biographical experiences relative to them. Moreover, their common past itself—a couple that can never come apart completely—will at least atrophy if their absence is prolonged. "If the absence is prolonged," observed Aristotle, who was the first to wonder at the commonplace, "it does seem to dim the memory of friendship itself. Hence the poet's words:

> 'How oft, alas, from sight and speech remov'd
> The *Friendship* passes with the *Friend* we lov'd!' "[6]

As we say today: "Out of sight, out of mind."

3. *Temporal Development*

The bonds that hold intimates together may also slacken as their relationship evolves over time. In the process of biological, psychological, and sociological aging, intimates may grow away from each other insofar as the characteristics that originally tied them together develop in different directions or at different rates. Since alterations in all of an individual's aspects are especially rapid during adolescence, few of his early intimacies survive this period; in fact, those who have been friends since childhood or who have married their childhood sweethearts are considered rare enough in our society to be worthy of at least a passing comment. Furthermore, the infrequency of lifelong friends testifies that changes in the magnetic components of individuals occur throughout the life cycle. Aging affects the intimate relation twice as much as it affects the intimates; since the attractive power of each connective force is determined by the degree to which one intimate's specific transmission matches the other intimate's specific reception, it will decrease when either becomes irrelevant to the other.

The physical beauty of their intimates is, for some people, the sine qua non qualifier of their love relationships. Their desire to preserve them, then, declines with the beauty of their aging intimates. Since Plato, would-be lovers have been warned against basing their relationships on so impermanent a foundation:

> Now the vicious lover is the follower of the earthly Love who desires the body rather than the soul; his heart is set on what is mutable and must therefore be inconstant. And as soon as the body he loves begins to pass the first

flower of its beauty, he 'spreads his wings and flies away,' giving the lie to all his pretty speeches and dishonoring his vows, whereas the lover whose heart is touched by moral beauties is constant all his life, for he has become one with what will never fade.[7]

(An association based on beauty will endure only if the aesthetic taste of the lover matures as his beloved matures or if it is underpinned by further linkages less subject to the scars of time.) Aristotle generalizes Plato's proposition when he points out that all qualifiers that can deteriorate will eventually undermine any relationship founded on them:

> These two forms of friendship then are grounded on an inessential factor—an 'accident'—because in them the friend is not loved for being what he is in himself but as source, perhaps of some pleasure, perhaps of some advantage. So parties are ready enough to dissolve their association when they themselves are changed. For if they are no longer agreeable or useful to one another, love dies a natural death. And as for utility, it is an impermament and protean quality. So with the disappearance of the motive, the friendship itself disappears, for it had no other *raison d'être*.[8]

Note, too, that the more the intimate's qualifiers (beauty, novelty, utility, etc.) decline over time, the more likely a better qualified third party will appear on the scene.

Once the frequency at which intimates see each other falls below a certain level, it is hard for them to raise it back up again. "Friendship, like love," Samuel Johnson has written, "is destroyed by long absence, though it may be increased by short intermission." The longer their relationship continues, the more likely intimates will eventually fall below this copresence threshold. Should one of them acquire a job, he may find he has cut down his time available for visiting the other.[9] Should he also acquire alternative sources of satisfaction in the meantime, he may come to feel he has better things to do with his free time than to spend it visiting his old intimate. Usually, however, he tends to blame his scarcity of time for what is actually caused by his satiety of pleasure ("I keep meaning to see him but I never seem to find the time anymore").

The relative proportion of intimate communications to acquaintance communications also seems to decline naturally as the relationship ages. A person must go out of his way to send most intimate, as opposed to most acquaintance, signals. Thus, touching demands more energy than not touching, kissing than not kissing, etc. Though the difference in wattage involved is small, nevertheless it builds up over time until more and more conscious effort is required to remember to telegraph i-n-t-i-m-a-c-y (which one person taps out to the other by touching him, hugging him, kissing him, etc.) rather than a-c-q u-a-i-n-t-a-n-c-e. Only when one person strongly wants his intimacy with the other to continue will he be willing to continue to generate the energy necessary to communicate it.

The fourth bond of an intimate relation that may deteriorate as it grows older is the informational one. As the relationship wears on, each intimate comes to learn the characteristics of the other—concealed at first acquaintance—that make him unsuitable as an intimate. Aristotle conjectures:

> Suppose another case. I have made a friend of a man in the belief that he is a person of good character, and he turns out—or one gets that impression—to be a scoundrel. Am I to go on treating him as a friend? Surely that is out of the question."[10]

If the frequency with which it is commented on can be taken as an index of its importance, then one of the most significant factors affecting friendship is the flux of fortune. When the ability of an individual to deal successfully with his environment is debiliated for social (disgrace), economic (bankruptcy), psychological (depression), or physiological (sickness) reasons, he not only strains his intimates' resources when he calls on them for aid, but becomes himself useless for them as a resource, at least in the immediate future. Since few friendships can survive such shocks, personal disasters are considered a de facto test of the value of the relationship (as contrasted with the planned tests noted in the previous chapters). There is a plethora of proverbs about the "fair-weather friends" who fail these tests: "Just as swallows are present in summer but in cold weather fly away, so false friends are at hand in fair weather but depart with the winter of fortune;" "Friends are the thermometers by which we may judge the temperatures of our fortunes;" "When fortune's fickle the faithful friend is found;" "In prosperity our friends know us, in adversity we know our friends." A friend who passes these tests, however, is awarded one of the highest adjectival honors the other can bestow: firm, loyal, constant, or tried-and-true. In general, a person often finds the crises of his life to serve the positive, if painful, function of sorting and grading his close relationships. Those that fail these tests are terminated, those that pass them are intensified.[11]

Finally, the communion between the intimates may be strained by the divaricating development of each of their self-components over time. Their material aspects—behaviors, habits, demeanor, etc.—may diverge:

. . .

—There you are, friends!—Alas, the man you sought
        You do not find here?
You hesitate, amazed? Anger were kinder!
I—changed so much? A different face and gait?
And what I am—for you, friends, I am not?
        . . .
Youth's longing misconceived inconstancy,
        Those whom I dreamed
Changed to my kin, the friends of whom I dreamed,
Have aged and lost our old affinity:
One has to change to stay akin to me.[12]

. . .

Their immaterial aspects—interests, attitudes, opinions, etc.—
may diverge:

> It seemed as though Butch and Danny and Kid weren't
> [interested in] doing the things we used to do, and they
> didn't want to do the things that I wanted to do. . . .
> After a while, I decided I wasn't going to hang out with
> Butch and Kid any more.[13]

Their environment to which they are responding—natural and
social—may diverge:

> One of the root causes of divorce in Western Civiliza-
> tion is the intellectual disparity between husband and
> wife. While the husband goes to work and broadens his
> intellectual ken, the wife remains home concentrating on
> housework and the rearing of children. . . . Dr. Guido
> Groeger, head of the Protestant Marriage Guidance
> Bureau in Dusseldorf, says: ". . . When the marriage
> partners come from limited cultural backgrounds, and the
> husband suddenly makes a successful career for himself,
> the wife, in many cases, is unable to keep up with him."[14]

An increasing status differential between the intimates is one of
the most common sources of stress on their intersubjective couples.
The intimate who succeeds or who fails moves into a different environment to which he must respond and with which he cannot
integrate his old friends. But, more important, since each intimate
achieves much of his identity by contrasting himself with the
other, the other's relative success or his own relative failure may
force him to acquire an identity that he does not appreciate, causing him to resent the other:

> Fame has made some changes in [Dustin Hoffman's] life
> style. Some old friends are not so friendly. "They've
> known you for ten years and suddenly you're way up

there and they don't seem to be getting anywhere. Some
people get bitter."[15]

"The path of social advancement," H. G. Wells maintained, "is,
and must be, strewn with broken friendships."

Termination Tactics

When third-party intrusion, spatial separation, or temporal
evolution undercuts a relationship that has already been crippled
by internal conflicts, both intimates will consider it no longer
worth saving. Without discussing the matter with each other, they
will take steps to finish it off by severing every one of their connections that are still intact.

1. When intimates have decided that the relationship has no
future, i.e., no potential to continue, they will no longer expend
the energy necessary to sustain it. Since this sustaining energy
is a main support of the relationship's other bonds, an intimacy
that declines below the stability threshold of its energy potential
will, from that point on, become autodisintegrating at an accele-
rated rate.

2. Intimates who are cutting their relationship apart spend less
time together, increase the interval between their encounters, and
specify the time of their next meeting more vaguely. Each intimate initiates contacts with the other less, while making it harder
for the other to initiate contacts with him. Their ratio of planned
to chance encounters decreases relatively, while their chance meetings dwindle absolutely as they unwind their intersecting routines.
The connection that consists of their ability to come together
easily should either ever want to meet the other again reaches its
lowest point when each crosses the other's name and number out
of his respective address book and discontinues informing the
other whenever he moves or has his number changed.

3. Intimates who want to become acquaintances switch back
each phileme family from intimate to acquaintance. First name
becomes formal name; endearments disappear; etiquette level increases; tone becomes colder; mutual silence becomes more em-

barrassed and less frequent. Kinesically, they look each other in the eye less often; they increase the distance at which they interact; they avoid touching.

4. Intimates who no longer want to be intimates intentionally reduce both their outputs and inputs of information to and from each other. On the one hand, each gradually ceases to keep the other informed of daily changes in his self and life. On the other hand, each gradually ceases to keep his image of the other up-to-date as he loses interest in the new mundane molecules that are added to the other's image and pays less attention to the other when he talks about major developments in his self and life.

5. Intimates who are becoming independent of each other reduce the number of favors they do for and ask from each other. On the one hand, each asks the other for favors less often in order to indicate that he has less need for the other's aid; on the other hand, each performs the favors the other asks him for less frequently or less well—either by giving an excuse why he cannot perform them at all or by performing them procrastinatingly, inadequately, or grudgingly—in order to indicate that he no longer wants the other to count or call on him for aid.

6. Intimates can retrench their relationship by uncoupling their intersubjective couples. Each can change his conduct or clothing. Each can alter his tastes, opinions, interests, personal culture, etc. Each can keep their common past from growing by no longer telling the other about his individual biography and by no longer having common experiences with the other. Each can curtain his Communication with the other. Each can select his own friends out of their common pool through differential association and can acquire new ones on his own. Finally, each can stop regarding the other as the point of reference against which he contrasts, and consequently creates, his individual identity.

SUDDEN DEATH

We have looked at the ways in which an intimacy may slide into oblivion slowly; we shall now see how it may slip into it suddenly. There are three ways in which an intimate relation can come to an abrupt end: (1) Both partners may gradually lose their intimacy but retain their relationship because certain of their bonds are difficult to break, until both are able to coordinate their efforts to cleave these obdurate connections quickly. (2) One partner may gradually lose his inclination to continue the intimacy while the other retains his, forcing the former to terminate their relationship unilaterally and precipitously. (3) Neither partner may wish to end their intimate relation, but, due to circumstances beyond their control, it suddenly ceases. In each of these cases, unlike those considered in the previous section, intimates must engage in one final—painful—conversation in order to conclude their affairs completely.

1. Two-sided Subsidence

Although the internal weakness of the relationship, as well as the factors enumerated in the previous section, may cause an intimacy to abate, both partners may have to continue to interact to a certain extent as long as they are chained together by unbreakable bonds.[16] Thus, siblings are periodically brought together at family functions whether they care to be or not. And friends who work together must continue to associate at a certain daily minimum long after their friendship has declined. Intimates may also be linked by bonds that neither can bend apart slowly by himself, but which both can break apart rapidly by coordinating their efforts. Bonds of commitment, for instance, are specifically designed to be impossible to attenuate on one's own, but possible to annul abruptly by mutual agreement. One of the characters in E. M. Forster's Howard's End complains about the difficulty in dismantling a relationship that has been hardened by commitment:

> "Can you break an engagement off slowly?" Her eyes lit up. "What's an engagement made of, do you suppose? I think it's made of some hard stuff, that may snap, but can't break. It is different to the other ties of life. They stretch or bend. They admit of degree. They're different."[17]

2. One-sided Subsidence

One intimate must also speak to the other about uncoupling their relationship when he discovers that, while he is actively striving to pull it apart, the other is actively striving to hold it together. Although friendships sometimes ebb unevenly, it is much more common for love relations to do so. In fact, in Western society today, love is often imputed to those who wish to continue the friendships their partners wish to discontinue (although their psychiatrists may euphemize it as "dependence" or "latent homosexual inclinations").

For social scientists as well as for laymen, the death of love is as mysterious an occurrence as its birth. Since it distorts time (as noted in Chapter 6) and since it is supposed to be "eternal" (according to modern ideology), those afflicted by love usually expect it to continue forever. Nevertheless, the lifetime of love, like the course of many physical diseases to which it exhibits marked similarities (see Chapter 6, note 33), is, for the most part, out of the lover's control; it passes according to the cycle of its own internal processes ("I tried to keep loving her, but I just couldn't"). A modern "romantic realist," Stephen Vizinczy, writes in his book In Praise of Older Women:

> We hang onto the hope of eternal love by denying even its temporary validity. It's less painful to think 'I'm shallow,' 'She's self-centered,' 'It's just physical,' 'We couldn't communicate,' than to accept the simple fact that love is a passing sensation, for reasons beyond our control and even beyond our personalities.[18]

But if the underlying epidemiology of love is obscure, its symptoms are clear enough. Having already noted in the foregoing chapters some of love's psychological and sociological consequences on intimates and their relationship, I will now consider the effect of its diminution on relationships that have been founded on it. I will first look at a declining love relationship from the point of view of the person whose love for the other is diminishing, and then from the point of view of the latter, whose love for the former is as strong as ever.

The diminishing of one person's love for another has repercussions on all the dimensions of their relationship—as the other soon becomes painfully aware. First, the person whose love is lessening no longer looks forward to an ever-more complete connection with the other, even losing interest in maintaining the connections they have already established ("He doesn't love me anymore," the other may be heard to complain). Second, his desire to see and be with the other diminishes as the latter ceases to be the meaning-generator of his life field at the center of his time and space coordinates ("He's never around anymore when I need him"). Third, performing the intimate linguistic and especially kinesic exercises with the other loses its previous appeal ("He never shows his affection for me like he used to"). Fourth, he stops looking at the other through rose-colored glasses and sees the latter's blemishes for the first time.[19] "Lovers," quipped La Rochefoucauld, "only notice their mistresses' faults when their mistresses' fascination has ended."[20] Furthermore, he no longer wants to continue imparting familiar, or particularly confidential, information to the other ("We don't seem to have anything to say to each other anymore—and he's become so secretive recently"). Fifth, he needs fewer favors from the other; consequently, he desires to do fewer favors for the other ("He won't do what I ask him anymore, and he used to be so prompt and willing"). Finally, he finds that the communion has drained out of his couples, leaving him bound to the other only by empty commitments ("I don't know what's happened, but the magic seems to have gone out of our marriage").

It is one thing to wish a love relationship were over; it is quite another thing actually to end it if the other party is actively trying to keep it going. "Those who have fallen out of love," our aphorist adds, "find it a sore problem to break off."[21] The one who no longer loves will find any termination talk he initiates to be a difficult script to direct, for it will force the one who still loves to revise his self-conception suddenly and drastically,[22] especially in regard to his estimation of his power to attract and hold others. And such sudden psychic readjustment can easily get out of control. On the one hand, the unloved lover may be unable to reassemble his shattered self-image; i.e., he may be unable to integrate his new self-conception (in which he now sees himself as a loser in love) with his old one (in which he had seen himself as a suave and successful suitor). On the other hand, the unloved lover may reassemble his self-image in the easiest possible way; i.e., he may see himself as the victim of the other's treachery and deceit. The unloving lover, who initiates a dramatic confrontation with the unloved lover then, will find he has to play the difficult dual role of both prosecutor and counsel. In the one role, he must disregard the latter's tears and entreaties while continuing to compel him to see that his present conception of himself and their relationship is untenable. In the other role, he must console the latter in order to help him reconstruct his self-conception. The unloving lover, in short, must keep the unloved lover both from the mental breakdown consisting of a self that is unassembled and unassemblable, and from the mental reconstruction consisting of a self that is reassembled around a conception of the unloving lover as an eternal enemy who, by breaking their implicit contract of mutual love in perpetuity, is responsible for the latter's present plight.

Needless to say, all this is a hard degradation ceremony to be master of, and few of those who have ceased to love would want to go through with it. Instead, it is easier for them to get their partners to initiate the relationship rupture and to take charge of the termination talk.[23] An unloving lover can get an unloved lover to be the first to suggest terminating their association by increasing its costs and decreasing its benefits for him. Thus, whenever their preferences are opposed, he can refuse to compromise with the other, making it necessary for the other to compromise himself more and more in order to continue the relationship. It is called "exploitation" when the unloving lover puts on this painful profit squeeze, but is careful not to make it bad enough to force the unloved lover to pull out.[24]

It is one of the most tragic aspects of intimate relations that the love of two individuals for each other does not often end at the same time. It is tragic in the sense that the conflict is irresolvable: the increasingly desperate desire of the intimate who has lost his love to terminate the affair is met by the increasingly desperate desire

of the intimate who is still in love to maintain it. All intimate relations are homeostatic systems—each partner continually readjusts
his own actions to offset the other's in order to keep the intimacy
level of their relationship stable—but love relations are especially
homeostatic. The lover, in particular, will do all he can to keep
their association alive and functioning smoothly by compensating
for his beloved's behavior. For instance, in order to keep their
contact frequency at a constant level, if the one he loves begins
to call and visit him less, he will begin to call and visit his loved
one more. Or, in order to elicit the amount of intimate communication from his partner to which he has become accustomed, if
the one he loves begins to communicate through less intimate philemes, he will begin to communicate through more intimate philemes, forcing his partner to match his raise.

> Love is not love
> Which alters when it alteration finds,
> Or bends with the remover to remove.
> O, no! it is an ever-fixed mark,
> That looks on tempests and is never shaken.[25]

Should his beloved be actively attempting to bring down their
association, however, his efforts to keep it up will contort him to
an increasingly agonized degree. The more he must bear sole responsibility for upholding the relationship, the more he must
lower himself. It is no easy matter for a person to maintain his
dignity while bending over backward to maintain his intimacy.

"Strength" is the term used for the unloved lover's ability to
put up with his unloving beloved's repulses, which increase the
relationship's costs for him, in order to retain its benefits ("O
Lord, give me strength to make it work"). Suffer for his beloved
the true lover will, but leave unbidden—never! Eventually, however, even he may reach the point where he can demean his demeanor no further and must initiate the have-it-out that he fears
may eventuate in termination talk. "Strength" is also the term
used for the unloved lover's ability to endure the loss of the re-

lationship's benefits, which he must give up in order to free himself from its increasingly intolerable costs ("O Lord, Give me strength to break it off").

Should the unloved lover not find the strength to kill off the affair and seem to have no minimum level of self-respect below which he cannot debase himself, the unloving beloved may take pity on him enough to be the one who initiates the termination. If the case in which the rejectee takes the initiative to terminate the relationship may be called *relational suicide* (in that he is destroying a large but languishing part of his self as well), the case in which the rejector takes the initiative to terminate the relationship may be called *relational euthanasia*.

3. Zero-sided subsidence

The ending of an intimate relation may be abrupt, coming as a complete surprise to both participants. Neither may want it to end, but both may suddenly find they can no longer continue to be the intimates they once were. Suddenly, unexpectedly, one intimate breaks a basic provision of the microsocial contract that underlies their association[26]—a provision the other feels is so basic that he cannot continue the relationship. The two most fundamental and irreparable provisions of the contract between intimates are that each will not harm the other's essential being and that each will uphold the interaction rules of their relationship that have become obligatory.

The first kind of breach of contract occurs when a have-it-out gets out of hand. Proverbial injunctions to be careful to keep arguments with intimates under control are legion. "It is difficult to win a friend in a year," goes a Chinese proverb; "it is easy to lose one in an hour." A dispute between intimates can come to an unexpected conclusion when, during its course, one attacks the other with intent to injure and suddenly finds he has—much more than he intended. Since intimates know each other's essential weaknesses, they are in a position to wound each other in the worst possible way. But any actual use of these ultimate weapons may result in *overkill*. Anyone who assaults his intimate with them will find he has struck their relationship a mortal blow from which it will not recover, despite his best efforts to resuscitate it through his profuse apologies.

Propelled by passion, one intimate may say and do certain things during the course of an argument that cannot be unsaid and undone. He may point out certain flaws in his partner that suddenly, painfully, and indelibly become' part of the latter's self-image. The fault-finding of have-it-outs in which each intimate portrays the other's flaws as inherent and incorrectable ("You're so goddam fat and ugly!") differs from the fault-finding of work-it-outs in which each intimate portrays the other's flaws as merely contingent and therefore correctable ("I think you should start taking better care of yourself. You've started to put on a little weight recently"). Or he may insult his partner's self-respect by categorizing him wholly by one of his lowly valued social statuses ("You goddam nigger [or kike, wop, etc.]!"). Or he may insult his partner by imputing to him a lowly valued social status that he does not even have ("You goddam bastard [or bitch, mother-fucker, etc.]!"). He may physically attack and attempt to destroy one of his partner's prized self-objectifications—pulling over her husband's record collection in a fit of rage, a wife stomps on the scattered albums, shattering discs and crumpling covers.[27] Or he may assault and attempt to batter that most accessible embodiment of his partner's self—his body. The party who feels that the attack on his self-conception, his self-respect, or his self-particularizations has penetrated into his essential being will be unwilling to continue to be the intimate of someone he had trusted not to wound him so deeply ("This time you've gone too far!").

Not all these attacks, of course, pierce a person to his core. The whereabouts of one's core varies with the person and, even for the same person, with the time. Even intimates, who know each other well, are likely to mistake the location of each other's shifting essences. Consequently, both the insulter and the injured can variously evaluate the effect of the same assault. One attackee may laugh off a slap; another (or the same one at a different time) may feel fatally struck. One attacker may expect his slap to be merely shrugged off; another may expect it to be lethal. The ambiguity of the effect of an assault allows the attacker to try to save the relationship by claiming in his apology that he was unaware that the vulnerable area in question had been designated a *demilitarized zone* when the treaty establishing their relationship was ratified[28] ("I'm sorry. I didn't mean it. I didn't know it would hurt you so much").

The obligation to engage in or to refrain from certain interactions or behaviors that affect each other indirectly constitutes a second provision of their compact, and a violation immediately voids their relationship. I have pointed out that intimates do not always observe their obligations to each other, but when they do not, they are careful to hide this nonobservance from each other. For instance, one intimate may maintain the appearance that he can be counted on for favors while dodging the doing of a particular favor by seeming to be out when the other comes or calls to ask for it. Or he may maintain the appearance that he is commited to exclusiveness while playing around with a multiplicity of mistresses by being discreet. However, it sometimes happens that his transgression techniques malfunction: his precautions prove inadequate, and the knowledge that he was not living up to his relationship obligations gets back to the other. Unless he can then excuse or explain his infraction of one of the fundamental rules of their relationship, his ability to abide by any of them is called into question. His intimate, unwilling to risk a close association with someone whose allegiance can no longer be assured, will immediately call off their relationship ("I'm certainly not going to associate with anyone who can't be trusted!").

In general, once one intimate has ruptured the relationship by breaking one of the basic articles of faith on which it rested (e.g., by being unfaithful), the other cannot take him back—no matter how much he may want to—and still maintain his self-respect. In other words, the offended party must choose between saving face and saving the relationship; unless he is so dependent on the continuance of the association that he will pay any psychological price to keep it going, he will usually find it easier to end the relationship than to reperceive himself as someone who permits himself to be crossed.

A relationship fractured in this way can be healed only if the wrongdoer can convince the offended party of his own ultimate innocence, and thus allow the dishonored to retain both his dignity and his intimacy. The wrong-doer may claim that the apparently infringed relationship rule was not actually basic or was not actually broken. Or he may claim that he did not know it was a rule, or that, though he did, he is now no longer the same person who broke it ("Oh, I've changed. I really have. Please take me back. I know better now. I would never do it again").

There are two other causes of the sudden cessation of an intimate relation; they do not concern its fundamental contract, insofar as this covenant was created without the knowledge of these factors. First, the intimates may come upon something in their common environment, such as a job or an award, that they both want but both cannot have. Their consequent competition will tear their relationship apart. One of the most common detonators that cause friendships to fission is a third party of the opposite sex whose single slotted opening for lover or spouse each friend would like to fill. Second, the intimates may also come upon something within themselves, such as an extreme difference of opinion, that cannot coexist within the confines of a close relationship. Should an issue that is suddenly brought to their attention reveal their core values (i.e., values each feels is an essential constituent of his self) to be at variance, each may feel he cannot continue to be the intimate of anyone whose essential nature he now sees to be so contrary to his own. In the late 1960s, for instance, the student revolts were said to have broken up many faculty friendships of long standing.

Finally, I should like to add one more cause of the sudden death of an intimate relation—namely, the sudden death of one of the intimates. Unlike those discussed above, this unexpected conclusion of a close association avoids the final aria of the termination talk; like them, it involves the survivor in many of the anticlimactic concerns to be considered in the Complications section of this chapter.

Termination Talk

Intimates who are so sewn together on each dimension that they cannot go silently their separate ways must engage in meta-intimate conversation about their relationship in order to untie their connective threads. The topic of all meta-intimate conversations in established personal relations is the unraveling of the fabric of the affair. But *termination talk* differs from the other forms of *serious talk* discussed in the previous chapter in that the latter are directed toward pulling the loose ends of the association together, whereas termination talk is directed toward cutting it apart.

The peroration of the relation begins with an inventory of the reasons why it can no longer continue. Its potential has been killed by too many little conflicts or by one big conflict. The intimate who initiates the termination talk gives the other a selective summary of the history of their relationship, emphasizing these conflicts. If the intimate to whom this historical lecture is directed also wants their relationship ended, he will add confirming instances of his own; if, however, he wants their relationship to continue, he will dispute the other's data by claiming that the bad times the other cited were not so bad as all that, and what about all the good times they had, which the other did not mention.

(Since any intimate relation—like this book, like all things—has both bad aspects and good aspects, it can be made to seem all bad or all good by playing up the former while playing down the latter or vice versa. In fact, intimates are continually rewriting the history of their relationship: at its high points, they recall only the past periods when their cohesion was at its peak; at its low points, they recall only the past periods when their cohesion was at its ebb.)

Should both intimates agree to part, or should one be adamant about leaving the other, they must discuss the techniques by which their association can be concluded completely. Having snapped the potential to continue their relationship (1), they must now meticulously unscrew the connections on each of the other five dimensions holding it together. The following specific disconnections will be either discussed or understood. (2) They will not plan to meet again, and they will unwind their intersecting routines in order to cut down the frequency of their chance encounters. (Note that termination talks often begin when one intimate is trying to set up his next meeting with the other and the latter decides that he cannot take any more encounters with the former, for the toxins of a festering relationship flow fastest when the intimates are face-to-face.) (3) They will no longer use any intimate philemes in their linguistic and kinesic communication. (4) They will no longer try to elicit public, but especially private, information about themselves from each other, nor will they volunteer any information about themselves to each other. (5) They will no longer aid each other in their dealings with their environment, nor will they ask each other for any more aid. (6) They will crack open their intersubjective couples. Thus, they will break up their common objects by giving back each other's gifts or by getting "custody" or "possession" of unsplittable common objects, such as children and house furnishings. They will bisect their social circle by telling its members that they have broken up, by breaking up in front of them, or by no longer interacting as intimates in their presence. Finally, if necessary, they will move out (break common space) and sue for divorce (break common time).

A *farewell address*, which speaks to the issue of severing the ties within every dimension of an intimate relation, might run as follows: "We just can't go on like this! I don't want to see you again. I don't want to speak to you again. Don't ask me what I'm going to do. Don't ask me for any more favors. Here's your ring back. You can have the house and the furniture. I'll take the baby. You'll have to call Tim and Ann and tell them we won't be able to come to dinner. I'll stay at a hotel tonight and send over tomorrow for my personal belongings. And you'll be hearing from my lawyer within a week. We're through!"

These termination procedures are subject to variation along two axes. First, the intimates must decide whether to ease out of their relationship gradually, by cutting only some of their connections at first, or whether to break out of it cleanly, by cutting all ties at once. Specifically, they may discuss whether they will still communicate with each other by telephone or by letter even though they agree not to visit each other anymore, or whether they should not attempt to communicate with each other again at all. Furthermore, they may discuss whether their termination should be probationary or permanent. That is, they may decide to have a *probationary period* in which to see how well each can exist apart from the other before completely cutting their commitments, just as they had a previous *probationary period* in which they saw how well each could exist together with the other before actually making their commitments. In breaking their commitment to common space, in particular, they must choose between a trial separation and a final separation.

Second, they must determine what their postintimate relationship is going to be. Will they remain "friends" (a euphemism ex-intimates use for acquaintances), or will they become "strangers" (i.e., enemies)? When they meet by chance, will they acknowledge each other as though they were acquaintances in order to indicate that they bear no enmity, or will they ignore each other as though they were strangers in order to indicate that they are enemies? Will they continue to communicate with each other the way acquaintances do, or will they "excommunicate" each other the way strangers do and cease to be on speaking terms, let alone on touching terms? Will they maintain the private knowledge they possess about each other's secret weaknesses, or will they put it into the public domain in an attempt to destroy each other? Will they still be willing to perform some favors for each other under certain conditions, even if not so many as before (for instance, will they be willing to "lend a hand" in an emergency, even if they are no longer willing to "lend a genital," as was their custom), or will they refuse to perform any favors for each other under any conditions, or will they even begin to perform "negative favors" to each other by making each other's environment even harder for him to cope with? Finally, will they try to retain their mutual friends or force them to choose sides?

It often happens that the termination talk itself is harder to terminate than the relationship, should one not want to lose the other as his intimate. As soon as the one who wants to retain the relationship realizes that this is his last chance to say everything he can to save it, he may *filibuster* to delay the adjournment of the terminal talk for as long as possible, eventually forcing the other to call for *cloture* and thus twist the sinew-severing knife he wields still deeper.

COMPLICATIONS

Those whose intimacy passes away by degrees experience little difficulty in ending their relationship effortlessly, for they have time enough to adjust to their new level of association. But those who suddenly find their intimacy dead are haunted on every dimension of their erstwhile relationship by a host of problems.

1. Intimates may not be certain that they want to break up. Should they fail to sever completely their potential to keep their relationship going, however, they are sure to suffer sorely. Their relationship is likely to modulate into a particularly unsatisfying and unstable state, which may be called "perpetual check," to borrow a handy chess metaphor. In this state of perpetual check, the intimates will continue to oscillate in and out of their relationship by alternatively increasing and decreasing the intensity of the forces holding it together, because they find neither the in-position nor the out-position tolerable enough to remain there for long. As soon as they begin to cut themselves apart, they become aware of how much they need each other and how little they can stand solitude; as soon as they begin to paste themselves together again, they become aware of how little they can stand each other and how much they dislike their relationship. They have neither the strength to break it off nor the strength to make it work. They can neither live without each other nor live with each other. Furthermore, as they must now continually be deciding whether to oscillate in or to oscillate out, they will find it more difficult to choose between two exclusive alternative strategies—each of which leads to a different bad situation—than to have a single bad situation they are forced to make the best of. Specifically, they will find it more difficult, on one hand, to choose between adjusting to loneliness or adjusting to each other than, on the other hand, to get used to the fact that

the rupture of their relationship is irreversible. At the end of the affair, it is easier to live with no hope than with some hope.

2. Kinematically, intimates who break up must expend a great amount of psychological energy in order to change the path of their daily movement over space; otherwise, the social inertia of their routinized course will cause them to continue to come together. Phenomenologically, intimates who break up will discover that their warm times and warm places take quite a while to cool off, i.e., to cease to be meaning-generating centers of orientation in the temporal flow and spatial stretch of their life field. Ex-intimates will experience some of their most poignant moments when they pass through the times and places when and where they had experienced together the peak points of their relationship. This phenomenological schema of the experiential end of an intimate relation may be used to interpret the song "Sunday Will Never Be the Same," sung by *Spanky and Our Gang*, which was popular in the late 1960s:

> I remember Sunday morning,
> I would meet her at the park.
> We'd walk together hand in hand
> Till it was almost dark.
> Now I wake up Sunday morning,
> Walk across the way to find
> Nobody waiting for me.
> Sunday's just another day.
> Sunday will never be the same.
> I've lost my Sunday song;
> She'll not be back again.
> Sunny afternoons that made me
> Feel so warm inside
> Have turned as cold and grey as ashes
> As I feel the embers die.
> No longer can I walk these paths
> For they have changed.
> I must be on, the sun is gone
> And I think it's gonna rain.

.I remember children
Feeding flocks of pigeons;
I remember sunshine
And you were mine.[29]

In a poem entitled "The Remedies for Love," the Latin poet
Ovid suggests several strategies ex-lovers can use to cut their kinematic and phenomenological connections that would normally
separate more slowly. He advises the lover who wishes to forget
his beloved to avoid the old sources of orientation that remind
him of her and to acquire new ones that do not. In order for the
sight of his beloved not to rekindle his fading fire for her, he
should try to keep from running into her accidentally by staying
away from where she is likely to be found.[30] And in order for
him to become oriented elsewhere, he should try to lose himself
in his work[31] or in his other woes,[32] or he should acquire a friend
who will attempt to distract him.[33] "Flight" is perhaps Ovid's most
important suggestion,[34] for it is certainly a piece of advice that has
been reiterated to losing lovers throughout the ages. "In love," said
Napoleon, who was an expert on winning and losing in both the
battlefield and boudoir, "the only victory is flight." A lover can
break both the kinematic and phenomenological aspects of the
congregational bond that ties him to his beloved by traveling to
another city or country, for his trip puts an immediate end to
their cycles of copresence, giving his warm periods and places an
opportunity to cool off without his being around to stumble into
them again and get burnt. Although the mobility of modern
societies makes it harder to get into good personal relations, it
makes it easier to get out of bad ones. E. M. Forster, however,
points out that the ability to avail oneself of this relatively pain-
less technique to terminate a relationship is differentially distributed by class:

> The poor cannot always reach those whom they want to
> love, and they can hardly ever escape from those whom
> they love no longer. We rich can. Imagine the tragedy
> last June if Helen and Paul Wilcox had been poor people

and couldn't invoke railways and motor-cars to part them.[35]

Difficulty in getting completely away from ex-intimates is one of the unsung sufferings of the poor.

Until ex-intimates find someone else who will service their joys and sorrows, their every pleasure will be diminished and their every pain will be intensified, for such emotions will remind them that their ex-partners are no longer available to amplify the one and alleviate the other. Montaigne mourns this aspect of their relationship, which his friend's death has killed:

> I have dragged out but a languishing existence, and even such pleasures as come to me, far from consoling me, redouble my grief for his loss. We were equal partners in everything, and I seem to be robbing him of his share,
>
> 'I have resolved to enjoy no pleasures, while he is not here to share them with me.'[36]
>
> (Terence)

He who grieves in this way over his ex-intimate must eventually confront the paradox that it is precisely the mundane pleasures and pains themselves—which at first seem to sharpen the sense of loss—that will eventually erase its memory. Unwillingness to face this paradox, I think, accounts for the long duration of the sadness of T. E. Lawrence's servant, who chose to do without his pleasures rather than to recall the friend with whom he shared them:

> The two had been friends from childhood, in eternal gaiety: working together, sleeping together, sharing every scrape and profit with the openness and honesty of perfect love. So I was not astonished to see Faraj look dark and hard of face, leaden-eyed and old, when he came to tell me that his fellow was dead; and from that day till his service ended he made no more laughter for us.... The others offered themselve to comfort him, but instead

he wandered restlessly, grey and silent, very much alone.[37]

3. Intimates who have broken up will experience difficulty in communicating with others insofar as they have developed a private language of words and gestures they alone have understood. Ex-intimates who have restabilized their relationship as acquaintances, moreover, often feel uneasy and awkward with each other, in part because they must now signal acquaintance philemes where once they sent intimate ones. Thus, lovers who still remain friends after ending their affair must now inhibit their previous predispostions to put their hands all over each other and may now be uncertain exactly what else to do with their hands. This discrepancy between communication that had been customary and communication that is now required does not make for unselfconsciousness or spontaneity.

4. Intimates who have broken up may face problems concerning the old information about each other they possess or the new information about each other they might possess.

To take the most extreme instance, a lover will still be drawn to his beloved on the knowledge dimension as long as he continues to "idealize" her, i.e., to sharpen her good features and blur over her bad. In order to avoid feeling he was a fool to give up someone so wonderful without a greater fight, he must now begin to reconceptualize her. Ovid suggests several techniques a lover can use to re-view his beloved as not so wonderful as he had thought and therefore not so great a loss:

Try to remember her deeds, her wicked, wanton behavior,
    Itemize, if you can, all she has cost you to date.
"She has this, she has that, she is never content with her
    booty,
    Even my household gods have to be mortgaged or sold!
She has sworn me true, and played me false in the
    swearing.
    How many times I have spent nights on the stone at
    her door!

Others she loves, but me—? She is much too nice to be
    bothered.
Any old peddler can have nights she refuses to me."
Let such memories set your feelings in gall and in worm-
    wood,
    Never forget to sow seeds of contempt in your mind.

. . .

One thing did me some good, a most repetitious insistence
    On every one of her faults; that brought effective relief.
I would say, "Look at her legs; did you ever see any that
    ugly?"
(That was a lie; her legs really weren't ugly at all.)
"What a runt!" (She was tall.) "How much she demands
    of a lover!"
    (That had a trace of the truth; that, mostly, helped me
    to hate.)

. . .

If she has full round breasts, call her *fat as a pig*; if she's
    slender
    Thin as a rail; if she's dark, *black as the ace of spades.*
If she has city ways, label her *stuck-up* and *bitchy*;
    If she is simple and good, call her *a hick from the farm.*

. . .

Sometimes it works very well to surprise her early some
    morning,
    Hardly expecting a call, when she's not fixed for the
    day.

. . .

What of the man who lay hid, and watched while the
    girl was performing
    Rites that custom forbids masculine eyes to behold?
God forbid that I should offer my patients such counsel!

. . .

So, compare your girl with the ones who really are
    beauties—
    It will be only a while till you regard her with shame.

. . .

Don't compare looks alone, but also character, talent,
Only, don't let your love bias the verdict you give.[38]

Ex-intimates will also still be drawn to each other as long as
each retains his desire to keep his cognitive portrait of the other
up-to-date. His curiosity about the other's activities, and especially
about the other's current opinion of him and of their relationship,
is notoriously slow to abate. For instance, a lover may continue
to thirst after knowledge about an old flame who left town long
ago, particularly information about interpersonally important transitions in *sociability status,* such as whether she has acquired a
new boy friend or has gotten married ("She married *him!*?"), for
these transitions affect the ever-lingering if small possibility of a
renewed affair as well as his ex-beloved's identity ("So that's what
she turned out to be!") and ultimately his own self-conception
("What an idiot I was to let her go!"). Usually, ex-intimates continue to acquire bits and pieces of information about each other
over the years by interrogating mutual friends and acquaintances.
Each ex-intimate cannot be too curious, however, for fear that the
news will get back to the other that his interest (and hence his
long for a revived relationship) still lives. It seems to be an
unwritten rule that a person demeans himself in wanting to resuscitate a relationship that has officially expired.

5. In Chapter 5, I showed how the intimates of an individual
function for him as another hand, eye, skin, etc., aiding his transactions with his environment. Here I would like to add that when
an intimacy is suddenly concluded, especially through the death of
one of the participants, each ex-intimate often describes the severing of their relationship in terms of the loss of a limb, that is, in
terms of the loss of an organ that made his environmental transactions easier ("He was my right hand. I don't know what I'll do
without him"). Sometimes, an individual who has lost his intimate
(like an individual whose leg has been amputated) still feels the
presence of his intimate (or his leg) and imagines him (or it) still
to be there and still to be capable of functioning for him as usual.

And it is only when he tries to act (or stand) on this false assumption that he falls into the nauseating awareness that what he had felt was only a *phantom limb* ("I know you're there, Wayne. Why don't you answer me? Why don't you answer me!").

An individual who has lost his intimate will often seek out his other, lesser, personal relations in order to try to obtain from them the services his intimate used to supply, especially such psychological ones as "support" (see Chapter 5). The end of an intimacy, therefore, will increase the stress on the ex-intimates' other personal relations, insofar as they are now called upon to supply services they are neither able, nor willing, to provide.

6. The intersubjective couples between intimates are the hardest bonds for them to break. Inner connections are always the most difficult and dangerous to disconnect.

Intimates may have so harmonized their conduct, their cognitions, their concerns, etc., that each discovers he cannot easily interact with others. He may have become so used to his intimate in these ways that he discovers he cannot readily readjust these aspects of himself to anyone else. He may have constructed with his old intimate so complex a common culture that he discovers he cannot completely rebuild one of equal intricacy with anyone new without spending months—even years—at the task.

Nor can ex-intimates easily detach themselves from the common past they shared. Remembrances of their relationship continue to haunt them, especially at night. But though ex-intimates cannot consciously obliterate the memory of their common past, they may be able to accelerate its natural period of decay. Two contrary strategies have been offered. On the one hand, Ovid suggests starving it to death by avoiding any revitalizing stimuli:

> Don't read over again those fondly cherished old letters;
>   Letters read over again move the most obdurant minds.
> Put them all in the fire, however reluctant your spirit,
>   Say, as you put them there, "This is the pyre of my
>   love."

· · ·

If you can do it, remove, as well, her portrait, or likeness;
Why let an image, mute, rouse the regret in your heart?
Places that say no word can hurt you; better avoid them,
Give them no chance to suggest days that are over and
gone,
Telling you, "Here she lay; we slept in that bedroom
together,
That was the place where, at night, she gave me
boundless delight."
Love is renewed afresh, and the wounds made worse, by
remembrance;
If you are weak you can be hurt by the slightest mistake.
Just as an ember, all gray, will crimson under the sulphur,
Springing to life again, flaming to ardor and fire,
So, unless you avoid whatever rekindles your passion,
Flames which were all but out presently flare up
again.[39]

On the other hand, Stendhal suggests indulging it to death by
gorging as much revitalizing stimuli as possible:

So far from trying to distract the lover bluntly and
openly, the rescuing friend should talk to him of his love
and of his mistress ad nauseam.... In order that absence
may be of any use, the rescuing friend ought always to
be on the spot to make the lover reflect as much as possible on the incidents of his love affair, and to try to make
these reflections boring by their length or inappropriate-
ness.[40]

If their remembered common past creates problems for ex-intimates because it is so difficult to destroy, their anticipated common future creates problems for ex-intimates because its destruction is so devastating. Suddenly gone is the temporal orientation
point of their future life together, which had provided so solid an
anchor for their phantasies. Cut adrift from his future plans, on
which much of the meaning of his present activities had de-

pended, each ex-intimate often begins to paddle aimlessly through the routines of his existence, which now seem pointless.

It is also difficult for intimates who are breaking up to break out of the social circle that encompasses them. Every member of their daily round defines them as intimates, creating another bond that holds them together. If the couple wish to separate completely, they must change this definition. From Lenny Bruce:

> And if you broke up and you go anywhere alone, there's always *momzas* that ask about your wife. Which is really a hang-up. Especially if you've been married about, well, ten years, say. And you're very tight with your old lady—you'd go everywhere together. And now, you start to go places solo—whether it's a supermarket, laundromat, or a Chinese restaurant:
> "Where's the missus?"
> "Oh, I got divorced—"
> There's an embarrassed silence, while the guy'll identify you—
> "Oh, you're a lovely couple. You should get together. She'll come back to ya."
> "Can I have my stamps? Yeah, I just wanna get the hell outta here."
>
> Chinese restaurant. Same waiter, week after week, for ten years. First time you go in alone, the waiter goes:
> CHINESE VOICE: "Where's maw-maw? How come you don't bring maw-maw in?
> Maw-maw sicka? Ah so, maw-maw velly sick. You better bring maw-maw home some cookies. Tell maw-maw say hello. Tell her say hello to her."
> "I'm divorced."
> "*Ohhhh. You bettuh awf.*"
> You bettuh awf. Christ, that's really going with the winner. What's he tell her?[41]

Breakups, even more than fights, have a negative effect on the interaction between the intimates and their social group. Not only does any failure to make their relationship work reflect adversely on their group reputation as competent interpersonal relators, but the collapse of their relationship also subjects to stress every member of the social group that held it together. Each ex-intimate may put every member of their social group who is involved in both sides of their relationship under opposing pressure to commit himself totally to one side or the other. Every group member, moreover, will find the polarizing confrontations between the ex-intimates to be especially agonizing whenever they are carried on jaw-to-jaw in his presence. Consequently, he is continually concerned with keeping them apart (for instance, by not inviting them to the same party) or, if he cannot, at least containing their conflict (for instance, by stepping between them should they come to blows). The physical battering he may receive while trying to separate them is merely a concrete manifestation of the psychological battering to which their breakup has already subjected him.

In Chapter 6, I showed that much of an individual's unique identity is created by his intimate insofar as the latter serves as the reference point against which he contrasts himself. When he breaks up with his intimate, therefore, his identity is threatened until he finds a new "specified other" to take the place of his intimate as his point of reference or until his old specified other gradually diffuses back into a "generalized other." In the meantime, however, he is likely to be confused and incoherent because he can no longer orient and clarify his thoughts vis-à-vis his accustomed conversation partner. He is usually aware that his thinking is deteriorating because his customary internalized conversations with his former intimate will never be externalized again, but he still cannot get his former intimate "off his mind."

Finally, intimates who break up will find their commitments to each other difficult to break apart because, as noted in Chapter 6, they were specifically designed to be difficult to break apart. The exclusiveness of their intimacy has made it difficult for each partner to be acquainted with others with whom to begin a new relationship. The common space they have created has made it difficult for one or both partners to move out and set up house elsewhere. And the common future they have forged through marriage has made it difficult for both partners to go through the complex and costly disengagement procedures of divorce.

What is the consequence of the collapse of all these intimate bonds? There is a good chance that the interpersonal breakup of a personal relation will lead to the intrapersonal breakdown of the persons involved. We have seen that those who become intimates so intertwine their selves and lives that they become a larger social, if not actually organic, unit. Should this unit suddenly disintegrate, each ex-intimate will feel he has been separated from half of himself. Montaigne concludes his eulogy of his dead friend thus:

> I have grown so accustomed to be his second self in everything that now I seem to be no more than half a man.

> 'If a premature death has taken away the half of my life, why should I, the other half, linger on, since I love myself less and have not survived whole? The same day destroyed us both.' (Horace)[42]

Each intimate has molded the other into the way he is and lives, and consequently constitutes part of the glue that holds him together, that keeps the various aspects of his self and life organized into a coherent whole. If it is the case—as I have contended in this book it is—that an individual who becomes the intimate of another gives up the smaller integrity of his individuality for the larger integrity of his intimacy, then we will expect that the decomposition of an intimate relation will lead to the decomposition of the intimates. Recalling the effect of the end of an affair on the ex-intimates we have known—and perhaps, too, on ourselves—should convince us that intimates who have "split up" sociologically are more than likely to "go to pieces" psychologically ("It's really sad. Ever since his wife left him, he's been all broken up about it").

Conclusion

IN PART ONE of this book, I attempted to describe how individuals construct an intimate relation: (1) the ways in which strangers lay the groundwork for a potentially close relationship by making each other's acquaintance; (2) the ways in which acquaintances who are becoming intimates set up cycles of corporeal copresence; (3) the ways in which they escalate intensity-indicating communications; (4) the ways in which they reciprocate increasing quantities of public and confidential information; (5) the ways in which they exchange greater and greater amounts of environment-alleviating aid; and (6) the ways in which they integrate more and more of their basic being. In Part II, I attempted to describe how an intimate relation, once constructed, is preserved and may eventually be destroyed: (7) the techniques those who have become intimates use to reintegrate their ever-disintegrating relationship; and, finally, (8) the causes that may ultimately wreck their relationship and the consequences of its collapse on those who built it. In general, I have attempted to enumerate the essential characteristics of an intimate relation throughout all phases of its existence: from birth, through maturity, to sickness and death.

To discuss an intimate relation in terms of the organic analogy of its conception, growth, decay, and destruction, however, is to use more than a mere metaphor, for what was begun as the deliberate construction of individual human beings soon acquires a literal life of its own. The architectural model must, therefore, be superseded by the biological. An intimate relation is a living thing insofar as it becomes a distinguishable, self-maintaining unit that drags around its occasionally unwilling creators in order to sustain its own existence, and that causes them to suffer great agony should it suddenly be wrenched apart. Whatever instinctual, emotional, or rational considerations induce a pair of individuals to procreate an intimate relation, its processes shortly acquire an inertia or structure of their own apart from its motivating force; and whenever this original vitalizing psychological impulse dies away, those who once were intimates may find the vitiated sociological skeleton of their relationship to be difficult to dismantle.

It is this fundamental if fragile social unit of the *intimate relation* that I have hoped here to establish as a domain of rigorous scientific inquiry without demeaning its aesthetic delicacy. Specifically, I have tried here to gather together enough empirical and theoretical materials involving intimacy to constitute a science of intimate relations—a subfield of sociology I have called PHILEMICS—which will investigate them both systematically and sensitively. The ordering of the profusion of empirical materials that I have made is only a preliminary one. I have attempted merely to induce concepts that discriminate the distinguishing features of the intimate relation—which at first seems so amorphous and protean a phenomenon—and to lay out the major dimensions along which these concepts are clustered. I have no theory of intimacy to offer, but only those of its variables that future theorists of intimacy may wish to take into account in constructing one. Much more empirical work, of course, remains to be done before this theoretical task can be fruitfully undertaken. Here are a few suggestions for further lines of research:

1. In order that the investigation of intimate relations cease to rely on the insightful but uneven productions of novelists and aphorists, case studies of particular relationships should be collected. Something between personal biography and social history

is needed. Since I have claimed here that intimate relations are as fundamental a unit of social life as individuals or institutions, we must have concrete chronicles of their course, focusing especially on such critical points as their origin, termination, transitions to higher and lower levels, outside influences, internal crises, and connections with the biographies of each of their participants, on the one side, and with the history of their society, on the other.

2. One means to understand intimacy is to discover how individuals are socialized into it. Further studies should be undertaken of how people come to learn what behaviors are appropriate for intimates and what behaviors are appropriate for nonintimates. Another means to understand intimacy is to look at those who fail to learn its ways properly: the lonely, the friendless, the losers in love. Still another means is to examine those who learn its ways all too well and use their knowledge to exploit their intimates: the roués who sexually exploit their loves, the con men who economically exploit their friends.

3. If the body of this book may be called a *microsociology*, it should be augmented by a *micropolitics* that stresses the strategies individuals employ to sustain their intimate relations while controlling their course.[1]

4. Since I have tried to portray only the normal pattern of intimate relations, its deviations still need to be described. (We may be assured that some pattern of intimate relations is considered "normal"—either in the sense of modal or stereotypical—by observing that intimates who vary from this pattern seem to recognize that they are straying from something standard, insofar as they find their divergence interesting and reportable. For instance, if cross-sexed intimates normally commit themselves to exclusiveness with each other before establishing common space, those who live together while still being allowed to date others will consider this feature of their affair to be worth mentioning whenever they discuss their relationship with third parties.)

The future of intimate relations? But prophecy has its perils, for the Owl of Minerva, blinded by the increasingly dazzling possibilities, usually loses its way whenever it tries to take wing at dawn. Nevertheless, two factors that will affect this future may dimly be distinguished: technological changes and social changes.

Most previous technological developments, such as trains and telephones, have facilitated the copresence and communication of intimates. But one imminent technological change may facilitate mutual monitoring too much. It appears that in the not too distant future we will all have telephones or even videophones that will be small enough to be carried around easily. Unfortunately, these portable communication systems will neutralize some of the contrivances we all use at one time or another to retard our interaction with our intimates without rending our relationships with them. At present, we can protect our privacy while maintaining our potential accessibility simply by not answering the telephone or doorbell, for our failure to respond in this case implies only that we certainly would have answered had we but been home to do so. In other words, it was only the accidental fact that we were not near our stationary communication systems that kept us from welcoming our intimates' attempts to get in touch with us. But when portable communication systems become our constant companions, we will have no such innocent excuse for not answering their ring; for whoever endeavors to contact us then will know that we are always carrying our receivers in our pockets. Should he ever be unable to get through to us, he will know it was because of our deliberate decision, for which we must bear full responsibility. Unless a new etiquette develops for the use of these portable phones, they will disrupt the subtle deceits that help to regulate the rhythms of solitude and sociability, the dynamics of all intimate relations.

Intimate relations in the future will also be affected by changes in the larger society. The cultural movement of the hippies and neo-rustics, the political movement of the New Left and liberation groups, and the psychological movement of the Encounter and Sensitivity schools constitute three types of social change whose influence on ordinary intimate relations is likely to grow (regardless of whether the movements themselves disappear). Many people have become members of these movements in order to avoid some of the problems of intimate relations in gesellschaft society noted in the Complications sections of the previous chapters. All of these gemeinschaftlike organizations emphasize relations among persons in groups rather than relations between persons in pairs. Each of these neo-communities, however, attempts to improve the quality of the relationships among their members in different ways. The cultural communes of the hippies and neo-rustics attempt to ensure the solidarity of their constituency by enhancing their common natural environment, endeavoring to make it more positive through the use of sensitizing drugs and through a retreat to beautiful natural surroundings. The political associations of the New Left and liberation movements attempt to ensure the solidarity of their constituency by deteriorating their common social environment, endeavoring to make it more negative through provoking selected functionaries in it and confronting the latter's repressive responses. The psychological groups of the Encounter and Sensitivity schools attempt to ensure the solidarity of their constituency by both deteriorating and enhancing their common internal structure, endeavoring first to make it more negative through intensifying the usual obstacles to intragroup communication, and then to make it more positive through overcoming these artifically intensified barriers. The rapid (if short-run) growth of these movements testifies to the effectiveness of these techniques in increasing the interpersonal pleasures of those who use them relative to the customary interpersonal pains of modern mass society. But how these and other social changes will affect the above-noted and other technological changes, and vice versa, as well as what their combined effect on the future of intimate relations will be, are presently impossible to predict.

There remains the task of locating these explorations of intimate relations in the province of social thought and in the more general realms of intellectual life.

The perspective on intimate relations put forward on these pages differs in certain respects from the customary psychological perspective and from the customary sociological perspective.

Psychologists, from classical Freudian to ultramodern T-group theorist, work from roughly the following propositions: (1) An individual has a drive or instinct for intimacy with others that is at bottom biological; (2) further, since an individual is a biological entity that is psychologically separate from others, he cannot actually be harmed by others biopsychologically; (3) consequently, whatever biopsychological pains he experiences in intimate relations are imaginary, or, at any rate, self-induced; (4) therefore, his fear of getting hurt in intimacy is irrational and ought to be overcome; (5) in praxis, since all intimacy is beneficial for an individual, he should not be afraid to become intimate with anyone.

For my part, on the contrary, I have proceeded from the following propositions: (1) an individual has a need or impulse for intimacy with others that is basically derived from social sources and historical conditions; (2) further, since an individual is a social entity that is not psychologically separate from others (for in intimacy, at least, he fuses essential segments of his self and life with theirs), he can actually be harmed (sometimes fatally) by others social-psychologically;[2] (3) consequently, whatever social-psychological pains he experiences in intimate relations are real; (4) therefore, his fear of getting hurt in intimacy is rational and ought to be enhanced (in the sense that he ought to be better able to distinguish those with whom an intimate relation would be ontologically dangerous for him); (5) in praxis, since indiscriminate intimacy is unsafe for an individual, he should be careful with whom he becomes intimate.

Sociologists seek the major determinants of a person's behavior in factors external to him (as opposed to inherent in him, though these external factors may be internalized), usually either in his general social statuses, which the structural-functionalist school of sociology emphasizes, or in his particular situations, which the symbolic-interactionist school of sociology emphasizes.[3] Here, however, I have claimed that his level of intimacy with his interaction partners has an effect on his behavior that is sociological in the sense of being essentially external to him, but is independent from the effects of his general statuses and of his particular situations. The more intimate the relationship, in fact, the more it generates its own moral reality that may, and often does, contradict other moral realities. The more intense the intimate relation, in other words, the more it can direct the intimates' behavior away from the behavioral imperatives of their statuses and situations. Intimacy, then, frees individuals from the tyranny of their sociological determinants—in particular, from the behaviors required by their statuses and situations whose normative rules they had no hand in making. Individuals who are isolated—either actually alone or effectively alone in stranger, role-, and acquaintance relations—have little choice but to obey the rules of their statuses and situations; only individuals who are intimates have the leverage (and courage) to break these normative decrees by playing off against them the rules of their own relationship. Since intimates themselves are responsible for the passing of these latter laws, they do not seem to them nearly so oppressive (most of the time[4]), for when individuals act in accordance with their own commands, they feel they are acting in accordance with themselves.[5]

How those who are becoming intimate come to set up the rules of their relationships, then, is a topic worthy of further sociological investigation. Recently, we have been witnessing, on the macrolevel, the supplementation of the static structural-functional analysis of institutional relations with a dynamic structuralism designed to account for their transformations. We ought now also to supplement, on the microlevel, the static symbolic-interactional analysis of interpersonal relations with an *evolutionary interactionism* designed to account for their development into something more.[6] For truly, intimacy is the child of interaction.

Expanding our vision beyond the borders of social inquiry, we can see unexpected isomorphisms between certain features of intimate relations and certain features of physical phenomena. On the one hand, laymen have often drawn on conceptions of natural processes to describe their interpersonal processes. For instance, they often talk about their "attraction," "repulsion," "friction," and "splitting up." On the other hand, natural philosophers have often described nature in interpersonal metaphors. For instance, Empedocles supposed "love" and "strife" to be the basic forces of nature, and early modern chemists like E. F. Geoffroy discussed chemical combinations in terms of the "affinity" of the component substances. Moreover, the same conceptual framework (consisting of various attractive forces) that has been so successful in classifying many observations in physics seems to be equally successful in classifying many observations in sociology. The six social forces that hold people together, which I have tried to describe in this book, seem to have the same fundamental stature in social science as the four natural forces that hold matter together[7] have in natural science. To account for these surprising similarities between social and natural processes, however, would take us into the sociology of knowledge or the philosophy of life—in either case, far beyond the boundaries of this book. It is best merely to note their presence, and pass on.

Finally, we have seen how each of the isolated individuals of mass society attempts to merge himself with others in order to recapture something of the satisfactions, security, self-stability, and selflessness his ancestors had obtained from the small communities in which they were submerged. We can now observe the remarkable resemblance between the social immersion of the individual in an intimacy and the mystic immersion of the individual in the universe. Individuals attempt to find in intimate relations the same things the devout attempt to find in the divine, and they use the same techniques to attain the one as to attain the other: the focusing of undirected yearning, the coming upon his (His) presence in sacred places, the ritual communications, the esoteric knowledge, the earthly benefits and inner resources, and ultimately the communion, contrariety, and commitment. So, too, a close relation with an intimate can be as fickle and frail, as in need of continual atonement and affirmation, as a close relation with the infinite. And both are subject to the same sorts of terminations, ranging from secularization and indifference in the one extreme to suffering and indignity in the other.

Today, in fact, many people actually consider their intimate relations to be a substitute for their celestial relations, and treat the former with the degree of awe and reverence as had heretofore been reserved solely for the latter.[8] Some of these people have complained to me that any sociology of intimacy such as I am attempting, which seems to secularize what they consider sacred, is somehow sacrilegious and should be condemned. But I say unto you "philophilers" who love love[9] that you should allow us "philosophers" who love truth a little leeway for our own amourous pursuits. We mean no harm. Allow us, friends—if I may call you that by now—the freedom to find our own path to perfection in whatever place we can. The corridors to the cosmos are many. There are more ways to the One than one.

Endnotes

INTRODUCTION

1. I chose to refer to my topic with the term "intimacy" because it had the widest reference for close interpersonal relations of any English term I could find—inclusive in particular of both friendship and love—even though it had the drawback of also implying the most intense aspect of these relations, whereas I intend to discuss their less intense aspects as well. I will use "intimacy" in approximately the same inclusive sense in which Martin Oswald, the translator and editor of Aristotle, *Nicomachean Ethics* (Indianapolis: Bobbs-Merrill, 1962), 214*n.*, claims the Greeks used "Philia": "The connotations of 'philia' are considerably wider than those of 'friendship'. . . . It designates the relationship between a person and any other person(s) or being which that person regards as peculiarly his own and to which he has a peculiar attachment. For example, in Homer . . . ['philia'] is frequently used . . . to describe the relation to one's wife and children. In [this] sense, [we] would [not] speak of 'friendship' in English. But, of course, as in English, the term also expresses (from Hesiod on) the relationship to a person to which one feels especially attached, i.e., to a 'friend.' On the other side of the scale, 'philia' constitutes the bond that holds the members of any association together, regardless of whether the association is the family, the state, a club, a business partnership, or even the business relation between buyer and seller.

Here again, we would not use the term 'friendship' in English, but expressions such as 'harmony' or 'good will.' "

2. "This entering of the whole undivided ego into the relationship may be more plausible in friendship than in love for the reason that friendship lacks the specific concentration upon one element which love derives from its sensuousness. . . . [Though] for most people, sexual love opens the doors of the total personality more widely than does anything else . . . the preponderance of the erotic bond may suppress . . . the opening-up of those reservoirs of the personality that lie outside the erotic sphere."—Georg Simmel, *The Sociology of Georg Simmel*, tr. K. Wolff (Glencoe: Free Press, 1950), 325.

3. On the minimal interactions between strangers, see Erving Goffman's notion of "civil inattention" in *Behavior in Public Places* (New York: Free Press, 1963), 83–88.

4. The standard work on this transition is Ferdinand Tonnies, *Community and Society*, tr. and ed. C. Loomis (New York: Harper, 1963). The essential features of the two types of gemeinschaften that Tonnies distinguishes are common spatial location, common culture ("geist"), and either common kinship or common work or calling. The conception of gemeinschaft implicit in my own discussion is somewhat more differentiated. See also Robert Nisbet, *The Sociological Tradition* (New York: Basic Books, 1965), 47–106, for related basic references, and Maurice Stein, *The Eclipse of Community* (New York: Harper, 1960), for contemporary American developments.

5. Robert Nisbet, *ibid.*, 101, in his discussion of Georg Simmel, remarks: "Just as the breakdown of traditional class structure makes men aware for the first time of the complexities and nuances of status, so the rupture of community leaves men preoccupied by the nature of friendship, the allowable boundaries of intimacy, the canons of discretion, and the limits of loyalty."

6. In fact, most novels, as opposed to other forms of literature, focus on personal relations. Ian Watt, in *The Rise of the Novel* (Berkeley: University of California Press, 1964), 185, points out, "The world of the novel is essentially the world of the modern city; both present a picture of life in which the individual is immersed in private and personal relationships because a larger communion with nature or society is no longer available."

7. This is not to say there was no individuality or role-playing in

the community, but only that whatever protoforms there were then are vastly more articulated today.

8. E. M. Forster, *Howard's End* (New York, Vintage, 1958), 261. See also Watt, *op. cit.*, 177, 185–186.

9. Guy Swanson, "The Routinization of Love: Structure and Process in Primary Relations," in S. Klausner, ed., *The Quest for Self-Control* (New York: Free Press, 1965), reviewing the work of J. Sarma and S. N. Eisenstadt, summarizes thus: "Both interpret the rise of friendship as signifying a relation which helps particular individuals in complex societies to thread their way among the many groups and institutions which make demands on their allegiance and which, often, set conflicting requirements for their behavior. The problem each individual faces has multiple facets which change from time to time, requiring a comparable many-sided and adaptable relationship to mediate them."

CHAPTER 1

1. This chapter is intended to supplement Erving Goffman's ground-breaking observations in *Behavior in Public Places* (New York: Free Press, 1963), especially Chapter 8, "Engagements Among the Unacquainted." Whereas Goffman focuses on those who are accosted and their fears, I will focus on those who accost others and their hopes.

2. The allure of a person's manifest qualifiers is the product of hereditary givens and (mostly, as fashion advertisements and magazines would have us believe) conscious creation. All fashion, in fact, is an attempt to mediate between natural endowment and socially valued appearance. More particularly, an individual makes up, grooms, ornaments, and dresses himself to appeal to the aesthetic standards of a certain social group, implicitly claiming to possess the less visible qualifiers valued by this group—in other words, to tempt all the members of this group to want to become his intimate.

3. Plutarch, *The Lives of the Noble Grecians and Romans*, tr. J. Dryden (New York: Random House, n.d.), 99–100 (stylistic emendations added).

4. Pierre Choderlos de Laclos, *Dangerous Liaisons*, tr. L. Bair (New York: Bantam Books, 1962), 175–176.

5. J. P. Donleavy, *The Ginger Man* (New York: Berkley, 1965), 22.
6. *Ibid.*, 22–23.
7. Helen Gurley Brown, *Sex and the Single Girl* (New York: Pocket Books, 1962), 55–56.
8. The first of these studies was J. H. S. Bossard, "Residential Propinquity as a Factor in Marriage Selection," *American Journal of Sociology*, XXXVIII (1932), 210–224. See Robert Winch, *The Modern Family* (New York: Holt, Rinehart & Winston, 1963), 324*n.*, for others.
9. An article in *The New York Times*, 4/6/69, 49, entitled "Young Unmarrieds Find a New Way of Life," reports the following: "The South Bay Clubs are a string of nine garden apartment complexes in California limited to single people between the ages of 21 and 40, but they sometimes seem more like cruise ships. ... When a resident gets married he is required to leave. ... Life in Los Angeles can be ... difficult, especially for the shy newcomer. There are no central business districts and no built-up apartment areas where young people gravitate. Practically everyone is from somewhere else. ... And few have relatives or school friends to fall back on. 'They're all strangers in some way,' said Ludmilla Anderson, the bubbly manager of the Mid-Wilshire South Bay Club. ... Doran Christie, a pixieish, dark-eyed girl from Bernardsville, N.J. ... and her roommate ... were playing pool together [at the South Bay Club] one evening. Unattached residents casually wandered in and out the brightly lit room. Several men stopped by and chatted, a few gave advice on how to hold a pool cue. 'This is a more relaxed atmosphere,' said Doran. 'You can be friends with people here. And you know they're not married,' she added with a grin."
10. "A person may deliberately seek out a particular alter because alter's personal or impersonal reputation suggests that he could provide role-support for a particular identity and would perhaps be a source of other rewards. Or other parties may 'bring the two together' on the basis of their reputations, for example, in the widespread practice of introducing eligible men and women to each other. ... The importance of reputation in bringing people together is often underestimated, for we seldom enter into sociable

encounters without already knowing something about alter."
G. McCall and J. Simmons, *Identities and Interactions* (New
York: Free Press, 1966), 180–181.

11. When members of one social category devalue the members of
the category against which they define themselves and fail to
socialize new members into their own category properly, the
new members will consider the members of the devalued second
category (who embody all the evil in the world, as far as the older
members of the first category are concerned) to be attractive
associates. Thus the appeal of lower-class blacks to young middle-
class whites.

12. Tamotsu Shibutaini, *Improvised News* (Indianapolis: Bobbs-
Merrill, 1966), 34, 100.

13. Georg Simmel, "Sociology of the Senses; Visual Interactions,"
reprinted in R. Park and E. Burgess, *Introduction to the Science
of Sociology* (Chicago: University of Chicago Press, 1921), 360.

14. "Single clubs: Where to meet the girl next door," *Boston After
Dark*, 9/18/68. However, Doran Christie, the girl quoted in
The New York Times (see note 9), goes on to complain that
these single clubs, at least those of the first variety, are not as
good for acquiring personal relations as they claim. Although
these clubs excel at overcoming clearance problems, they make it
difficult both to sustain a conversation around integrating topics
and to evaluate each other's total self from what they see of each
other's come-on self. "Manhattan Beach is a big place to meet
guys, but you're going to be picked up, that's why you're there.
I don't go for that. I have nothing against meeting people in bars,
but they're usually so packed you can't carry on a conversation.
You have no idea what it's like. All you do is shout at each other
over the noise, and if you leave together, you know nothing about
each other. Everyone is always putting on airs, trying to impress
each other. You never get down to the essentials of the kind of
people you are."

15. Helen Gurley Brown, *op. cit.*, 33–34.

16. An excellent portrait of a Jewish matchmaker can be found in
the title story of Bernard Malamud's *The Magic Barrel* (New
York: Farrar, Straus & Giroux, 1958).

17. "Autumn Brings Bicycle Traffic Jams to Central Park Path,"
The New York Times, 10/12/68, p. 67.

18. "Some age-combinations are forbidden, like that between a mature man and a twelve-year-old girl. Love between a young man and a women who 'might be his mother' is frowned upon as slightly pathological. A marriage between a woman who has come of age and a man who might be her grandfather seems to be more acceptable, unless there is suspicion of an ulterior motive on the woman's side. While these age combinations are considered to be deviant, or at least not ideal, they have been exploited by artists to emphasize the strength of love, breaking down the barriers of age. Such is one critical interpretation of *Lolita.*" Vihelm Aubert, "A Note on Love," in *The Hidden Society* (Totowa, N.J.: Bedminster Press, 1965), 231.

19. Visitors to a foreign country often have a difficult time meeting the natives. Since the former are enmeshed in the concerns and problems of *visiting* while the latter are enmeshed in the concerns and problems of *everyday life,* visitors and natives have no obvious common relevances and interests. Personal identity, therefore, is usually overwhelmed by collective nationality. Because each becomes for the other only a representative-of-his-respective-country, he has nothing to say to the other beyond exchanging opinions about the other's country and his own. Note, however, that foreigners from different countries visiting the same country are able to meet each other more easily than either could meet natives because they have the same minority status of "foreigner" and, consequently, common concerns and problems.

20. Helen Gurley Brown, *op. cit.*, 40.

21. In general, the old intimates of an individual—lovers, friends, and family—may make it more difficult for him to contract new intimacies. J. Mayer, "The Self-Restraint of Friends: A Mechanism of Family Transition," *Social Forces* (March, 1957), 237 *n.*, suggests, "The physical separation of the couple from their customary social relationships may be viewed as an alternative mechanism that effectively shelters them from adverse opinion. In this connection it is often held that people do fall in love more readily when away from home, their circle of friends, and their community. In a similar connection it is of interest that movies frequently portray the central characters as unhampered by family connections."

22. Although the *potential* for an intimate relation is the most ineffable of interpersonal bonds, some people find it the most

powerful. They see no reason to continue any relationship whose potential for increased intimacy has ended. Their constant search for new intimacies and their high *turnover rate* for old relationships indicate that they prefer this bond to all others.

On the other hand, "lack of *potential*" itself can sometimes facilitate the development of an intimate relation. For example, a shy young man may become quite close to a married woman precisely because she is already married, as in Goethe's *The Sorrows of Young Werther*, tr. C. Hutter (New York: New American Library, 1962). Having nothing to gain often dispels the fear of having something to lose.

CHAPTER 2

1. Francis Bacon, "Of Friendship," in *The Complete Essays of Francis Bacon* (New York: Washington Square Press, 1963), 70.
2. *Ibid.*, 70.
3. *Ibid.*, 72.
4. See Erving Goffman's "On Face-Work," *Psychiatry*, XVII, 3 (Aug. 1955), 216 ff, for his discussion of this aspect of the self (which here he calls "face-work") and the rest of his article for the techniques by which the self withstands and overcomes opposition.
5. Erving Goffman defines an "encounter" in "Fun in Games," *Encounters* (Indianapolis: Bobbs-Merrill, 1961), 17–18, as "a single visual and cognitive focus of attention; a mutual and preferential openness to verbal communication; a heightened mutual relevance of acts; an eye-to-eye ecological huddle that maximizes each participant's opportunity to perceive the other participants' monitoring of him." In his article, Goffman deals primarily with the encounters of acquaintances. In this chapter, I attempt to specify how the encounters of intimates differ from the standard form of encounters that he discusses.
6. Aristotle, *Ethics*, tr. J. A. K. Thomson (Baltimore: Penguin, 1953), Bk. IX, Chap. 12, 284–285.
7. "Time Essay: The Pleasures and Pains of Single Life," *Time*, 9/15/67.
8. Philippe Ariès, *Centuries of Childhood*, tr. R. Baldich (New York: Vintage, 1962), 399.

9. *Ibid.*, 399.
10. *Ibid.*, 390.
11. *Ibid.*, 391. See also Lewis A. Coser, *Men of Ideas* (New York: Free Press, 1965), 11–25.
12. Shakespeare, *As You Like It*, I, 3, 75–78.
13. Some societies and historical periods have provided few private places in which intimates can meet; others few public places. Philippe Ariès, *op. cit.,* 391–398, suggests that French society in the seventeenth century was an instance of the former; Morton Hunt, *The Natural History of Love* (New York: Minerva Press, 1959), 67, suggests that Rome at the time of the Empire was an instance of the latter.
14. Discothèques, however, so overload all the senses with stimuli that they often seem to be without any. Perhaps baseball games or horse races, where extreme amounts of stimuli occur only intermittently, would be better examples of public places in which external diversions are maximized but small talk is possible.
15. Each time individuals attend cocktail lounges, night clubs, restaurants, bars, pubs, or cafés, they must pay "rent" to the establishment to be allowed to lease part of the space it owns for a certain period of time. Rent may be collected directly in the form of a minimum or cover charge, but more often it is indirectly added to the price of the food and drink bought, which accounts for much of their markup over the cost of equivalent cuisine consumed at home. When payment for the leased space has not been sufficient or the metered time that has been paid for has run down, such meter-maids as waitresses or such meter-men as managers may evict the overtime parkers ("No loitering!"). The fact that their lease has expired and they have to "buy more" to keep it in effect or leave is especially annoying to those who have come to meet, not eat. Thus, high school students often find themselves at cross-purposes with the proprietors of drugstores and soda shops, and college students often have similar conflicts with the managers of all-night cafeterias and diners.
16. Henry David Thoreau, *A Week on the Concord and Merrimack Rivers* (Boston: Houghton Mifflin, 1893), 359.
17. Aristotle, *op. cit.*, Bk. VIII, Chap. 5, 237.
18. Henry David Thoreau, *op. cit.*, 358.
19. Compare Goffman's notion of "interaction tonus" in *Behavior in Public Places* (New York: Free Press, 1963), 25–30.

20. For a background to my assertion, see Erving Goffman, *The Presentation of Self in Everyday Life* (Garden City: Anchor, 1959), and Daniel Miller's distinction between "core identity" and "persona" in "The Study of Social Relations: Situation, Identity, and Social Interaction" in S. Koch, ed., *Psychology: Study of a Science* (New York: McGraw-Hill, 1963), Vol. 5, 674.

21. John Barth, *End of the Road* (New York: Avon, 1958), 57–58. Note also what Nietzsche has to say of solitude: "But here you are at your own hearth and home; here you can utter everything and pour out every reason, nothing is here ashamed of hidden, hardened feelings." In Nietzsche, *Thus Spoke Zarathustra*, tr. R. J. Hollingdale (Baltimore: Penguin, 1961), 202.

22. There are two extreme social types who live half-heartedly, in the sense that they operate on only half of this cycle. On the one hand, *hermits* are those who seem to feel the psychological pressures to get away from people intensely, while experiencing the pressures to get together with people not at all. On the one hand, those who seem to feel the psychological pressures to get together with people intensely, while experiencing the pressures to get away from people not at all, may be called *gregarians*, for want of a better English term. Hermits, who are always found alone, perform solo recitals of their views and experiences to themselves; gregarians, who are always found at parties and other public occasions, chant theirs to others.

23. In times past, everyone seems to have had this problem. Philippe Ariès, *op. cit.,* 398, points out, "Until the end of the seventeenth century, nobody was ever left alone. The density of social life made isolation virtually impossible, and people who managed to shut themselves up in a room for some time were regarded as exceptional characters." But then, in those progesellschaft days, personal relations were also quite different.

24. Marvin Scott and Stanford Lyman, "Accounts," *American Sociological Review,* Vol. 33, 1 (Feb., 1968) 47, make a useful distinction between "justifications," in which "one accepts responsibility for the act in question, but denies the pejorative quality associated with it," and "excuses," in which "one admits that the act in question is bad, wrong, or inappropriate but denies full responsibility."

CHAPTER 3

1. Roger Brown and Albert Gilman, "The Pronouns of Power and Solidarity," in Thomas Sebeok, ed., *Style in Language* (Cambridge: M.I.T. Press, 1960), 254. The authors report, however, p. 261, that in modern Europe the use of this phileme family seems to be dying out, as the 'T' form of the pronoun is more and more applied to everyone indiscriminately.

2. Paul Friedrich, "Structural Implications of Russian Pronominal Usage," in Bright, ed., *Sociolinguistics* (The Hague: Mouton & Co., 1966).

3. Brown and Gilman, *op. cit.*, 255ff.

4. Pierre Choderlos de Laclos, *Dangerous Liaisons*, tr. L. Bair (New York: Bantam Books, 1962), 248.

5. André Gide, *The Counterfeiters*, tr. D. Bussy (New York: Modern Library, 1955), 137.

6. Friedrich, *op. cit.*, 219.

7. T. Beidelman, "Terms of Address as Clues to Social Relationships," in Gouldner and Gouldner, eds., *Modern Sociology* (New York: Harcourt, Brace, 1963), 308–315. Philippe Ariès, *Centuries of Childhood*, tr. R. Baldich (New York: Vintage, 1962), 26–27, reports that at the beginning of the eighteenth century "child" was a common term of address in friendship, and also that, at the time, the notion of childhood was bound up with the notion of dependence.

8. Leo Tolstoy, *The Kreutzer Sonata*, tr. Aylmer Maude, reprinted in *The Death of Ivan Ilych and Other Stories* (New York: New American Library, 1960), 214.

9. Martin Joos, *The Five Clocks* (New York: Harcourt, Brace, 1967), 23–32.

10. *Ibid.*

11. Basil Bernstein, "Elaborated and Restricted Codes: Their Social Origins and some Consequences," in J. Gumperz and D. Hymes, eds., *The Ethnography of Communication*, Special Issue: *American Anthropologist*, Vol. 66, #6, Part 2 (1964), 60–61. (Italics mine.)

12. T. H. Holmes, *et al.*, *The Nose*, cited by Paul Moses in T. A. Sebeok *et al.*, eds., *Approaches to Semiotics* (The Hague: Mouton & Co., 1964), 46.

13. "Vocalization at intimate distance plays a very minor part in the communication process, which is carried mainly by other channels.

A whisper has the effect of expanding the distance."—Edward Hall, *The Hidden Dimension* (Garden City: Doubleday, 1966), 110. "Although actions are condoned, or even completely accepted, verbal representations may be prohibited. Lovers may do something together about which they cannot speak without violating a sense of modesty or even without altering the nature and meaning of the act. Verbal reserve can be combined with physical abandon."—Vilhelm Aubert, "A Note on Love," in *The Hidden Society* (Totowa, N.J.: Bedminster Press, 1965), 209.

14. See Guy Swanson, "The Routinization of Love: Structure and Process in Primary Relations," in S. Klausner, *The Quest for Self-Control* (New York: Free Press, 1965), 183; Albert Schefflin, "The Significance of Posture in Communication Systems," *Psychiatry*, Vol. 27 (1964), 327; and Robert Sommers, "Sociofugal Space," *American Journal of Sociology*, Vol. 72 (1967), 657.

15. Schefflin, *op. cit.*, 328.

16. Helen Carlton, "Uniworld of His & Hers," *Life*, 6/21/68, 87.

17. Georg Simmel, "Sociology of the Senses; Visual Interaction," reprinted in R. Park and E. Burgess, *Introduction to the Science of Sociology* (Chicago: University of Chicago Press, 1921), 358.

18. Claude Brown, *Manchild in the Promised Land* (New York: New American Library, 1965), 72.

19. Pierre Choderlos de Laclos, *op. cit.*, 164.

20. Edward T. Hall, *The Hidden Dimension* op. cit., 108ff.

21. *Ibid.*, 113.

22. *Ibid.*, 110–111.

23. "The acquaintance responds almost entirely to the standardized meaning, the face value of the person's gestures in situations as socially defined. Good friends and intimates . . . respond to the face value of the gesture, but they also are more or less keenly responsive to the 'personal meaning' of the gesture. That is, they grasp something of its role as an expression of a total pattern of personal integration."—Herbert Fingarette, *The Self in Transformation* (New York: Harper, 1963), 275–276. See also Alfred Schutz, *Collected Papers* (The Hague: Martinus Nijhoff, 1964), Vol. II, 55–56.

24. Harry Crockett, Jr. and Lewis Levine, "Friends' Influences on Speech," *Social Inquiry*, Vol. 37 (1967), 109–128.

25. Alfred Schutz, *op. cit.*, Vol. I, 219–221; Vol. II, 109–110, dis-

cusses some of the features of interpersonal communication that occur when individuals are in a "face-to-face relationship."

26. In this connection, it is interesting to compare Sartre's myopic view of "the look," *Being and Nothingness* (New York: Washington Square Press, 1953), 340ff, 474ff, with Simmel's farsighted one, cited in footnote 17.

27. "Some of the most trenchant communication involves the combination of one spoken pronoun with paralinguistic features of body movement and intonation that would normally accompany the covert unspoken pronoun; thus, an explicit 'Vy' combined with paralinguistic 'Ty' (warmness of tone, and so forth), could often signal a felicitous union of personal respect and an affection whose strength was not mitigated by overt restraint; an overt, spoken 'Vy' when conjoined with the modulations and gestures usual for certain 'Ty' bonds could often signal revilement and disgust in the most painful manner."—Friedrich, *op. cit.*, 251.

28. Nat Hentoff, quoted in J. Cohen, ed., *The Essential Lenny Bruce* (New York: Ballantine, 1967), 261. See also Oscar Lewis cited in Beidelman, *op. cit.*

29. Tom Burns gives a somewhat different interpretation of *banter*, which he defines as "to play at being hostile, distant, unfriendly, while intimating friendliness" and contrasts it with *irony*, which he defines as "to play at being friendly . . . while intimating enmity, rejection." See Tom Burns, "Friends, Enemies, and the Polite Fiction," *American Sociological Review* (December 1963), 655, 657. Gregory Bateson *et al.* in the famous article, "Towards a Theory of Schizophrenia," *Behavioral Science* (October 1956), 251–264, discussed the harmful effect on children of the kind of contradictory communication Burns would call "irony."

30. Denis de Rougemont, *Love in the Western World*, tr. M. Belgion (New York: Fawcett, 1956), 126 & note.

31. Whatever the specific sequence of phileme families through which lovers progress over the course of their relationship, they seem to repeat it sometimes in the preliminaries to each of their sexual encounters. Lovers reiterate the order of their intimate discourse in the preface to their sexual intercourse because this series consists of their ongoing movement through the psychological embodiments they consider more and more sacred. On the social level, their particular advance toward coition reproduces their general progression toward intimacy in the same way that, on the

biological level, the development of the embryo reproduces the evolution of the species. In brief, *foreplay recapitulates philogeny* in the same way that *ontogeny recapitulates phylogeny*. I must stress, however, that the extent of these correlations between the development of the particular and the evolution of the general is by no means clear at either the social or the biological level.

32. For the notion of "saving face," and the techniques by which it is done in other than intimate situations, see Erving Goffman, "On Face-Work," *Psychiatry*, Vol. 18 (1955), 213–231.

33. Stendhal, *The Red and the Black*, tr. L. Bair (New York: Bantam Books, 1959), 63–65.

34. Vladimir Nabokov, *Nabokov's Dozen* (New York: Popular Library, 1958), 25–26.

35. André Gide, *op. cit.*, 78.

36. Hall, *op. cit.*, 111–112.

37. "Was Mrs. Wilcox one of the unsatisfactory people—there are many of them—who dangle intimacy and then withdraw it? They evoke our interests and affections, and keep the life of the spirit dawdling round them. Then they withdraw. When physical passion is involved, there is a definite name for such behavior—flirting—and if carried far enough, it is punishable by law. But no law—not public opinion, even—punishes those who coquette with friendship, though the dull ache that they inflict, the sense of misdirected effort and exhaustion, may be as intolerable."—E. M. Forster, *Howard's End* (New York: Vintage, 1958), 79.

38. Georg Simmel, *The Sociology of Georg Simmel*, tr. K. Wolff (Glencoe: Free Press, 1950), 50.

39. Helen Gurley Brown, *Sex and the Single Girl* (New York: Pocket Books, 1962), 74–75.

40. Marya Mannes, "New Bites by a Girl Gadfly," *Life*, 6/12/1964, laments: "The art of flirtation is dying. A man and woman are either in love these days or just friends. In the realm of love, reticence and sophistication should go hand in hand, for one of the joys of life in discovery. Nowadays, instead of progressing from 'Vous' to 'Tu,' from Mister to Jim, it's 'darling' and 'come to my place' in the first hour."

41. In *The Red and the Black*, *op. cit.*, 333, Julian Sorel devises the following safeguards to keep himself from being taken in and teased when Mademoiselle de la Mole sends him a serious love letter. First, he secretly posts it to a friend for safekeeping; then

he sends her this reply: "What, mademoiselle! . . . Can it be true that Mademoiselle de la Mole has sent, through her father's servant Arsène, a seductive letter to a poor sawyer from the Juras, no doubt in order to ridicule his simplicity."

CHAPTER 4

1. Laurence Sterne, *The Life and Opinions of Tristram Shandy* (Baltimore: Penguin, 1967), 41.
2. "One of the most valuable functions of dating is the chance it gives young people to learn something about each other's character, opinions and plans for living—a need which hardly existed in the stable smalltown life of earlier centuries, when every young man was known, or known about, by nearly every young girl he was likely to court."—Morton Hunt, *The Natural History of Love* (New York: Minerva Press, 1959), 359.
3. "The 'intimate' character of certain relations seems to me to derive from the individual's inclination to consider that which distinguishes him from others, that which is individual in a qualitative sense, as the core, value, and chief matter of his existence."—Georg Simmel, *The Sociology of Georg Simmel*, tr. K. Wolff (Glencoe: Free Press, 1950), 126.
4. *Ibid.*, 334–335. Simmel's whole discussion of interpersonal secrecy is relevant to this chapter. See especially pp. 307–38.
5. "The peculiar color of intimacy exists . . . if its whole affective structure is based on what each of the two participants gives or shows only to the one other person and to nobody else."—*Ibid.*, 126.
6. "The practice of life urges us to make the picture of a man only from the real pieces we empirically know of him, but it is precisely the practice of life which is based on those modifications and supplementations, on the transformation of the given fragments into the generality of a type and into the completeness of the ideal person. In practice, this fundamental process is only rarely carried to completion."—Georg Simmel, "How is Society Possible?" in *Georg Simmel: 1858–1918*, tr. K. Wolff (Columbus: Ohio State University Press, 1959), 344.
7. Erving Goffman, *The Presentation of Self in Everyday Life* (Garden City: Anchor, 1959), and *Behavior in Public Places* (Glencoe: Free Press, 1963), 112–113.

8. See H. A. Hodges, *The Philosophy of Wilhelm Dilthy* (London: Routledge & Kegan Paul, 1952); *Max Weber on the Methodology of the Social Sciences,* tr. E. Shils & H. Finch (Glencoe: Free Press, 1949); *Georg Simmel, 1858–1918, op. cit.;* G. H. Mead, *Mind, Self and Society* (Chicago: University of Chicago Press, 1934); Alfred Schutz, *Collected Papers* (The Hague: Martinus Nijhoff, 1962, 1964).

9. For other comparisons between everyday and scientific approaches to the social world, see Alfred Schultz, "Common Sense and Scientific Interpretations of Human Actions," reprinted in his *Collected Papers, op. cit.,* Vol. I, 2–47; and Harold Garfinkel, "Common Sense Knowledge of Social Structures: the Documentary Method of Interpretation in Lay and Professional Fact Finding," and "The Rational Properties of Scientific and Common Sense Activities," both reprinted in his *Studies in Ethnomethodology* (Englewood Cliffs: Prentice-Hall, 1967), 76–103, 262–283.

10. See index under "typification" in Vols. I & II of Alfred Schutz, *Collected Papers, op. cit.*

11. Sidney Jourard, *The Transparent Self* (Princeton: Van Nostrand, 1965), 178.

12. "We may communicate . . . private feelings, moods, and motives in intimate relations. . . . And as we do so we are learning about ourselves. As we tell our motives to others we become aware of new aspects of ourselves. For by telling them even to one significant other, we may justify having them or seek relief from them. . . . Thus making others understand us, we can understand ourselves and reconstruct our image of self."—H. Gerth and C. W. Mills, *Character and Social Structure: The Psychology of Social Institutions* (New York: Harcourt, Brace, 1953).

13. "Previously uninterested politically, [a wife] now identifies herself as a liberal. Previously alternating between dimly articulated religious positions, she now declares herself an agnostic. Previously confused and uncertain about her sexual emotions, she now understands herself as an unabashed hedonist in this area."— Peter Berger and Hansfried Kellner, "Marriage and the Construction of Reality," *Diogenes* (1964), 14.

14. Although the etymology of these phrases is unknown, I suggest that the first may be derived from "come along," which one person would say to his companion who is walking along with him when the latter has become so involved in a performance or position that he has stopped. I suggest that the second may be

derived from "Come off the stage [platform, soap box]," which one person would say to his companion when the latter has become so involved in his performance or position that he is no longer engaged in a dialog but merely in the monolog of a professional actor or public orator.

15. Goffman thinks not. He feels that sincerity too is merely a mask. ". . . reserving the term 'sincere' for individuals who believe in the impression fostered by their own performance," he says in *The Presentation of Self in Everyday Life, op cit.,* 18. Goffman tends to identify what a person really is with the techniques he uses to manufacture his mask and to defend it. Here, however, I am conceiving of what a person really is as what he takes himself to be, which is *what* he uncovers and covers over rather than *how* he presents and protects. What a person takes to be his "real self" is the one he needs the least psychological energy to present (See Chap. 2, p. 48) and the most to protect. Since one's real self is so enjoyably effortless to put forth, yet so dangerously vulnerable to any attack, it can be shown only to intimates who are trusted not to harm it.

16. "Under the rubric of acquaintance, one knows of the other only what he is toward the outside, either in the purely social-representative sense, or in the sense of that which he shows us."— Georg Simmel, *The Sociology of Georg Simmel, op. cit.,* 320.

17. Erving Goffman provides some of the following examples in his two main works dealing with concealment: *The Presentation of Self in Everyday Life, op. cit.* and *Stigma* (Englewood Cliffs: Prentice-Hall, 1963). Sidney Jourard, *op. cit.,* provides some of the others.

18. Stendhal, *The Red and the Black,* tr. L. Bair (New York: Bantam Books, 1959), 101, contains a nice example: "There were times when, in spite of his habits of hypocrisy, [Julian] found extreme pleasure in confessing his ignorance of all sorts of little social usages to the noble lady who admired him. . . . There were times when he, who had never loved or been loved before, found such sweet pleasure in being sincere that he was on the point of confessing to Madame de Rênal the ambition which until then had been the very essence of his existence."

19. Even the father of psychoanalysis might have done well to consider why he was concealing from the world what he was confessing to his intimate: "During the most significant period of

his life Freud confided to Fliess in a uniquely free and uninhibited manner not only his ideas but also the internal struggles, hopes, and discouragements that accompanied his relentless efforts to create a new psychological theory of the human personality."— Franz Alexander and Sheldon Selesnick, *The History of Psychiatry* (New York: Mentor, 1968), 238.

20. For an intriguing description of how an ex-man conceals the fact that she has not always been a normal woman, see Harold Garfinkel, "Passing and the Managed Achievement of Sex Status in an Intersexed Person," *Studies in Ethnomethodology, op. cit.,* 117–185; 285–288.

21. David Bakan, "Eros and Knowledge," *Chicago Today*, 48, 50.

22. Freud, like all great founders, should not be held responsible for the follies of his followers. According to Bakan in *Sigmund Freud and the Jewish Mystical Tradition* (New York: Schocken, 1958), 280, Freud "was well aware of the relationship between knowledge and sexuality." Bakan supports his case by quoting Freud himself: ". . . the instinct for knowledge or research . . . cannot be counted among the elementary instinctual components, nor can it be classed as exclusively belonging to sexuality. Its activity corresponds on the one hand to a sublimated manner of obtaining mastery, while on the other hand it makes use of the energy of scopophilia." Thus, Freud sees the cognitive drive and the sexual drive as two independent sources of human motivation. Though this position is more accurate than that of his followers who derive the desire for knowledge from the desire for sex, it is still far from the cognigenic position put forth in this chapter, in which *Eros* is derived from *Logos*.

23. Perhaps children are socialized into thinking that their sexual parts are their essential parts because these parts are considered too shameful even to be named. Witness parents who say to their children, "Hide yourself; you're open," or "Stop playing with yourself."

24. Stendhal, *On Love* (New York: Anchor, 1947), 69.

25. José Ortega y Gasset, *On Love* (Cleveland: Meridian Books, 1957), 136.

26. Goffman seems to make approximately the same distinction between the kinds of things he deals with in *The Presentation of Self in Everyday Life, op. cit.,* and the kinds of things he deals with in *Stigma, op. cit.*

27. Goffman, *The Presentation of Self in Everyday Life, op. cit.,* 112.
28. Natsume Soseki, *Kokoro,* tr. E. McClellan (Chicago: Gateway, 1957), 6, 7, 11, 14, 18.
29. Friedrich Nietzsche, *Beyond Good and Evil,* tr. W. Kaufmann (New York: Viking, 1966), 92.
30. Friedrich Nietzsche, *Thus Spoke Zarathustra,* tr. R. J. Hollingdale (Baltimore: Penguin, 1961), 83.
31. Natsume Soseki, *op. cit.,* 187–188.
32. "Completely reversing his earlier strategy of presenting only the most impressive parts of his self, he now flaunts his weaknesses. Having first impressed us with his Harvard accent and Beacon Hill friends, he may tell a story that reveals his immigrant background. After having talked only of the successes he has enjoyed in his career, he may let us in on the defeats he has suffered. Having earlier carefully protected himself against ridicule or even made jokes at the expense of others, he may relate an incident that makes us laught at, as well as with, him. Whatever the contents of his remarks, they show him as a person willing to admit his shortcomings. . . . Self-depreciating modesty does not make one attractive, it merely activates already existing feelings of attraction by reducing the reluctance to express them. Therefore unless the weaknesses a person admits are less salient qualities than those with which he has impressed others, he will not have demonstrated that he is approachable as well as attractive but, instead, will have provided evidence that he is, all things considered, really unattractive."—Peter Blau, "A Theory of Social Integration," *American Journal of Sociology* (1960), 549–550.
33. Aristotle, "Rhetorica," in *The Basic Works of Aristotle,* ed. R. McKeon (New York: Random House, 1941), Bk. 2, Chap. 4, 1388.
34. Michael Radomisli "Love, Friendship and Aim-inhibited Aggression," *The Psychoanalytic Review* (Spring 1968), 59–60.
35. Nietzsche, *Beyond Good and Evil, op. cit.,* 217.
36. "Yet such complete intimacy becomes probably more and more difficult as differentiation among men increases. . . . Except for their earliest years, personalities are perhaps too uniquely individualized to allow full reciprocity of understanding and receptivity, which always, after all, requires much creative imagination and much divination which is oriented only toward the other. It would

seem that . . . the modern way of feeling tends more heavily toward differentiated friendships, which cover only one side of the personality, without playing into other aspects of it."—Georg Simmel, *The Sociology of Georg Simmel, op. cit.,* 326.

37. Ralph Waldo Emerson, "Friendship," in *The Complete Essays and Other Writings of Ralph Waldo Emerson,* ed. B. Atkinson (New York: Modern Library, 1949), 225.

38. J. Mayer, in "The Self-Restraint of Friends," *Social Forces* (1967), 236 *n.,* points out, "The racial bigot and the romantic lover are not entirely unrelated; where the former is blind to the virtues of certain groups, the latter cannot see the faults of his beloved." Love differs from bigotry, however, in that *love* is individuating and gives a positive valence to the unique aspects of the beloved, whereas *bigotry* is generalizing and gives a negative valence to the common features of the group bigoted against. Although all "beloveds" certainly exhibit some common features, no one sees "beloved" as constituting a natural class.

39. Stendhal, *On Love, op. cit.,* 7.

40. Lucretius, *De Rerum Natura,* tr. A. Wimspeare (New York: Harbor Press, 1955), Bk. IV.

41. Georg Simmel, *The Sociology of Georg Simmel, op. cit.,* 127.

42. Lenny Bruce, *How to Talk Dirty and Influence People* (Chicago: Playboy Press, 1966), 52.

43. E. M. Forster, *Howard's End* (New York: Vintage, 1958), 122.

44. R. D. Laing, *The Divided Self* (Baltimore: Penguin, 1965), 126.

45. José Ortega y Gasset, *op. cit.,* 136–137. The translator has rendered the key word in this passage as "flirtation," but the context plainly demands "seduction."

46. Pierre Choderlos de Laclos, *Dangerous Liaisons,* tr. L. Bair (New York: Bantam, 1962), 108–109.

47. Nietzsche, *Beyond Good and Evil, op. cit.,* 92.

48. Choderlos de Laclos, *op. cit.,* 166.

49. Matthew 26:14–16.

50. Plato, "Phaedrus," in *Plato: The Collected Dialogues,* ed. E. Hamilton and D. Cairns (New York: Bollingen Foundation, 1963), 481–482.

51. Blaise Pascal, *Pensées,* tr. W. Trotter (New York: Dutton, 1958), 101.

52. Leo Tolstoy, *The Kreutzer Sonata,* tr. Alymer Maude, reprinted

in *The Death of Ivan Ilych and Other Stories* (New York: New American Library, 1960), 207.
53. *The New York Times*, 9/3/67. The *Boston Globe*, 3/19/67, reported that in Boston friends and relatives accounted for 30 of the 40 explained homicides and two-thirds of the aggravated assaults.

CHAPTER 5

1. Ralph Waldo Emerson, "Friendship," in *The Complete Essays and other Writings of Ralph Waldo Emerson*, ed. B. Atkinson (New York: Modern Library, 1949), 230.
2. Henry David Thoreau, *A Week on the Concord and Merrimack Rivers* (Boston: Houghton Mifflin, 1893), 350–351. Thoreau, in fact, feels that physical services have little place in intimacy, for he says later (370–371): "Few things are more difficult than to help a Friend in matters which do not require the aid of Friendship, but only cheap and trivial service, [as] if your Friendship wants the basis of a thorough practical acquaintance. . . . It is as if, after the friendliest and most ennobling intercourse, your Friend should use you as a hammer, and drive a nail with your head, all in good faith; notwithstanding that you are a tolerable carpenter, as well as his good Friend, and would use a hammer cheerfully in his service."
3. Francis Bacon, "Of Friendship," in *The Complete Essays of Francis Bacon* (New York: Washington Square Press, 1963), 75.
4. *Ibid.*, 75.
5. Natsume Soseki, *Kokoro*, tr. E. McClellan (Chicago: Gateway, 1957), 94.
6. For a study of patronage in the academy, see Theodore Caplow and Riece McGee, *The Academic Marketplace* (New York: Basic Books, 1958), Ch. 6.
7. Claude Brown, *Manchild in the Promised Land* (New York: New American Library, 1965), 69.
8. Bacon, *op. cit.*, 73–74.
9. Aristotle, *Ethics*, tr. J. A. K. Thomson (Baltimore: Penguin, 1953), Bk. 8, Chap. 1, 228.
10. I Samuel XVIII–XX.
11. See Howard Feinstein, "Hamlet's Horatio and the Therapeutic

Mode," *American Journal of Psychiatry* (1967), 803–809. In comparing Horatio's relationship with his friend Hamlet and the ideal therapist's relationship with his patient, Feinstein emphasizes Horatio's efforts to validate Hamlet's perception: "Throughout the play Horatio is a man who is ready to perceive and verify his friend's world even if it leads to conclusions which may be painful or dangerous. He does not shield Hamlet from the truth. . . . Instead, he concludes 'Let us impart what we have seen tonight unto young Hamlet.' " See also the discussion of the part experiential validation plays in marriage in Peter Berger and Hansfried Kellner, "Marriage and the Construction of Reality," *Diogenes*, 46 (1964), 3–4.

12. John XV, 13.
13. Eccles. VI, 14.
14. Brown, *op. cit.*, 264.
15. For a poignant example of job protection in the academy, see Vladimir Nabokov, *Pnin* (New York: Atheneum, 1966), Chap. 6, Sect. 1 & 12.
16. Eccles. VI, 16.
17. Eccles. IV, 10.
18. Brown, *op. cit.*, 79.
19. Edward Albee, *A Delicate Balance* (New York: Pocket Books, 1967), 123.
20. Rex Reed, "Breakthrough by 'The Boys in the Band,' " *The New York Times*, 5/12/68, Sect. 2, D11.
21. Jane Brody, "When Illness Follows a 'Giving up,' " *The New York Times*, 4/7/68, E11, reports: "The Rochester studies suggest that if a person responds to an event or events in his life with a sense of helplessness, hopelessness or giving up, he may somehow initiate a biological change that fosters the development of an already present disease potential." It seems, then, that once one section of an individual's foundation begins to crumble, his other pillars begin to give way, and there develops a cycle that, unless it is stopped, becomes increasingly vicious.
22. Job III, 20–22.
23. Job II, 11.
24. Cicero, "On Friendship," tr. Frank O. Copley, in *On Friendship and On Old Age* (Ann Arbor: University of Michigan Press, 1967), 72.
25. Job II, 12–13.

26. So that each intimate may empathize with the other more exactly, each usually asks the other about, or the latter volunteers, information concerning the precise circumstances that upset him. Thus, each seems to "take the emotion of the other" in the same way that the inhabitants of George Herbert Mead's purely cognative and behavioristic world "take the role of the other." See G. H. Mead, *Mind, Self and Society* (Chicago: University of Chicago Press, 1934). In both processes, each individual does not empathize with the other's emotion or role in general, but only as it appears in a concrete situation. In order to enter into the emotion or role mentally, then, he must reconstruct the situation that caused it or in which it was played out, in as much particularity as possible.

27. Those who are good at minimizing another's discomfort through expressing it for him in this way are called "warm." Perhaps, then, the reason some people consider Northern Europeans and others to be "cold" is not that the latter are unable to sympathize with suffering, but that, because they do not express their own reactions to pain through visual and verbal cues that are obvious to these people, they do not generate in these people this feedback process. Among themselves, however, Northern Europeans and others are likely to be capable of discriminating the more subtle symptoms by which they manifest their emotions; thus, they may reciprocally relieve each other's sorrows, and hence do not find each other particularly "cold."

28. Erving Goffman, "On Cooling the Mark Out," *Psychiatry*, XV, 4 (Nov. 1952), 454–455.

29. Hugh Sidey, "Seeking Solace amid the Dissent," *Life*, 11/17/67, 40.

30. Erving Goffman, *Asylums* (Garden City: Anchor, 1961), 56, 136–139.

31. Shakespeare, *Julius Caesar*, IV, 13.

32. Friedrich Nietzsche, *Thus Spoke Zarathustra*, tr. R. J. Hollingdale (Baltimore: Penguin, 1961), 83. Also Alexander Pope:
    "Trust not yourself; but your defects to know,
    Make use of ev'ry friend—and ev'ry foe."

33. The axiom that an individual defines himself in terms of another, and especially in terms of his intimates, is basic to both Gabriel Marcel—see the passages of his *Being and Having* excerpted on pp. 209–210 of M. Friedman, *The World of Existentialism* (New

York: Random House, 1964)—and Martin Buber—see *I and Thou* (New York: Scribner, 1958).

34. La Rochefoucauld, *The Maxims of La Rochefoucauld*, tr. L. Kronenberger (New York: Vintage, 1959), #410.
35. Thoreau, *op. cit.,* 363–364.
36. Brown, *op. cit.,* 35.
37. Michel de Montaigne, "On Experience," in *Essays,* tr. J. M. Cohen (Baltimore: Penguin, 1958), 359.
38. Cicero, *op. cit.,* 55, 56.
39. Nelson Foote, "Love," *Psychiatry,* XVI, 3 (August 1953). Martin Buber's 'I–Thou' relationship is similar to Foote's definition of love in that the 'I' allows for the dynamic development of the 'Thou,' unlike the 'I–It' relationship in which the 'I' fixes the 'It' in time as a static object. See *I and Thou, op. cit.* Sartre's view of love also seems to be similar in that the lover does not reify his beloved but allows her to retain her possibilities; unlike the nonlover, who reifies others and strips them of their possibilities. See his discussion of the "loving look" in *Being and Nothingness* (New York: Washington Square Press, 1953), Part 3, "Being for Others." Both Buber and Sartre, however, are pessimistic about the possibility of sustaining this state.
40. Aristotle, *op. cit.,* Bk. 9, Chap. 12, 285.
41. "Lust combined with the need for intimacy frequency drives the victim towards correcting certain warps in personality and towards developing certain facilities, certain abilities, in interpersonal relations."—Harry Stack Sullivan, *The Interpersonal Theory of Psychiatry* (New York: W. W. Norton, 1953), 270.
42. Thoreau, *op. cit.,* 342.
43. Morton Hunt, *The Natural History of Love* (New York: Minerva Press, 1959), viii–ix.
44. Cicero, *op. cit.,* 73.
45. J. P. Sartre, *op. cit.,* 481.
46. Cicero, *op. cit.,* 62.
47. Pierre Choderlos de Laclos, *Dangerous Liaisons,* tr. L. Bair (New York: Bantam Books, 1962), 58, 238.
48. In a provocative article, Harold Searles contends that the continued refusal on the part of the intimates of an individual to verify what he has perceived will cause him to doubt his own senses and may eventually drive him crazy. See "The Effort to Drive the Other Person Crazy—An Element in the Aetiology and

Psychotherapy of Schizophrenia," *British Journal of Medical Psychology,* XXXII, 1 (1959), especially p. 4.

49. R. D. Laing, *The Divided Self* (Baltimore: Penguin, 1960), 52–53, points out the even more extreme possibility that an individual might become dependent on his intimates for his sense of existence: "In this lesion in the sense of personal autonomy there is . . . a failure to sustain the sense of oneself as a person. . . . It is a failure to be by oneself, a failure to exist alone. As James puts it, 'Other people supply me with my exisence.' . . . It means . . . feeling that one is in a position of ontological dependency on the other (i.e. dependent on the other for one's very being)."

50. Confucius, *Analects,* tr. A. Waley (London: George Allen & Unwin Ltd., 1938), IV, 26 (my stylistic emendations).

51. For a somewhat different approach to the problem of jealousy, see Georg Simmel, *Conflict and the Web of Group Affiliations* (Glencoe: Free Press, 1955), 50–55.

52. R. J. Hollingdale, *Nietzsche: The Man and his Philosophy* (Baton Rouge: Louisiana State University Press, 1965), 16–17.

53. The "basic works" of Exchange Theory include Marcel Mauss, *The Gift* (London: Cohen and West, 1954); George Homans, "Social Behavior as Exchange," *American Journal of Sociology,* LXII (1958), 597–606; Alvin Gouldner, "The Norm of Reciprocity," *American Sociological Review,* XXV (1960), 161–178; and Peter Blau, *Power and Exchange in Social Life* (New York: Wiley, 1964). However, one of the best discussions of the exchange problems of personal relations is still to be found in Aristotle, *Ethics, op. cit.,* Bks. VIII–IX.

54. Ian Watt, *The Rise of the Novel* (Berkeley: University of California Press, 1957), 161.

55. "One expresses unfriendliness through gift giving by breaking the rule of approximate reciprocity (returning a gift in near, but not exact, value of that received). Returning 'tit for tat' transforms the relation into an economic one and expresses a refusal to play the role of grateful recipient. This offense represents a desire to end the relationship or at least define it on an impersonal, nonsentimental level. An exact return, then, is essentially a refusal to accept a 'token of regard,' which is to Mauss, 'the equivalent of a declaration of war; it is a refusal of friendship and inter-

course.' "—Barry Schwartz, "The Social Psychology of the Gift," *American Journal of Sociology*, LXXIII, 1 (1967), 6.

56. Vihelm Aubert, "A Note on Love," *The Hidden Society* (Totowa, N.J.: Bedminster Press, 1965), 222.

57. ". . . we help others to make sure they will help us under similar circumstances, and the services we render them are, properly speaking, benefits we store up for ourselves in advance." La Rochefoucauld, *Maxims, op. cit.*, #264.

58. See Peter Blau, *op. cit.*, 79–84.

59. Injunctions against lending money to friends are legion in proverbial lore. A few examples: "When I lend I am a friend, when I ask I am a foe." "Lend your money and lose your friend." "Neither a borrower nor a lender be; for a loan oft loses both itself and friend." The last homily appears in Shakespeare's *Hamlet*, I, 3. Polonius, of course, speaks it.

60. The value of lendable items depends on their cost, rarity, sentimental associations, or degree of personalization. Those who lend these items often worry that those who borrow them will damage or destroy them. Confucius, however, feels that we should value these lent items less than we value the friends to whom they are lent: "I should like to have carriages and horses, clothes and fur rugs, share them with my friends, and feel no annoyance if they were returned to me the worse for wear." *Analects, op. cit.*, V, 25 (my stylistic emendations).

61. La Rochefoucauld, *op. cit.*, #83.

62. Cicero, *op. cit.*, 71.

63. Michel de Montaigne, "On Friendship," in *Essays, op. cit.*, 99–100.

CHAPTER 6

1. Ferdinand Tönnies, *Community and Society*, tr. & ed. C. Loomis (New York: Harper, 1963), 42–43.

2. Michel de Montaigne "On Friendship," in *Essays*, tr. J. M. Cohen (Baltimore: Penguin, 1958), 97–98.

3. Georg Simmel, *The Sociology of Georg Simmel*, tr. K. Wolff (Glencoe: Free Press, 1950), 58.

4. Aristotle, *Ethics*, tr. J. A. K. Thomson (Baltimore: Penguin,

1953), Bk. 9, Chap. 8, 274. The original source of this proverb is probably Homer's *Iliad*, Bk. 16, line 267. See Alexander Pope's translation.

5. *Ibid.*, Bk. 9, Chap. 4, 267.

6. Cicero, "On Friendship," tr. Frank O. Copley, in *On Friendship and On Old Age* (Ann Arbor: University of Michigan Press, 1967), 80.

7. Aristotle, *op. cit.*, Bk. 9, Chap. 4, 266.

8. Sigmund Freud, *Civilization and Its Discontents*, tr. J. Strachey (New York: W. W. Norton, 1961), 12–13.

9. Harry Stack Sullivan, "Conceptions of Modern Psychiatry" (Washington: William Alanson White Psychiatric Foundation, 1947).

10. Erik Erikson, *Childhood and Society* (New York: W. W. Norton, 1963), 128.

11. Plato, "Symposium," found in *Plato: The Collected Dialogues* (New York: Bollingen Foundation, 1963), 542–545.

12. "Under conditions of physical contiguity—between mother and child, lover and beloved—the pulse can also be directly transmitted. This fosters a feeling of intimacy."—Peter Ostwald, citing J. Meerloo, "Rhythm in Babies and Adults," *Arch. General Psychiatry* (1961), 169–175, in T. Sebeok et al., eds., *Approaches to Semiotics* (The Hague: Mouton & Co., 1964), 18.

13. Violette Leduc, *Thérèse and Isabelle* (New York: Dell, 1966), 45.

14. See Erving Goffman, "The Nature of Deference and Demeanor," *American Anthropologist* (1956), 489–493.

15. Claude Brown, *Manchild in the Promised Land* (New York: New American Library, 1965), 168.

16. Ralph Waldo Emerson, "Friendship," in *The Complete Essays and other Writings of Ralph Waldo Emerson*, ed. B. Atkinson (New York: Modern Library, 1949), 225.

17. See Marcel Mauss, *The Gift* (London: Cohen and West, 1954), 11, and Erving Goffman, *The Presentation of Self in Everyday Life* (Garden City: Anchor, 1959), 253.

18. *I Samuel*, XVIII, 3–4.

19. I first heard this notion during an unpublished lecture given by Erving Goffman at Brandeis University in the Spring of 1967.

20. Aristotle, *op. cit.*, Bk. 8, Chap. 9, 244. The proverb is attributed to Pythagoras.

21. *Ibid.*, Bk. 8, Chap. 12, 252. See also Peter Berger and Hansfried Kellner, "Marriage and the Construction of Reality," *Diogenes* (1964), 16–17. The imaginary child in Edward Albee's *Who's Afraid of Virginia Woolf?* seems to serve the same function.

22. Peter Berger and Hansfried Kellner, *ibid.*, 15.

23. Natsume Soseki, *Kokoro*, tr E. McClellan (Chicago: Gateway, 1957), 128.

24. For instance, Cicero, *op. cit.*, 75: ". . . are there any circumstances in which new friends, found worthy of friendship, should be put ahead of old friends, as, for example, we commonly put fresh young horses ahead of old, worn-out ones? No man worthy of the name will feel any hesitation here, for we have no right to get tired of friendships as we do of other things. It is always true that the old and familiar, like wines which can stand aging, is bound to have the best savor."

25. This phrase is basic to Mead's discussion of communication in *Mind, Self and Society* (Chicago: University of Chicago Press, 1934). See especially his comments on the "significant symbol."

26. From an interview with an LSD user reported in Anne de Saint Phalle's "Harvard and your Head," *Harvard Crimson Supplement*, 3/4/68.

27. Montaigne, *op. cit.*, 98–99.

28. Alfred Schutz's whole discussion of face-to-face relations is relevant to this paragraph. See his *Collected Papers* (The Hague: Martinus Nijhoff, 1962, 1964), especially Vol. I, 219–221; Vol. II, 109–110.

29. Violette Leduc, *op. cit.*, 8.

30. There are several phenomenological descriptions of interpersonal communication that parallel parts of the one I have given. See the passages of Merleau–Ponty's *The Phenomenology of Perception* and Marcel's *Reflection and Mystery* excerpted on pages 200–201, 211 of M. Friedman, *The Worlds of Existentialism* (New York: Random House, 1964). See also Martin Buber, *I and Thou* (New York: Scribner, 1958), 9, 12, 30, 78, and R. D. Laing, *The Self and Others* (London: Tavistock, 1961), 128.

31. Denis de Rougemont, *Love in the Western World* (New York: Fawcett, 1956), 153–154. See also José Ortega y Gasset, *On Love* (Cleveland: Meridian Books, 1957), 44–51.

32. Emerson, *op. cit.*, 213–214.

33. "Antiquity has left no record of an experience akin to the love of Tristan and Iseult. It is well known that the Greeks and Romans looked on love as a sickness—the expression is Menander's— whenever it went, no matter how little, beyond the sensual pleasure which was considered to be its natural expression."— Denis de Rougemont, op. cit., 62.

Considering the extreme physical symptoms exhibited by those who are in love, it is amazing that love has not been studied—to my knowledge—as a medical problem. (Instead, medicine has shunted love off to the speciality of psychiatry, where it became something to be assumed rather than something to be explained.) The physical symptoms that erupt in the lover as soon as the beloved is present—blushing, sweating, dizziness, nausea, etc.— resemble nothing so much as an allergic reaction. In the light of recent advances in the study of pheromones, it might be profitable for future medical research to consider love as a specific allergy.

34. La Rochefoucauld, The Maxims of La Rochefoucauld, tr. L. Kronenberger (New York: Vintage, 1959), #136. Stendhal has an amusing passage in The Red and the Black, tr. L. Bair (New York: Bantam, 1959), 318, in which one of his heroines has to recall all the descriptions of love she has ever read about in order to determine whether the slight passion which she feels warrants that designation.

35. Vladimir Nabokov, The Eye (New York: Pocket Books, 1965), 33–34.

36. See Peter Berger and Hansfried Kellner, op. cit., 10–11; Barry Schwartz, "The Social Psychology of the Gift," American Journal of Sociology (1967), 11; and G. McCall and J. Simmons, Identities and Interactions (New York: Free Press, 1966), 175–176.

37. Georg Simmel, op. cit., 405–406.

38. Ibid., 380.

39. R. J. Hollingdale, Nietzsche: The Man and his Philosophy (Baton Rouge: Louisiana State University Press, 1965), 62.

40. Ernest Jones, The Life and Work of Sigmund Freud, ed. L. Trilling and S. Marcus (New York: Anchor Books, 1963), 80.

41. For showing how "true" intimacy enhances individuality, Martin Buber's thought is paradigmatic. He carefully distinguishes what he calls the 'I–Thou' relationship from mysticism, stressing that in the former a person does not merge totally with anyone, but rather becomes aware, accepts, and confirms the essential

difference between himself and others. The theme that people are essentially different from one another and that in their personal relations they should emphasize, not deny, these differences pervades the entire corpus of his work. Perhaps its clearest statement can be found in the following passage from *The Knowledge of Man* (quoted in M. Friedman, *The World of Existentialism*, *op. cit.*, 232): "The chief presupposition for the rise of genuine dialog is that each should regard his partner as the very one he is. I became aware of him, aware that he is different, essentially different from myself, in the definite unique way which is peculiar to him, and I accept whom I thus see. . . . To be aware of a man . . . means in particular to perceive . . . the dynamic center which stamps his every utterance, action, and attitude with the recognizable sign of uniqueness."

42. Peter Berger and Hansfried Kellner, *op. cit.*, 16, have pointed out that a person usually conceives of the changes that occur in his character under the impact of his personal relations not as an actual transformation of the elements of his individuality but as his deeper appreciation of what his unique elements have always been: "Re-constructed present and reinterpreted past are perceived as a continuum, extending forwards into a commonly projected future. The dramatic change that has occurred remains, in bulk, unapprehended and unarticulated. And where it forces itself upon the individual's attention, it is retrojected into the past, explained as having always been there, though perhaps in a hidden way. Typically, the reality that has been 'invented' . . . is subjectively perceived as a 'discovery.' Thus the partners 'discover' themselves and the world, 'who they really are,' 'what they really believe,' 'how they really feel, and have always felt, about so and so.'"

43. An individual can sharpen his identity against that of his intimate only if his intimate's identity is relatively coherent, as Cicero, *op. cit.*, 85, perceived: ". . . the essence of friendship consists in the fact that many would, so to speak, become one, and how can that take place if even in the one individual the soul is not single and forever the same, but various, changeable, kaleidoscopic?"

44. See G. H. Mead, *op. cit.*, 152–156.

45. See, for instance, Erving Goffman, *The Presentation of Self in Everyday Life, op. cit.*, 9–10.

46. Montaigne, *op. cit.*, 97. Simmel makes a similar observation, *op. cit.*, 406: "In the stage of first passion, erotic relations strongly

reject any thought of generalization: the lovers think that there has never been a love like theirs; that nothing can be compared either to the person loved or to the feelings for that person. An estrangement . . . usually comes at the moment when this feeling of uniqueness vanishes from the relationship."

47. Erving Goffman, *The Presentation of Self in Everyday Life, op. cit.,* 50.

48. There is a close parallel to this idea in Alfred Schutz, *Collected Papers, op. cit.,* Vol. II, p. 111.

49. "So a man ought to have a sympathetic consciousness of his friend's existence, which may be attained by associating with him and conversing and exchanging ideas with him. For that is what is meant when human beings speak of 'living together'—it does not mean grazing together like a herd of cattle." writes Aristotle, *op. cit.,* Bk. 9, Chap. 9, 280.

50. William McWhirter, "The Arrangement at College," *Life,* 5/31/68, 62.

51. Erik Erikson, *op. cit.,* 261–263, defines 'identity' both in terms of psychosocial integration and temporal organization. Since he then defines 'intimacy' as a merging of identities, he must therefore conceive of intimates as uniting both their psychosocial integrations and their temporal organizations.

52. See Peter Berger and Hansfried Kellner, *op. cit.,* 15.

53. R. J. Hollingdale, *op. cit.,* 47.

54. R. D. Laing, *The Divided Self* (Baltimore: Penguin Books, 1965), 44. See also Erikson, *op. cit.,* 263–264.

55. Ralph Waldo Emerson, *op. cit.,* 235.

56. Claude Brown, *op. cit.,* 147.

57. Intimate relations sometimes makes strange bedfellows. Both Sartre and Buber find themselves in rare agreement on this point. "[The 'we-relation' is extremely unstable.] It comes and disappears capriciously, leaving us in the face of others-as-objects or else as a 'they' who look at us." writes Sartre, *Being and Nothingness* (New York: Washington Square Press, 1934), 404. "But this is the exalted melancholy of our fate, that every 'Thou' in the world must become an 'It,'" concurs Buber, *I and Thou, op. cit.,* 16.

58. See Simmel's discussion of the effect of the intrusion of a third person into a dyadic conversation, *op. cit.,* 135–136.

59. "Jealousy . . . stems from our knowledge or our fear that some of

these intimate facets are not being given to us and to us alone."—
G. McCall and J. Simmons, *op. cit.*, 177.
60. Leo Tolstoy, *The Kreutzer Sonata*, tr. Aylmer Maude, reprinted in *The Death of Ivan Ilych and Other Stories* (New York: New American Library, 1960), 227.
61. *Ibid.*, 199.
62. Claude Brown, *op. cit.*, 15.

CHAPTER 7

1. Georg Simmel, "Conflict," in *Conflict and the Web of Group Affiliations*, tr. K. Wolff (Glencoe: Free Press, 1955). See particularly 17–18, 87–107.
2. Lewis Coser, *The Function of Social Conflict* (Glencoe: Free Press, 1956), 33–38, 87–110. See also the forthcoming work of Jerome Boime, to whom I am indebted for clarifying some of the ideas expressed in the following discussion.
3. Denis de Rougemont, *Love in the Western World* (New York: Fawcett, 1956), 43 (italics his).
4. *Ibid.*, 291, 298.
5. Roger Brown and Albert Gilman, "The Pronouns of Power and Solidarity," in Thomas Sebeok, ed., *Style in Language* (Cambridge: M.I.T. Press, 1960), 261.
6. First suggested, I believe, by Jerome Boime.
7. Eugenia Ginzburg, *Journal into the Whirlwind*, quoted in *The New York Review of Books*, 1/4/68, 15.
8. Erving Goffman, *Asylums* (Garden City: Anchor Books, 1961), 285.
9. Erving Goffman, "Role Distance," in *Encounters* (Indianapolis: Bobbs-Merrill, 1961).
10. Sigmund Freud, *Totem and Taboo* (New York: W. W. Norton, 1950), 140ff. Phillip Slater, *Microcosm* (New York: Wiley, 1966), expands Freud's thesis. See index under "Revolt, and intermember solidarity."
11. Erving Goffman, "Fun in Games," in *Encounters, op. cit.*, 63.
12. Freud, *op. cit.* Freud's most extended discussion of identification with leaders and with institutions can be found in *Group Psychology and the Analysis of the Ego* (New York: Bantam Books,

1960). See Slater, *op. cit.*, 74ff for the phasing in groups of unification through identification and unification through revolt.

13. A less common form of imbalanced intimacies, one that is almost the inverse of a Platonic relationship, occurs when individuals perform intimate kinesics with each other without the prerequisite intimate kinematics. "Casanova reported in his *Memoirs*," reports Morton Hunt, *The Natural History of Love* (New York: Minerva Press, 1959), 272–273, "that when he visited England, a strange lady once offered him a lift in her carriage, and though she refused to tell her name, allowed him to proceed from a squeeze of the hand to an inevitable conclusion before the ride was over; some time later, when he met her in someone's home and asked if she had forgotten him, she frostily replied: 'I remember you perfectly, but a frolic does not constitute an introduction.'"

14. Natsume Soseki, *Kokoro*, tr. E. McClellan (Chicago: Gateway, 1957), 39.

15. Claude Brown, *Manchild in the Promised Land* (New York: New American Library, 1965), 127.

16. Ernest Jones, *The Life and Work of Sigmund Freud*, ed. L. Trilling and S. Marcus (New York: Anchor, 1963), 73, 74.

17. For an extensive analysis of the arguments between intimates from the psychological perspective, see George Bach and Peter Wyden, *The Intimate Enemy* (New York: William Morrow, 1969).

18. Georg Simmel, *op. cit.*, 44–45 (italics his).

19. *Ibid.*, 17–18, 43–48. Coser, *op. cit.*, 67–86.

20. Jones, *op. cit.*, 84, 89. Ultimatums can also function as a *bordermark* for the relationship. The phrase "I just won't stand for it anymore" puts "it" out beyond the limits of behavior allowed in the relationship, and in so doing circumscribes these limits more clearly.

21. Leo Tolstoy, "The Kreutzer Sonata," tr. Aylmer Maude, in *The Death of Ivan Ilych and Other Stories* (New York: New American Library, 1960), 184–185.

22. *Ibid.*, 186, 187.

23. *Ibid.*, 206–207.

24. *Ibid.*, 207–208.

25. *Ibid.*, 209.

26. *Ibid.*, 209.

27. Jones, *op. cit.*, 89.

28. For a general discussion of why all sorts of social constructions must appear successful whether or not they actually are, see Erving Goffman, *The Presentation of Self in Everyday Life* (New York: Anchor, 1959), particularly his treatment of "teams," 77–105.

29. Emile Durkheim, *The Elementary Forms of Religious Life* (New York: Collier, 1961), especially 337–461.

30. *Ibid.*, 419–420. Durkheim also calls these ceremonies "representative."

31. Jones, *op. cit.*, 71.

32. *Ibid.*, 81, 82.

33. Brown, *op. cit.*, 201.

34. Violette Leduc, *Thérèse and Isabelle* (New York: Dell, 1966), 22. My discussion of the foreboded "death" of an intimate relation may be seen as an extension of Georg Simmel's discussion of the foreboded "death" of an intimate dyad. See *The Sociology of Georg Simmel*, tr. K. Wolff (Glencoe: Free Press, 1950), 123–124.

35. Durkheim, *op. cit.*, 434–435.

36. *Ibid.*, 378.

37. Philippe Airès, *Centuries of Childhood*, tr. R. Baldich (New York: Vintage, 1962), 245–246.

38. Pierre Choderlos de Laclos, *Dangerous Liaisons*, tr. L. Bair (New York: Bantam Books, 1962), 91–92.

39. José Ortega y Gasset, *On Love* (Cleveland: Meridian Books, 1957), 90–91.

40. Perhaps with the relentless advance of quantification, intimates might someday express the *passion-power* of their personal relations in precise statistics. One can imagine the romantic phrasing of the complaints about the ups and down of their affairs to which unsure lovers in the future will give voice: "An 82! But it was an 88 yesterday!"

41. Dan Greenburg, *How to Make Yourself Miserable* (New York: Random House, 1968). Greenburg's humor comes from the technique of having an individual himself initiate the interactions destructive to himself and his relationships, which are usually initiated by others. Another of his examples of these self- and relationship-destructive interactions begins with the simple request for a reassurance ritual:

You	Mate
Do you love me?	Of course I love you.
Do you *really* love me?	Yes, I really love you.
You really *really* love me?	Yes. I really really love you.
You're *sure* you love me—you're absolutely sure?	Yes. I'm absolutely sure.
(Pause) Do you know the meaning of the word love?	(Pause) I don't know.
Then how can you be sure you love me?	(Pause) I don't know. Perhaps I can't.
You can't, eh? I see. Well. Since you can't even be sure you love me, I can't really see much point in our remaining together. Can you?	(Pause) I don't know. Perhaps not.

You've been leading up to this for a pretty long time, haven't you?

42. William Shakespeare, *Timon of Athens,* I, ii, 15–18.
43. William Shakespeare, *Julius Caeser,* IV, ii, 13–23.
44. Though it is, of course, dangerous to generalize from interpersonal relations to international relations, students of foreign affairs often conceive of nations as individuals whose interactions exhibit many of the characteristics of affairs between persons. The following dispatch from *The New York Times,* 10/13/67, is especially interesting in the light of future developments:

> "*East Germans Irk Their Red Allies*
>
> "Reliable Communist informants say that many Eastern European officials are complaining bitterly about the behavior of the Government of Communist East Germany. . . . "The reason, say [the informants], is the almost psychotic craving of the regime headed by Walter Ulbricht for constant proofs of 'solidarity' by the other Communist governments.
>
> "The East Germans' demands of their Communist allies have steadily mounted as a result of the overtures of friendship to the East Europeans by Chancellor Kurt Kiesinger's West German Government.

"The informants said that what began as simple requests for (shows) of solidarity with East Germany, such as mutual support treaties, had undergone a qualitative change.

" 'Now the East Germans are openly intervening in our internal affairs,' said a Czech Communist."

CHAPTER 8

1. Peter Berger and Hansfried Kellner, "Marriage and the Construction of Reality," *Diogenes* (1964), 11–12.
2. "The arrival on the scene of attractive alters may come to dominate one's thinking to such an extent that these new people become vitally incorporated into his imaginations of himself in a particular social role. . . . Other audiences may suggest important new activities or qualities that should pertain to his image of himself in the social role. Whatever the cause of such change in the content of a role-identity, the change itself is often of such nature or magnitude that the other party is no longer willing or able to support ego's role-identity, at least at a competitive cost. As a result, ego becomes less interested in continuing to seek out alter."—G. McCall and J. Simmons, *Identities and Interactions* (New York: Free Press, 1966), 197.
3. Claude Brown, *Manchild in the Promised Land* (New York: New American Library, 1965), 130.
4. Ernest Jones, *The Life and Work of Sigmund Freud,* ed. L. Trilling and S. Marcus (New York: Anchor, 1963), 79–80.
5. Alfred Schutz, "The Homecomer," in *Collected Papers* (The Hague: Martinus Nijhoff, 1964), II, especially 111–113.
6. Aristotle, *Ethics,* tr. J. A. K. Thomson (Baltimore: Penguin, 1955), Bk. 8, Chap. 5, 236.
7. Plato, "Symposium," in *Plato: The Collected Dialogues* (New York: Bollingen Foundation, 1963), 537. See also "Phaedrus," *ibid.,* 482.
8. Aristotle, *op. cit.,* Bk. 8, Chap. 3, 232.
9. William Foote Whyte, in his classic sociological study of a streetcorner gang, *Street Corner Society* (Chicago: University of Chicago Press, 1955), 42, reports: ". . . the Nortons began to disintegrate. . . . Danny's job kept him busy at Spongi's all afternoon and evening. He was no longer able to hang out on the corner."

10. Aristotle, *op. cit.*, Bk. 9, Chap. 3, 265.

11. Conversely, those who wish to become intimate or more intimate with someone have a conflict of interest concerning his well-being, for the worse off he becomes, the more rewarding the test they can pass. "We are easily consoled for the misfortunes of our friends if they give us a chance to prove our devotion."—La Rochefoucauld, *The Maxims of La Rochefoucauld*, tr. L. Kronenberger (New York: Vintage, 1959), #235.

12. Friedrich Nietzsche, "From High Mountains: Aftersong," *Beyond Good and Evil*, tr. Walter Kaufmann (New York: Viking, 1966), 243, 245.

13. Claude Brown, *op. cit.*, 107–108.

14. "Recuperation Homes for Mothers," *Boston Sunday Parade*, 6, *Boston Globe*, 8/18/68.

15. "The Rise of Dustin Hoffman," *Boston Globe Magazine*, 48, *ibid.*, 5/19/68.

16. "Some relationships . . . in which the bonds of ascription, commitment, or investment are very strong, are not allowed to become attenuated unchecked, no matter how unrewarding they may be. . . . Beyond some point attenuation is forbidden. These persons are required to interact and exchange with each other at some specified minimal level, no matter how mutually painful or unprofitable it may be for them. The relationship has become an empty round of duties, and we speak of the members as having become *alienated* from it."—G. McCall and J. Simmons, *op. cit.*, 199.

17. E. M. Forster, *Howard's End* (New York: Vintage, 1958), 10–11.

18. Stephen Vizinczey, *In Praise of Older Women* (New York: Ballantine Books, 1966), 163.

19. "The illusions of love may be sweeter, but who does not know that they are also less durable? And what dangers are brought by the moment that destroys them! It is then that the slightest defects seem offensive and intolerable, by their contrast with the idea of perfection which had misled the two lovers before their marriage. Yet each thinks that only the other has changed, and that he himself still has all the qualities that were attributed to him in a moment of error. He is surprised to see that he no longer exercises the attraction he has ceased to feel; he is humiliated by this: wounded vanity embitters the mind, increases faults, produces ill-humor and gives birth to hatred; and frivolous pleasures are

finally paid for by long misfortunes."—Pierre Choderlos de Laclos, *Dangerous Liaisons*, tr. L. Bair (New York: Bantam Books, 1962), 225.

20. La Rochefoucauld, *op. cit.*, #545.

21. *Ibid.*, #351.

22. See Erving Goffman, "On Cooling the Mark Out," *Psychiatry* (1952), especially, 456.

23. "Unlike relationships that effectively end by fading away, those whose members are alienated from them end only through confrontations and unpleasant scenes in which the members overtly sever the remaining ties, at considerable psychological cost. . . . Very often the actual break is made not by the offender but by the offended—the party who became alienated only through the signs of alienation given off by the other. The hurt to one's pride is so great that few people can admit to themselves that they have been jilted or that the partners have broken off the relationships. Consequently, the offended one may strike first, as far as the *overt* break is concerned, on the theory that the best ego defense is a good offense."—G. McCall and J. Simmons, *op. cit.*, 199–201.

24. In a study of lesbians in prisons, D. Ward and G. Kassebaum, "Homosexuality: A Mode of Adaption in a Prison for Women," *Social Problems* (1964), 171, note: "Exploitation, when it does occur in these relationships, comes when one of the parties is tiring of the other."

25. Shakespeare, *Sonnets*, #116.

26. Of course, this contract does not actually exist, but is merely a social fiction; nevertheless, the intimates themselves usually feel they have achieved some sort of "understanding" with each other that functions like a contract and to which they often appeal ("But I thought we were supposed to . . ."). They become conscious that their relationship is based on a contract, however, only when it is infringed. Their contract's lack of clarity accounts for the unique difficulties of interpersonal litigations.

27. "In June, 1918, [André] Gide eloped to England with Marc and left his wife alone at home, in wartime. When she found herself deserted in the big house, she took out all the letters he had written to her and burned them. In the autumn, on his return, when he was writing his autobiography . . . , he asked to see the letters to refresh his memory, and then she told him what she had done. He was heartbroken that she should have done this to him,

and he felt that she had killed their child—his and hers—and that these letters had been the best things that he had ever written." Enid Starkie reviewing George Painter's *André Gide, New York Times Book Review*, 6/23/68, 8.

28. Conversely, the person who was attacked can claim "overkill"— even when there was none—merely as a tactic to terrorize his attacker (by threatening to end their relationship). If the attacker can be convinced he went too far, he can be coerced not only into surrendering his position in the original argument, but also into providing reparations for excess damage.

29. "Sunday Will Never Be the Same." Words and Music by Gene Pistilli and Terry Cashman. (New York: Pamco Music Inc., 1966 & 1967). Recorded by *Spanky & Our Gang* on Mercury Records.

30. Ovid, "The Remedies for Love," in *The Art of Love*, tr. Rolfe Humphries (Bloomington: Indiana University Press, 1957), 200, 202.

31. *Ibid.*, 185.

32. *Ibid.*, 198.

33. *Ibid.*, 199.

34. *Ibid.*, 187.

35. E. M. Forster, *op. cit.*, 61.

36. Michel de Montaigne, "On Friendship," *Essays*, tr. J. M. Cohen (Baltimore: Penguin, 1958), 103.

37. T. E. Lawrence, *The Seven Pillars of Wisdom* (New York: Dell, 1962), 506.

38. Ovid, *op. cit.*, 190, 191, 194, 203.

39. *Ibid.*, 203.

40. Stendhal, *On Love* (New York: Anchor, 1947), 129–130.

41. J. Cohen, ed., *The Essential Lenny Bruce* (New York: Ballantine, 1967), 197–198.

42. Montaigne, *op. cit.*, 103.

CONCLUSION

1. Recent literature by the women's liberation movement is a step in the direction of developing such a micropolitics, but it still needs to be generalized to include all intimate relations in which power is unequally distributed.

2. The very fact that the self of an individual is diffuse, is composed of components that can be given or taken out of his control (e.g., his body, possessions, reputation, and other aspects enumerated especially in Chapter 6), which can cause him so much satisfaction in some circumstances, can cause him so much suffering in others—depending on who or what it is that obtains control over these self-components. To present aspects of one's essence to an intimate who is dedicated to its betterment is one thing; to surrender them to an institution that is dedicated to its destruction is quite another. For an analysis of the destructive consequences of institutions on the same kind of self on which I have here considered the constructive consequences of intimates, see Erving Goffman's *Asylums* (Garden City: Anchor, 1961), especially 12–48.

3. Erving Goffman, the leading spokesman for this latter school, has enumerated an enormous number of rules for classes of "situations," "settings," "gatherings," and "occasions." These situational determinants, he asserts, usually influence a person's behavior far more than any of his status determinants. "More than to any family or club, more than to any class or sex, more than to any nation, the individual belongs to gatherings." *Behavior in Public Places* (New York: Free Press, 1963), 243.

4. The exceptions occur because intimates cannot always amend the rules of their relationship fast enough to keep up with changing conditions. Variations in sentiments inside the relationship and in enticements outside the relationship, whether temporary or permanent, sometimes cause intimates to feel that their personal freedom has been curtailed in the present by the interpersonal obligations they themselves had freely contracted for in the past.

5. Perhaps the continuing controversy over whether the conception of man in modern sociology is "oversocialized" (and consequently "underindividualized")—the contending positions are most clearly stated in Denis Wrong's, "The Oversocialized Conception of Man in Modern Sociology," *American Sociological Review* (1961), 183–193—can best be clarified if we distinguish two types of sociological determinants of an individual's behavior: (1) those an individual did not choose or create and (2) those he did. We can now see that an individual (for individual reasons) sometimes consciously attempts to escape the influence of the former (e.g., certain of his statuses and situations) by choosing or creating the latter (e.g., certain close relationships). In this way, sociologists

can still analyze his behavior in terms of determining sociological factors, while recognizing that his being determined by certain particular sociological factors rather than others is largely his own doing. But sociologists should note further that the individual's intimate relations may also function as that *fulcrum* with which he can move society, with which he can change the very forms of social statuses and situations.

6. Symbolic Interactional Analysis, of course, is not static in the same sense as Structural Analysis is, for it focuses on processes, not structures. But it is still relatively static in the sense that it sees these processes as *repetitive* rather than *evolutionary*.

7. The four fundamental forces in physics today are gravity and electromagnetism on the superatomic and atomic levels, and what are called "weak interactions" and "strong interactions" on the subatomic and intranuclear levels.

8. This is one of the themes of Denis de Rougemont's *Love in the Western World* (New York: Fawcett, 1956).

9. Love—like certain drugs, the threat of death, religious ecstasy, and revolutionary activity—is a phenomenological stimulant. Those who live at certain times and places seem to need more intense experiences than those who live at other times and places do. Today, I believe, it is the mass media—constantly bombarding the individual with the high points of human experience—that has caused him to find his everyday life less than real and, therefore, to seek to increase his feeling of reality by the above methods. But I do not know why some individuals should choose to intensify their experience in one of these ways rather than in another.